DOING THEOLOGY

Jared Wicks, SJ

PAULIST PRESS
New York • Mahwah, NJ

This book's cover depicts theologians of different eras who exemplify important ways of doing theology. They are, clockwise from the right, John Henry Cardinal Newman (1801–90), Martin Luther (1483–1546), St. Athanasius (295–373), St. Thomas Aquinas (1225–74), and Yves Congar (1904–90). The reader can find accounts of their theological work on the pages specified for each in the Index.

Photograph of Rev. Yves Congar, OP, courtesy of the Dominican Friars of the Province of France.

The scripture quotations contained herein are from the New Revised Standard Version: Catholic Edition Copyright © 1989 and 1993, by the Division of Christian Education of the National Council of the Churches of Christ in the United States of America. Used by permission. All rights reserved.

Cover design by Sharyn Banks.

Copyright © 2009 by Detroit Province, Society of Jesus.

Library of Congress Cataloging-in-Publication Data

Wicks, Jared, 1929-
    Doing theology / Jared Wicks.
        p. cm.
    Includes bibliographical references and index.
    ISBN 978-0-8091-4564-5 (alk. paper)
    1. Theology–Methodology. 2. Catholic Church–Doctrines. I. Title.
    BR118.W567 2009
    230'.2–dc22

                                                    2009019327

Published by Paulist Press
997 Macarthur Boulevard
Mahwah, New Jersey 07430

www.paulistpress.com

Printed and bound in Canada.

Dedicated to my colleagues of 1979–2004
on the Gregorian University Theology Faculty in Rome,
who were exemplary in doing theology well

Contents

Abbreviations

BDCT   *Biographical Dictionary of Christian Theologians.* Edited by Patrick J. Carey and Joseph T. Lienhard. Westport, CT: Greenwood, 2000, and Peabody, MA: Hendrickson, 2002.

DFT   *Dictionary of Fundamental Theology.* Edited by René Latourelle and Rino Fisichella. New York: Crossroad, 1994.

NAB   The New American Bible.

ND   Neuner-Dupuis. *The Christian Faith in the Doctrinal Documents of the Catholic Church.* Edited by Joseph Neuner and Jacques Dupuis. 7th revised and enlarged edition. Staten Island: Alba House, 2001.

Documents of Vatican Council II

AG   *Ad Gentes.* Decree on the Church's Missionary Activity.

DH   *Dignitatis Humanae.* Decree on Religious Liberty.

DV   *Dei Verbum.* Dogmatic Constitution on Divine Revelation.

GS   *Gaudium et Spes.* Pastoral Constitution on the Church in the Modern World.

LG   *Lumen Gentium.* Dogmatic Constitution on the Church.

NA   *Nostra Aetate.* Declaration on the Church and Non-Christian Religions.

OT   *Optatum Totius.* Decree on the Training of Priests.

UR   *Unitatis Redintegratio.* Decree on Ecumenism.

Introduction

WHILE TEACHING AT the Gregorian University in Rome, the author brought out a book on method in theology published in 1994, with editions in both English and Italian.[1] The present book is a thoroughly reworked version of that earlier text. After the author moved to John Carroll University near Cleveland, it became clear that this work needed updating to give references to more recent writings in theology. It also needed revising with a view to better serve students of religious studies and theology in North America.

These pages are offered to men and women who are beginning the theological quest. They speak about the life that theology *is,* especially by putting the readers in contact with a remarkable set of companions. Readers will meet early Christians like Irenaeus of Lyons, Origen of Alexandria, and then Thomas Aquinas and his lesser known Dominican confrere Melchior Cano.

The bishops and theologians of Vatican Council II (1962–65) speak repeatedly in this volume, and there is a silent but influential presence of figures like Henri de Lubac and Yves Congar. Along with others, like the Belgian and German experts of the Council, these were the advance scouts of twentieth-century Catholic theology on the path of *ressourcement,* that is, drawing in a fresh way on scripture and the Church Fathers to gain insights from which to reformulate and revitalize the Catholic doctrinal heritage.[2]

The Council was *the* great ecclesial event of the twentieth century, and Pope Benedict XVI affirmed its continuing relevance when he began his Petrine ministry on April 20, 2005:

> I too wish to affirm with force my decided will to pursue the commitment to enact Vatican Council II.... With the passing of time the conciliar documents have not lost their timeliness; their teachings have shown themselves to be especially pertinent

to the new exigencies of the Church and the present globalized
society.[3]

The Council is present here, both in the text and in the Appendices, where one may learn of the vision of the popes of the Council,
John XXIII and Paul VI, and come to know about the contributions
made to Vatican II by theological experts and consultants.

These pages invite the reader to join the company of those pursuing
the theological quest, both by coming to know classic and recent
theologians and by taking up the task of prolonging their quest well
into the twenty-first century.

God's Revelation

This book follows the guidance given by Vatican II in understanding
the word and work of God's revelation of himself and of the truth
that we need for humane and holy living. God's word of revelation
is what faith accepts and what a person then seeks to penetrate and
envision coherently while doing theology. One does theology, most
fundamentally, by extending faith's personal hearing of God's revealing word into an active inquiry into the meaning given by revelation,
which conveys to us the truth about God, his good news ("Gospel")
to humankind, and about our human vocation.

To be sure, many people think spontaneously of "revelation" as
the unveiling of a heretofore hidden wisdom about which ordinary
people have little or no inkling or awareness. Persons communicating such lore may claim to have visited the spiritual realm and seen
all reality under divine light, as did Emanuel Swedenborg (1688–
1772), or to have received a new sacred text such as Joseph Smith's
Book of Mormon (1830), or to have had access to the ancient root
of all other faiths, as did Helene Blavatsky in her *Secret Doctrine*
(1888).[4]

But mainstream Christian theology has not worked from reports
issued by exponents of esoteric doctrine conveyed to chosen initiates.
What has prevailed instead is revelation taken as God's communication given in history and prophecy to ancient Israel and in the deeds
and words of Jesus, as the scriptures of the Old and New Testaments
attest these in a final way. The message and meaning of this revelation

has been and is still being passed on publicly by commissioned and empowered spokespersons. In this way God is informing the human family about himself, his gracious and saving work in human history, and his call to come close to his light and goodness. Such revelation shows to the submissive mind the loving face of God and points out the way to come to God in communities gathered by witnesses serving his saving intentions for the whole human family.

For recent Catholic thought, the First Vatican Council of 1870 set forth an "instructional" notion of God's word of supernatural teaching, and then countless textbooks of theology presented revelation in this way in the years that followed that Council.[5] But this does not suffice today, after the mid-twentieth-century revisitation of the basic sources. The emphasis placed on *revealed knowledge* and on the authority of its bearers can easily lead to an impoverished notion of faith as docile submission in order to receive supernatural knowledge. Faith does involve knowing, and it does lay hold of God's work and word in doctrines, but the doctrines arise in a matrix of experiences neglected by Catholics in the years before Vatican II.

Today, as confirmed by the Vatican II Constitution on Revelation, *Dei Verbum* (1965), a holistic notion prevails concerning God's approach to humans in saving solidarity and in his word of call and grace. God speaks to us lovingly with a call out of the chaos of sin to communion with himself in friendship. Scripture relates how God acted in history and then spoke to men and women to rescue them from isolation and lead them to sharing life with himself, as occurred paradigmatically in Jesus' gathering of his band of disciples. God's revelation creates *communion,* both between God and ourselves and among those who share with each other their faith's vision of God.

God reveals so "that all should have access to the Father, through Christ, the Word made flesh, in the Holy Spirit" (DV 2). Jesus brings the culminating revelation, because he introduces his followers into life in relation to his Father in their Spirit. In this setting, valuable new knowledge of God and his saving work arises, especially in the Gospel message that God is near to save us from sin and raise us to life in him. Faith becomes certain of this, when a human heart gives its grateful Yes to God's good news and gift of himself in life to be shared.[6]

Theology and Doctrines

In the wake of Vatican II, Catholic theology cannot be satisfied to simply restate more systematically the revealed doctrines of faith founded on scripture and formulated in the dogmatic definitions of councils and popes. The doctrines expressed in the creed and articles of faith do make known how God frees us from sin and death to draw us into communion with himself. Doing theology involves pondering these magnificent truths and their consequences for life, but it begins with an exploration of their grounds in the original and originating experiences of believers in Israel and in the circle of Jesus' followers.

The prophets of Israel, Jesus, and his apostles all testified to God's gift of communion with himself, and their witness makes up a privileged theological topic. The theological quest for insight into their message and explanations leads in time to articulating doctrine in an ordered manner, but the systematic schemes of theology stand or fall on their capacity to lead persons into fuller communion with the Father, through Christ, in the Holy Spirit.

Vatican Council II, in the original inspiration and guidance given by Pope John XXIII, was oriented to the *pastoral* renewal of the Catholic Church.[7] The measuring rod with which the bishops of the Council evaluated proposals on teaching, worship, and life was their potential to lead Catholic believers to greater holiness, fuller participation in the worship of God, and more effective witness in this world to the Gospel concerning God's gracious gifts and ongoing saving presence.

Thus, doing theology under the inspiration of the Council will be a service of God's word, working toward making it a *viva vox evangelii* ("living voice of the Gospel," DV 8), for a renewed apostolic and transforming evangelization of our world. Theology has to constantly test itself regarding its potential to serve Christian proclamation and promote Christian service in the particular socio-cultural region in which the theology originates (AG 22).

Grasping deeply God's good news, which fosters communion of life with him, remains the pearl of great price that theology sets out to acquire. We ponder repeatedly an apostolic heritage, the *depositum fidei* (deposit of faith), but with a strong sense of its enveloping *depositum vitae* (deposit of life) that still exists to foster communion with God and the service of his saving purposes today.

The Structure of This Book

In what follows, this book first reviews selected examples of goals and methods marking the theological quest in the past and then takes up the directives and impulses given by Vatican Council II to doing theology (chapter 1). It then turns to God's normative and inspired scriptures, which call for attentive listening and ordered interpretation (chapter 2). The listening to God's word that is central here, leading to reflective investigation, takes place in the context or stream of Catholic tradition (chapter 3) and under the light of church teaching, which the theologian weighs, examines, and opens up by drawing on its sources (chapter 4). But since God reveals himself as Savior of human beings and generous giver of communion, theology must look to life to draw wisdom from lived experiences of God's grace and thereby to enrich human living (chapter 5). In these chapters, sections 1.3 and 5.1 state briefly the ways and means of doing theology presented in more detail in the other chapters and sections.

The conviction underlying the chapters of this book is that the theological quest does not aim at acquiring apocalyptic or gnostic lore, for it concerns *life* and draws on testimonies proven to be wellsprings of humane and holy living. The biblical and ecclesial sources witness to a life that, in Christ, entered once and for all into our human history. Hearing these testimonies, one is called to communion of life with the witnesses and with the Triune God, in much joy (1 John 1:1–4).

At the end of each of the five main chapters, as well as after this Introduction, "Review Questions" have been provided that can be used as study aids by individuals or in a class context. "Projects for Further Study" offers suggestions that the professor may wish to assign for more advanced study where appropriate.

A Note on Theological Genre

This book is a work of *fundamental theology*, which has its place among the theological subject areas as Appendix 7 sketches this below. In this theological area, this book draws conclusions about doing theology from contemporary Catholic positions concerning God's revelation, faith, and the communication about God's action and word by the scriptures, tradition, Catholic magisterial teaching, and the witness of Christian lives.

Review Questions

1. Why were Henri de Lubac and Yves Congar major figures in twentieth-century Catholic theology?

2. At the fundamental level, how does doing theology relate to believing by faith?

3. In mainstream Christian theology, where is God's revelation found?

4. How do the two Vatican Councils differ in their accounts of God's revelation?

5. What does theology seek to do when it deals with doctrines?

Projects for Further Study

1. In Appendix 4 below (page 181), study Vatican II's chapter on "Divine Revelation Itself." *How* does God reveal? *What* does God principally reveal? *To what end or goal* does God offer his revelation? *What role* does Jesus Christ have in God's revelation?

2. In the *Dictionary of Fundamental Theology*, study pages 930–34, by R. Latourelle, on specific features of Christian revelation. How is revelation *historical*? How does it combine *event and commentary*? Give examples of revelation's dialectic of *promise and fulfillment*. How is God's revelation *centered in Christ*?

Chapter One

Theology in History and the Church

THIS OPENING CHAPTER moves toward a basic organizing principle of doing theology in a methodical way. But we approach this basic principle by first reviewing six suggestive examples of how theology has been practiced in the Christian past (section 1.1). Second, Vatican II will offer four guidelines for doing theology (1.2). Then, at the level of basic principle, the text will describe the two kinds of intellectual activity that give a basic organization to theological work, namely, *listening* to what the sources say as they convey God's saving word and then *explaining* the meaning of what the believing listener has grasped about God and about humane and holy living (1.3).

But this approach to doing theology methodically starts with an initial short reflection on the goal of all these activities of doing theology.

THEOLOGY AND MEANING

The theologian's passion is meaning. Doing theology is to probe the sense of what God has given to believers by the message they accept and by the new life into which God leads them. Ultimately, theology is about the meaning of God's word addressed to all human beings. When believers accept this word, the universe becomes meaningful as God's creation, and human lives gain meaning from God's saving grace in Christ, leading to guidance for living given by God's word and the Holy Spirit. Such a word of meaning is a call to a life of discipleship that believers try — with different degrees of success — to live out. Theology, centrally, is the search for the meaning

7

of God's word and of the life of faith.[1] Theological questions concern the meaning of what God has revealed of himself as he lovingly invites believers into communion of life with himself (DV 2). Doing theology involves examining God's disclosure of himself in successive stages, first, as he dealt with Israel through Moses and the prophets; second, as God's saving action culminated in Jesus Christ; and, third, as the Gospel of Christ was proclaimed once-for-all by Jesus' apostles and is still announced and lived out in the church. From this, theology works to draw out the sense and significance of God's word and of the new life that that word engenders.

In the history of Christianity, this theological quest has taken on a variety of forms and followed quite different methods. Theologians have sought meaning in very different contexts, for example, in the ancient world both before and after Constantine (Roman emperor, AD 306–37), in medieval Western Christendom, in early modern Europe divided by Protestantism and the Catholic Counter Reformation, and in our era marked by secularization, dialogue between the world's religions, and the Catholic Church's reform and redefinition of itself at Vatican II.

As the setting of theological work changed, also the motives and methods of the theological search came to be reshaped according to different priorities. This chapter, therefore, will first review how the theological search has been understood by some significant individuals who have done theology before us.[2]

1.1. THEOLOGY IN PAST ERAS OF CHRISTIANITY

This section is not a review of the whole history of Christian theology. Instead it selects notable examples of how believers have searched and found meaning in God's word, which they hold in faith. The aim is not to give complete coverage, but instead to present several theological projects that serve well to broaden our own horizons by learning how important thinkers before us carried out the theological task.

Two Early Fathers: Irenaeus and Origen

One useful reference work calls St. Irenaeus "the first great Catholic theologian."[3] Irenaeus, the bishop of Lyons in Gaul (d. ca. AD 200), wrote his two surviving works, *Adversus Haereses* (Against the Heresies) and *The Demonstration of the Apostolic Preaching,* in the last decades of the second Christian century, when persecution menaced the church from the outside and doctrinal turmoil raged within. Irenaeus worked out a coherent and well-grounded alternative to the doctrinal speculations of Christian "gnostic" masters like Valentinus and Basilides.[4] Long passages of Irenaeus's *Adversus Haereses* recount the teachings on God, creation, and redemption that these masters claimed to have received as saving knowledge (*gnosis*) from an oral transmission going back to conversations with the Risen Jesus in appearances not recounted in the canonical Gospels.

Against the secret doctrines transmitted by the gnostic masters, Irenaeus affirmed forcefully what was taught openly and from the beginning as the "rule of truth" in the churches founded by the original apostles of Jesus. This "rule" will come up in chapter 3 below as an early form of the church's doctrinal tradition. In Book III, chapter 3, of *Adversus Haereses,* Irenaeus ascribed a special, universal validity to one church's doctrinal rule, namely, "that tradition derived from the apostles, of the very great, very ancient, and universally known church founded and organized at Rome by the two glorious apostles Peter and Paul."[5]

Irenaeus appealed to the content of public instruction in the churches. The doctrinal tradition of the apostolic churches can be summarized in the three fundamental articles of belief in God the Father and Creator, the Son and Redeemer, and the Holy Spirit sent to sanctify us and reveal the plan of salvation. While the different gnostics spin out ideas often at variance with one another, the church's faith is a matter of universal consensus and from this it has its power to convince.

> The church, having received this preaching and faith, although scattered throughout the whole world, yet, as if occupying one house, carefully preserves it. She believes these points of doctrine, just as if she had one soul and one and the same heart, and she proclaims them, teaches them, and hands them down with perfect harmony, as if she possessed only one mouth. Although the languages of the world are different yet the import of the

> tradition is one and the same.... Just as the sun...is one and the same throughout the whole world, so also the preaching of the truth shines everywhere, and enlightens all people willing to come to knowledge of the truth. Nor will anyone of the rulers of the churches, however gifted he may be in eloquence, teach doctrines different from these.[6]

Irenaeus seemed to sense that his appeal to tradition might seem to impose a deadening weight upon the human mind. So he went on to explain that inside the house of faith there is ample space for exercising an inquiring and reflective mind. The fundamental preaching, once accepted and professed, opens up its own terrain for exploration and research.

> One may bring out the meaning of those things spoken in parables and accommodate them to the one scheme of the faith; and explain the operation and dispensation of God connected with human salvation;... and understand for what reason God, though invisible, manifested himself to the prophets under one form, but differently to different individuals; and show why it was that more covenants than one were given to humankind; and teach what was the special character of each of these covenants; and search out for what reason "God has imprisoned all in disobedience, so that he may be merciful to all" (Rom 11:32); and gratefully describe on what account the Word of God became flesh and suffered; and relate why the advent of the Son of God took place in these last times...rather than in the beginning; and unfold what is contained in the scriptures concerning the end and the things to come.[7]

For Irenaeus, theology is an intellectual activity situated within the coordinates of the "one scheme of the faith" taught and embraced in the church by believers. The theologian explores revelation, remaining ever attentive to what has come from the apostles and been received in one's heart as the content and structure of belief in God as manifested in the missions of the Son and the Spirit.

If Irenaeus of Lyons is the first great exponent of theology who linked it to the church's instructional tradition, Origen of Alexandria (ca. AD 185–254) is his counterpart, because of his orientation to the text of scripture. This teacher of the first half of the third century held that because the biblical texts are inspired by God's Spirit, they should be interpreted with a view to uncovering their "spiritual" meaning, that is, what the inspiring Spirit intends to say in and through them.[8]

According to Origen, all believers admit that scripture discloses "certain mysterious dispensations" through narratives and symbols chosen by the Spirit to convey deeper religious truths. A human being has the three component parts, body, soul, and spirit, as Paul suggests in 1 Thessalonians 5:23, and Origen saw in the text of the Bible a similar three-part structure of meaning. The "body" is the surface meaning of what the Bible narrates; the "soul" is the instruction given to those advancing in the life of faith; the "spirit" is the hidden wisdom of God's ways, about which hints are now offered until all is finally revealed in heaven. Origen explains this in the first three chapters of his *On First Principles,* chapter 4. In the midst of this passage, Origen speaks like Irenaeus on how understanding of scripture takes guidance from the church's rule of faith received from the apostles. The Preface of *On First Principles* had set forth the main tenets of that doctrinal tradition.[9]

Convinced that the biblical authors were inspired by God while they wrote, Origen approached his work of interpretation sure that he would find instruction even in texts that at first glance promise little. Chapter 33 of the book of Numbers seems to be only a list of the obscure oases that served the Israelites as campsites on their journey from Egypt to Sinai and on to the Jordan across from Canaan. But for Origen there is much more in Numbers 33. First, he notes that Israel's journey was made in forty-two stages, a fact that obscurely foreshadows the forty-two generations listed in Matthew 1 between Abraham and Jesus the Messiah. Even more engaging is the symmetry between Israel's journey to the promised land and the soul's progress in this life, under training by God's law and testing by temptation, as it grows toward deeper union with God.[10]

In Irenaeus and Origen, therefore, we meet two different styles of doing Christian theology. Both were searchers into meaning who worked to formulate and communicate what God has disclosed about himself and about his project of human salvation.

Irenaeus found content and structure in "the one scheme of the faith" taught in the apostolic churches. He then posed typical theological questions. What then is the sense of the tradition? How do the covenants fit together? What can we say about the comings — past, present, and future — of Christ? Irenaeus begins with the single content of basic belief and then turns to the many texts of scripture to probe into the "whys" and "hows" of God's meaningful dealings with humankind.

Origen of Alexandria was convinced that the Holy Spirit had prepared a fruitful and ample store of meaning in Scripture. He approached every biblical text assured that the Holy Spirit was there speaking to believers about Jesus and about their life in the Lord. Today many interpreters find parts of Origen's spiritual interpretation strained and fanciful, but one can surely still share his central conviction, namely, that God offers abundant wisdom and guidance in the Bible. If theologians will only interpret the written word rightly, they, along with other believers, will be enriched profoundly.

Irenaeus and Origen expressed these two fundamental orientations, which then were taken over in different combinations by many other Church Fathers. Further on, section 3.2 will sketch what the Church Fathers have to contribute to doing theology. But it remains basic to theology to draw on tradition as Irenaeus did and to study Scripture with the passion of an Origen. Therefore, later parts of this book will treat the theologian's work with the canonical and inspired text of Scripture (chapter 2) and sketch the several ways in which good theology interacts with the ongoing tradition of the church (chapter 3).

Theology at the Beginning of the Modern Age: Luther and Cano

Whereas Irenaeus and Origen exemplify orientations to different sources of theological meaning, our next two examples show Christian theologians choosing between tightly concentrated work around a single central topic or, instead, drawing on a wide and various series of sources. In the sixteenth century, Martin Luther expressed the ideal of theological concentration on a single central truth, while the influential Dominican methodologist Melchior Cano set forth the ideal of a panoramic breadth of attention to a notable number of theological sources.

Luther (1483–1546) is best known for his polemics against elements of the Catholic tradition and for his claim that there was only one source for doctrine and guidance in living, *sola Scriptura* (scripture alone). But there is more to Luther. Today, researchers in the Catholic tradition are working out an ecumenical rapprochement with many aspects of his positive teaching.[11] Here we attend to Luther's remarks on doing theology rightly and beneficially. We know that Luther had an impact on many believers and that his work changed the course of history. But what basic orientation and focus did Luther gave to his theology?

One reason for the power of Luther's teaching is his constant insistence on a single basic truth. Luther learned from St. Paul that without Christ we humans are inextricably caught in sin and guilt. But in Christ we encounter freely given forgiveness, justification before God, and new freedom. Luther attributes extraordinary importance to justification, that is, to a person's coming, by the Gospel word and unmerited grace, to be set in the right relation to God. For Luther justification is both a set of doctrines with definite contents and a principle to apply when treating practically all other theological questions.

In his *Lectures on Galatians* (delivered 1531, printed 1535), Luther claimed that one who loses the true doctrine of unmerited, freely given justification thereby loses all of Christian doctrine, for justification is the *caput et summa* (head and summary) of all Christian teaching.[12] Luther went so far as to say he would revere the pope and tolerate all the Roman church's abuses if pope and church would only admit that God justifies us solely by his own grace through Christ.[13] The theologian, according to Luther, must focus total attention on the themes that make up the doctrine of justification. It is the lens for viewing God and humankind in a truly theological way.

> Let no one, therefore, ponder the divine majesty, and what God has done and how mighty he is; or think of a human being as the master of property, the way a lawyer does, or of his healing, the way a physician does. But think of human beings as sinners.

> The proper subject of theology is the person guilty of sin and condemned, and God the justifier and savior of the sinner. Whatever is asked or discussed in theology outside this subject is error and poison. All scripture points to this, that God commends his loving-kindness to us and in his Son restores to righteousness and life the nature that has fallen into sin and condemnation.[14]

Theological work focuses on the drama of sin and grace as the heart of the Bible's teaching. Across the broad field of doctrinal and ethical questions, that drama is the constant point of reference and the pole star. Doing theology means constant attention to God's action to save human beings by his unmerited gift of justification and new life.

For Luther, theology rests on the spiritual experience of sin and forgiveness, of death and life. In a table remark in 1531, he went so far as to say, "Experience alone makes a theologian." Luther has in mind experiences given in prayer, meditation on scripture, and struggling with temptation.[15] Luther did not reduce theological explanations to only what a person has felt, nor did he make his own personal experience a norm or criterion of truth. When Luther gave instruction, as in his catechisms of 1529, he explained the traditional components, namely, the commandments, the creed, the Our Father, and the sacraments. But Luther also gave these well-known texts a freshness and vigor from what he had lived through personally in encountering God's gracious action to save his otherwise lost human creatures.[16]

The Catholic Church formulated its official response to the challenge posed by Luther and the Protestant reforms in the doctrines and decrees issued by the Council of Trent (1545–63). But just as the Council was finishing its work, the Spanish Dominicans of Salamanca brought out a book, *De locis theologicis* (on the fields of theology), by Melchior Cano, OP, which became the premier methodological treatise of modern Catholic theology. Cano had died in 1560 before he could write the final chapters. But this did not diminish the impact of the book, which was reprinted thirty times down to 1890.[17]

Cano provides a suggestive ideal that many Catholic theologians have followed, even when they have not read *De locis*. Cano sets forth the *loci*, or "places," that are the documentary fields in which the theologian discovers evidence in support of what will be set forth as arguments to support one's own position or explanation and/or to refute other doctrines as wrong. The main trait of theology in the style of Cano is the breath and number of the resources, what we can call the true catholicity of the bases on which such work draws. This theology may lack the concentration practiced and recommended by Luther, but it often impresses by the variety of fields in which it moves.

Cano's influential work on method presupposes an unfolding and development of the original Christian tradition from its essential beginning by Jesus and its transmission by his apostles into the sources from which a Catholic theologian draws material. Certain rules govern work with each *locus* (place), showing how to derive specific testimonies to God's revealed truth in the manner appropriate to the place or source. Cano borrowed from Cicero's *De oratore* and called the *loci* the "domiciles" of all those elements with which one carries on theological argumentation.[18]

Cano places holy scripture first among the *loci* and explains its truth and canonical authority. The second theological *locus* is the complex of fundamental traditions of doctrine, life, and worship that come from Christ or from the Holy Spirit's instruction of the apostles and belong to the perennial heritage of Catholic teaching and spiritual guidance. The first two "places," scripture and apostolic tradition, are the fundamental sources that give a primordial witness to God's word of revelation.

What one finds in the first two *loci* is then interpreted, protected, and developed by what the theologian comes to find in five further expressions of God's truth in the life of the church: the faith of the universal body of believers, synods and councils, the Roman Church and its bishop, the Fathers, and the scholastic theologians. When investigated properly — according to rules based on the nature of each — these first seven *loci* give testimony to God's revelation. Each can provide a proper and authoritative witness to the content of Christian doctrine.

Cano, as a Dominican disciple of St. Thomas, did not construe theological work as exclusively and narrowly dependent on authority, but instead went on to list three further fields in which one should find materials relevant to doing theology. These *loci* are the "annexes" of the main dwelling places of theological evidence, but they have their specific contribution to make. Cano thus listed as the final three *loci* the arguments of natural reason, the views of philosophers, and the lessons of human history.

After Cano, and usually with an explicit nod in his direction, Catholic fundamental theology, in its account of God's revelation and of how we come to know God's word, has regularly undertaken an exposition of the doctrinal sources, much as the further chapters of this book will do. Such a "doctrine of principles" is the natural complement of the primary topics of fundamental theology, that is, God's revelation, the signs that recommend a mediator of revelation as credible, the response of faith, and the transmission of the Gospel in the church for the world.

A contemporary doctrine of the *loci*, or sources, will introduce areas not found in Cano, such as the witness of the liturgy, the meaning that breaks forth from lives outstanding in holiness, and the experience of regional and local churches. But Cano's presentation retains its relevance for two principal reasons.

His account is first a salutary warning against constricting the scope of the theological search for meaning, as for example by attending only to the actuality of special experience or by looking for preemptive certitude, which might come from recovering the literal sense of scripture or from citing a text issued by the church's magisterium. Cano indicates the proper breadth of a Catholic theologian's *auditus fidei* ("hearing in faith," as Paul indicates in Rom 10:17). No single locus may claim a monopoly as a witness to truth and meaning.

Second, the system of numerous *loci* indicates that the Gospel does in fact impinge on the believer "in many and various ways" (Heb 1:1). The witnesses to revealed truth speak with voices of different pitch and timbre, which a Christian worker in theology seeks to compose into a symphonic whole. Other combinations and configurations are obviously possible. But good theology attracts and charms precisely by reason of the harmonious interaction of its diverse components.

Thus, two early modern figures, Luther and Cano, gave notably different guidelines on doing theology. Luther would have theology focus on the main truth that we are saved by God's grace in Christ. Cano, then, gives the salutary reminder not to reduce the myriad ways in which God's revelation and its meaning come to us. A person setting out to do theology in the early twenty-first century can learn from both of these early modern exponents of doing theology rightly.

Theology in 1870 and 1950: Vatican I and Pope Pius XII

Documents of authoritative Catholic teaching treated theology's aims and tasks in the years 1870 and 1950. The first statement formed part of the First Vatican Council's Dogmatic Constitution on the Catholic Faith, *Dei Filius* (April 24, 1870; given in Appendix 4 below).

Vatican I defines the act and attitude of *faith* as the graced acceptance of what God has revealed about himself and what he intends for us. In faith, the human person submits to God by accepting as true what God communicates about himself and the plan of salvation he has decreed for humankind (*Dei Filius,* chapters 2–3). Scripture and the traditions coming from the apostles contain this revelation, and the church sets it forth for faith's acceptance.

But faith, according to Vatican I, is not blind submission to authority, because God has surrounded his revealed truths with a coherent web of "signs of credibility," such as the miracles worked by Jesus, the prophecies he fulfilled, and the remarkable qualities of holiness and stability shown forth in the church founded by Jesus. To be sure, the word of revelation calls human beings to go beyond perceptible evidence and rational conclusions, to lay hold of mysteries like the Trinity of divine persons, the divine Word's incarnation and redemptive death on the cross, and the grace-giving sacraments, but human inquiry can discover a framework in which the message and faith's submissive listening has a logic of its own and clear coherence with the rest of life (*Dei Filius,* chapter 3, nos. 2 and 6–7).[19]

Faith, in itself, is submissive and docile. It accepts amazing truths as a gift and this leads to a gratitude, much like what Jesus once expressed in prayer: "I thank you, Father, Lord of heaven and earth, because you have hidden these things from the wise and intelligent and have revealed them to infants; yes, Father, for such was your gracious will" (Matt 11:25–26). But faith also leaves room for the mind's inquiry. The theological search has its place *in* the life of faith, as the Council of 1870 set this forth.

In a subtly constructed paragraph, Vatican I then described some central approaches that the theological search takes inside the house of faith. For one can attain an "understanding of the mysteries," that is, an intellectual penetration of the truths expressing God and his saving work, but this does not dissolve their mysterious character:

> If reason illumined by faith inquires in an earnest, pious, and sober manner, it attains by God's grace a certain understanding of the mysteries that is most fruitful. This arises from grasping the analogy with objects of the mind's natural knowledge, from the connection of the mysteries with one another, and from their relation to the ultimate end of human beings. But reason does not become capable of understanding the mysteries in the way it grasps the truths that constitute its proper object. For divine mysteries by their very nature so excel the created intellect that, even when communicated in revelation and received in faith, they remain covered by the veil of faith itself and shrouded as it were in darkness, because as long as we are in this mortal life, "We are away from the Lord, for we walk by faith, and not by sight" (2 Cor 5:6–7).[20]

Here, Vatican I indicated three ways by which the inquiring mind of one doing theology may reach a limited yet helpful understanding of the meaning of God's revelation. There is, first, the exploration of the analogies or similarities between what scripture and dogma teach and the structures of created reality that we know by study and reflection. Where revelation witnesses to God's redemptive work of rescuing and saving sinners, for example, theology has explored how this is like the actions, known in past societies, by which slaves were given their freedom. A simple but profound similarity given in scripture links Christian baptism with being born into the life of our human family, for pondering the latter leads to insight into the first of the sacraments.

A second path to understanding is to work out the relations that the revealed mysteries have with one another. One can, for instance, connect the three fundamental parts or "articles" of the creed by reference to the Father's creation of a world good in itself but then damaged by sin, to the Son's fundamental restoration of goodness and right order, and to the Holy Spirit's work of inculcating in all people a right relation to the Father–Creator until the Son returns. Vatican II reflected the interconnectedness of the mysteries in its teaching on biblical inspiration, by which divine wisdom takes on written form, which is related by similarity to the mystery of the divine word assuming a human nature by the work of the Holy Spirit.[21] Such theological reflections on the teachings of faith assume that revelation is coherent, so that theology can set forth interior harmonies between different contents of revelation.

Third, theology should take seriously that God's whole revelation is "for us and for our salvation," as the creed says of Christ's first coming. What is revealed is not simply imposed upon unsuspecting human beings from above, for it comes to strike a chord in our human hearts and fulfill our deep yearnings for meaning and wholeness. So theology studies the relation of the revealed mysteries with "the ultimate end of human beings." One theologian alert to this human dimension of faith is St. Thomas Aquinas, who in a striking passage of his *Summa of Theology* worked out how humankind needs to be saved precisely by God's Word becoming incarnate. In five ways the incarnation promotes the human good; in five related ways it takes away evils that diminish human beings.[22] The theological search is thus linked with the more fundamental search of human minds and hearts for freedom and for their own fulfillment in God.

Vatican I's declaration of 1870 sketched three fruitful procedures for the search for meaning in God's word and later dogmas. One is to ponder how revealed truths correlate with each other and with the world and human life as we know them. Coherently with the Council's recommended method, Leo XIII (pope, 1878–1903) issued in 1879 the encyclical *Aeterni Patris* endorsing St. Thomas Aquinas as model and norm of Catholic theological thought, because his works exemplify both the positive interrelation of reason and faith and the concern for an integrated study of doctrine that Vatican I had recommended.[23]

But the everyday work of Catholic theologians in the time between the two Vatican Councils (1870–1960), we have to say realistically, was only rarely marked by the universal quest of wisdom characteristic of St. Thomas. The textbooks of theological instruction used in

Catholic universities and seminaries in the first half of the twentieth century were more influenced by the principles of Melchior Cano
than by Aquinas. Dogmatic theologians were children of their pos-
itivist age, and so they tried above all to amass evidence from the
sources to support the doctrines of divine instruction that they presented in carefully worded theses. Typically, a chapter of a theological
manual of that era began with the precise statement of the church's
most recent teaching on a particular point. Then follow the proofs,
drawn from scripture, tradition, and rational argument to show the
grounds for the doctrine being treated.

What the theological manuals were doing even received official
approval from Pius XII (pope, 1939–58) in three points of his encyclical *Humani generis* (1950). This document first confirmed the close
bond of the Catholic theologian with the teaching authority of the
church. The church's magisterium of its councils, bishops, and the
pope is for those doing theology the "proximate and universal norm
of truth, because Christ entrusted the scriptures and apostolic tradition to this authoritative office for their defense and interpretation."[24]
Theology pursues an understanding of what is believed, but the starting point of its quest is found in the doctrine of the church's living
magisterium.

Second, the preemptive authority of the teaching office did not
mean that in doing theology a person only repeats the contents of
church documents. Pius XII also insisted on immersion in the life-
giving waters of the original sources, for pure speculation is sterile,
while scripture and tradition give fresh vigor to theological work:

> Theologians must always return to the sources of divine reve-
> lation.... Each source of divinely revealed doctrine contains
> so many rich treasures of truth, that they can really never be
> exhausted. Hence it is that theology through the study of its
> sacred sources remains ever fresh; on the other hand, specula-
> tion which neglects a deeper search into the deposit of faith,
> proves sterile, as we know from experience.[25]

In a third point of *Humani generis*, Pius XII then specified the
direction taken by proper theological work in its movement between
the official, authoritative norm of truth and the original sources of

doctrine. The theologian should begin from the present-day teaching of the church and from it he or she goes back to show how this teaching was originally expressed in the language and thought-forms of scripture and then developed in different ages in the teaching of the Fathers, classic theologians, and earlier magisterial documents. The biblical and traditional sources are to be read in accord with what is taught and believed in the theologian's own day. The specific task of the theologian is, therefore, "to point out how the doctrine of the living magisterium is to be found either explicitly or implicitly in the scriptures and in tradition.... For together with the sources of positive theology God has given to his church a living magisterium to elucidate and explain what is contained in the deposit of faith obscurely and implicitly."[26]

Under the direction of Pius XII, Catholic theology practiced a "regressive" method, that is, it moved back from a starting point in present church teaching to find the origins of this teaching in the older, at times more primitive, formulations of the sources. Present-day convictions guide the theologian's quest of the meaning of earlier texts, helping one to find implications perhaps only obscurely present in the sources. The underlying conviction is that the substance of the faith has not changed over time and that theology can show coherence and continuity between earlier formulations and the faith of the church articulated by its teaching authority today.[27]

Looking back at this section on six different models of theological work, we can see in Melchior Cano and in the directives of Pius XII the outlines of "positive theology." This is the phase of drawing out of the sources the doctrines that are held to be true, are defended, and are then further explained. With Pius XII's encyclical, however, the church's magisterium took over the first place among the *loci* (fields) of theology in its positive phase.

Following logically after such research in the sources, the theological quest moves to a reflective or "speculative" phase sketched by Irenaeus and Origen and then concisely sketched by the First Vatican Council. Here the mind seeks further understanding of what one holds in faith, by integrating particular truths into larger schemes of coherence and meaning.

1.2. THEOLOGY IN THE LIGHT OF
THE SECOND VATICAN COUNCIL

The Second Vatican Council of 1962–65 is for present-day Catholic theology an ongoing source of guidance and inspiration.[28] The Council enriched all the sectors of theology, especially with four impulses toward doing theology well. These are (1) the initial call of Pope John XXIII to reformulate the doctrinal heritage so that it might bring good news and salutary benefits to humankind; (2) the Council's fresh presentation both of the theological sources, of tradition and scripture, and of the magisterium of the church; (3) the recognition that theological expositions have to take account of doctrinal changes through the course of history; and (4) the structuring of particular doctrines according to the "hierarchy of truths" under faith in Jesus Christ.

Doctrine Reformulated
to Benefit Human Beings (John XXIII)

The bishops who gathered in Rome for the Second Vatican Council received innovative instructions from Pope John XXIII (pope, 1958–63) in his opening discourse of October 11, 1962. The pope's address exuded optimism about engaging the world saved by Christ. Pope John expressed the church's confident possession of a doctrinal heritage passed down through the ages, especially by its Ecumenical Councils. The bishops should see themselves as stewards of a reality of potential benefit to human beings in all sectors of their lives on earth. Christian teaching, which the Council will set forth in a fresh way, can radiate blessings into the lives of individuals and families, and into the whole of society.

John XXIII's first words at Vatican II are, unfortunately, not found in some English editions of the Council documents, such as the otherwise fine edition edited by Austin Flannery, OP, so it is given as Appendix 1 below. This papal discourse is, in fact, the Council's first great text.

According to John XXIII, the times call for a fresh penetration of the heritage and a leap forward in formulating Catholic doctrine to make it more fruitful in bringing forth sanctity and truly humane living. The Council should rearticulate the treasure that the church bears within itself for the benefit of the whole human family. This is the context of Pope John's famous distinction between the substance of the doctrinal tradition and the changeable ways in which the same teaching is expressed and transmitted: "The deposit of faith is one thing, namely, the truths contained in our venerable teaching, but the manner in which they are formulated is another, always keeping the same meaning and same understanding." As Vatican II opened, this simple contrast came to have an operational relevance, for because of it the Council, through fresh study and deeper penetration of the Catholic heritage, went on to reformulate important parts of the Catholic tradition to make it more beneficial to believers and all people.[29]

John XXIII's call to reformulate the heritage was accepted by Vatican II and came to inspire its sixteen documents on doctrine and church practice. The Council echoed John XXIII's word in its Decree on Ecumenism, which says that Christ calls the church to an ongoing and thorough reformation, including the updating of its teaching, so as to show greater fidelity to revelation and promote unity among Christians (UR 6).

Vatican II's Pastoral Constitution on the Church in the Modern World, *Gaudium et spes* (1965), is the Council's principal statement on human dignity and on the light of Christ as beneficent for human living in the world (see, especially, what GS 10 confesses about Christ). But the encounter between the church and human culture has not always been a happy one. The face that the Catholic Church has shown to the world has at times expressed so much disapproval and censure as to impede the radiation of the saving influence of Christ and his Spirit. Here theologians have to contribute to a suitably contemporary communication of the message of faith. They can do this, because as John XXIII stated when opening the Council, what the church has received as the legacy of Christ and his apostles is one thing, while another thing is the variable manner of formulating this selfsame meaning for the people of a given era (stated also in GS 62).

New Light on Tradition, Scripture, and the Teaching Office (Magisterium)

Vatican II's Constitution on Divine Revelation, *Dei Verbum*, was adopted after numerous revisions on November 18, 1965, three weeks before the Council ended. This dense text treats in chapter 1 (DV 2–6) revelation and faith, by which God enters into loving conversation with human beings and through Christ and in the Holy Spirit draws them into communion of life with himself.[30] Chapter 2 (DV 7–10) explains the communication of revelation through scripture, tradition, and the church's magisterium. The rest of the constitution, chapters 3–6, treats sacred scripture in an ample way, in terms of the Bible's inspiration and interpretation (DV 11–13), the Old Testament (DV 14–17), the New Testament (DV 18–20), and the many-sided contribution that scripture should make to the lives of believers in the church (DV 21–26).

Dei Verbum offers a fresh understanding of the *tradition* given over by Jesus' apostles to the first Christians and then further transmitted in a vital way in the church. In the churches they founded, the apostles announced the good news of the Gospel, and by this they communicated divine gifts to all people. The apostles' ministry included preaching, exemplifying life as Jesus' disciples, and founding the basic institutions of the communities. All this was based on their experience of Jesus, for they handed on what they had heard him say, how he acted, and what they had gained by living in close contact with him (DV 7). The New Testament, made up of books composed in the apostolic churches, shows that just as Jesus had done before them, the apostles probed the scriptures of Israel and drew on them in their instructions on God's plan of salvation that culminated in Jesus.

Thus the apostolic "deposit" or legacy of founding tradition, upon which all Christian theology draws, is more than just a systematic body of doctrines. It comes from Jesus and his Gospel; it entails a way of life in community. The books of the New Testament set down in written form the main themes and norms, but the tradition is more than what is written. Christian theology has a larger reservoir upon which to draw:

> What was handed on by the apostles comprises everything that
> serves to make the people of God live their lives in holiness and
> increase their faith. In this way the church, in her doctrine, life,
> and worship, perpetuates and transmits to every generation all
> that she herself is, all that she believes. (DV 8)

The apostolic heritage is not reducible to a single component. A
Catholic theologian draws on a whole complex of resources for religious living. The meaning of what the apostles transmitted cannot be
articulated all at once, but has to be drawn out gradually over time
by contemplation based on scripture, by study and insight, by lived
experience, and by the preaching of those called to pastoral leadership (DV 8). Because theology's quest for meaning is based on the
apostolic tradition, it is also oriented to the whole life of the church,
where tradition continues as a vital activity. Chapter 3 of this book
will treat the interrelation of tradition and the theological quest more
extensively.

Dei Verbum's teaching on scripture is fairly extensive. The Bible
is, first, the message of salvation in Christ committed to writing by
the apostles and their immediate co-workers (DV 7). But the apostolic
writings have sense only in relation to the word of God first addressed
to Israel, "For whatever was written in former days was written for
our instruction, so that by steadfastness and by the encouragement
of the scriptures we might have hope" (Rom 15:4, cited in DV 14).
Vatican II offers a set of principles of biblical interpretation in DV 12,
giving a sophisticated account of the origin and composition of the
Gospels in DV 19, but what appears most remarkable is the high
evaluation of the biblical books expressed by the Council:

> Since they are inspired by God and committed to writing once
> and for all, they present God's Word in a fixed form, and they
> make the voice of the Holy Spirit resound again in the words of
> the prophets and apostles. Therefore all preaching of the church,
> as indeed the Christian religion itself, should be nourished and
> ruled by sacred scripture. (DV 21; translation by J. Wicks)

With a certain natural sequence, the Council moves from this
global commitment to scripture to speak of the Bible in the life of

the church, for instance, as a permanent foundation of all theological work, with the study of scripture being "the very soul of sacred theology" (DV 24). Chapter 2 below will develop the relationship of theological work to the biblical word of God.

On the church's magisterium, or office of teaching, *Dei Verbum* makes two declarations that relate the teaching office to the revealed Word of God, directly witnessed in tradition and scripture, which those holding this office then serve in a dependent and subordinate manner. Even at the beginning of its treatment of the transmission of revelation, the constitution refers to bishops as succeeding to the teaching office of Christ's apostles "in order that the Gospel might be preserved completely and vitally in the church" (DV 7). The magisterium's service thus is to serve an integral and life-giving work of evangelization.

Chapter 2 of *Dei Verbum*, on the transmission of God's revelation, concludes with a concise paragraph on the magisterium (DV 10), which first refers to God entrusting his written and transmitted word to the whole church, people and pastors, who profess the apostolic faith handed on from the apostles and strive to live it out. Within the church, the magisterium then has a role to play in service of the transmitted word.

> The task of authentically interpreting the written or transmitted Word of God is entrusted solely to the living magisterium of the church, which exercises its authority in the name of Jesus Christ. But this magisterium is not over the word of God, but is in its service, for it teaches only what is transmitted. Its role, by divine mandate and assisted by the Holy Spirit, is to listen devoutly, guard religiously, and faithfully expound the word. All that it proposes as divinely revealed for acceptance in faith is derived from this one deposit of faith. (DV 10)

Official church teaching is thus bound to the written scriptural testimony and the vital ethos that is the church's tradition. The magisterium is less a creative agency within the church than a protective and interpretative ministry dedicated to communicating the original message and meaning given once and for all by the prophets and apostles.

In DV 12, the Council set down guidelines for those who work at "exegesis," that is, a disciplined and methodical interpretation of the biblical books. Biblical studies are seen in the end to contribute to the maturing of the magisterium's grasp of the revealed message and teaching.

> It is the task of exegetes to work according to these rules toward a more accurate understanding and exposition of the meaning of sacred scripture, so that their work, in the phase of preparatory study, might contribute to the maturing of the church's judgment. (DV 12)

Here, for the first time in history, reference is made in a church document to the teaching office being in process and moving from one stage to a more advanced or mature stage. The magisterium has thus spoken about its own work as marked by the passage of history, as its judgments on what to teach undergo a "maturing."

Further on, our chapter 4, on theology and magisterium, will develop more in detail this mutual relationship. For the present, DV 10 makes clear that the magisterium offers to believers, including theologians, an interpretation of God's word. But, because the magisterium first "listens devoutly" to the word and then moves gradually toward a mature judgment, theology has a contribution to make to the teaching office. In this book, Appendix 5 relates how theologians helped prepare Vatican II and then during the Council gave competent assistance to the Council members, the bishops, as they carried out their magisterial work.

Doctrine in History

Vatican II began in 1962 with Pope John XXIII's word about the imperative of doctrinal adaptation and reformulation. In 1965, the Council's decree on priestly formation included a paragraph that resonates with the pope's opening words by, first, insisting on how theologians should commit themselves to focusing on the historical development of doctrines in history and, then, to expressing church teaching in a fresh way for the benefit of their contemporaries.

The far-reaching consequences of this paragraph, *Optatum totius* 16, can be obscured by its inclusion of quite traditional references to theology dealing with the "eternal truths" of revelation. Also, the abundance of perspectives from which to consider doctrine, namely, biblical, patristic, historical, speculative, liturgical, and practical, can distract from the innovative character of the passage. But the paragraph on doctrine is part of a larger chapter on the renewal and restructuring of studies for church ministry. OT 16 looks toward a mode and method of theological teaching that is to differ from preconciliar practice.[31]

Vatican II's main statement on method in systematic theology espouses a genetic and progressive order of consideration resting on the conviction that doctrine has developed in the life of the church. Theology should reflect the gradual development and several adaptations of the church's teaching to new situations. Any given doctrine comes from a certain line of historical development; every doctrine, once understood, should then lead to a meaningful and beneficent dialogue with those who are immersed in an ever-changing set of present social conditions.

> Dogmatic theology should be taught in accord with the following order: biblical themes should have the first place; then students should learn what the Fathers of the Church, both of East and West, have contributed to the faithful transmission and elucidation of the different truths of revelation; the further history of dogma should be traced, with attention to its relation to the broader history of the Church; then, to elucidate as far as possible the mysteries of salvation, the students should learn to examine them more deeply and see their interconnection, in accord with St. Thomas's teaching; they should learn to see the same mysteries present and operative in the liturgical actions and whole life of the Church; finally, they should learn to seek the solutions of human problems in the light of revelation, to apply its eternal truths to the changing conditions of human affairs, and to express them in a language that people of their world can understand.[32]

Thus, scripture gives to the work of systematic theology a fixed basis and anchors its discourse in the testimonies of Moses and the prophets, in Jesus' words and deeds, and in the apostles' transmission of the Gospel. The Fathers of the Church show the modern theologian how the scriptures were fruitfully read in quite different cultural contexts, such as Syria, Hellenistic Alexandria, and the Roman Empire. The Councils issued dogmatic teaching at particular moments in history in response to problems and questions which historical research can ascertain. Thomas Aquinas shows us a reflective understanding of the faith (*intellectus fidei*) making use of concepts and thought forms offered by the best secular wisdom of his day, when Aristotle's works were newly accessible. But theology orients itself ever again to the life of the community — its worship, its testimony, its practice of service amid suffering. Finally, the theological penetration of revelation opens itself to the communication of meanings that are capable of enlightening human life amid the struggles of a given era with its dominant problems and needs.

Theology, in this formulation of Vatican II, is aware of the genesis of the formulations in which it enshrines the meaning it has found in God's word. Theological discourse emerges from a given history. But theology also pivots toward the future, for it is an intermediate stage between the original "sacred page" of biblical narrative and teaching and the contemporary retelling of God's work in history for the well-being of all men and women.

The Hierarchy of Truths

A further contribution of the Second Vatican Council to method in doing theology is in the Decree on Ecumenism, on the practice of ecumenical dialogue (UR 5–12). The decree urges dialogue participants to search for deeper meanings, to use a language intelligible to those of other traditions, and to be sensitive to the interrelations between particular doctrines of the church. The third point is clearly applicable to all theology. The truths of faith and doctrines should not be treated as isolated atoms but as parts of a complex, organic whole.

Catholic belief should be explained more profoundly and precisely, in such a way and in such terms that our separated brothers and sisters can also really understand it.

Moreover, in ecumenical dialogue, Catholic theologians, while holding fast to the teaching of the Church, should join their efforts with those of separated Christians in searching further into the divine mysteries, always with love of the truth, charity, and humility. When comparing doctrines with one another, they should remember that there exists an order or "hierarchy" among the truths making up Catholic teaching, since doctrines vary in their relationship to the foundation of the Christian faith.[33]

One can discover different principles for organizing Christian doctrines in a hierarchical order. The bishop who introduced this idea during Vatican II, Andrea Pangrazio of Gorizia, Italy, attributed a primacy of origin within the hierarchy of truths to the Triune God and the incarnation of the Word, while seeing as dependent and derived the ordinary means of our salvation, such as the sacraments of the earthly church. In the New Testament, the fundamental announcement, the *kerygma,* of Jesus' death and resurrection (1 Cor 15:3–4; Acts 2:22–24, 36) is of first importance in preaching and belief. Scripture also speaks of the "great commandment," which must pervade the believer's practice of obedience to God in all other parts of life (Matt 22:34–40).

Different hierarchical orders can be constructed that show the organic character of what God has revealed. The point is to treat particular truths so as to show them complementing, supporting, and illuminating one another in meaningful ways. Good theological teaching fosters appreciation for the inherent order between all that faith lays hold of and professes.

1.3. THE TWO PHASES OF THEOLOGICAL METHOD

Stepping back from our six historical examples (section 1.1) and from the four orientations given by Vatican II (section 1.2), we can now mark out the two fundamental activities that make up good theological work.

Sound theology moves like a pendulum between attentive listening and the active intellectual elaboration of the meaning of what one has heard. Theology is rhythmic, as the theologian passes back and forth between (1) consulting the sources out of a desire to lay hold of the message enshrined in them and (2) then explaining constructively and systematically what their witness means both in itself and for the faith and life of believers today.

Theology first probes the communications of God's word, namely, the varied expressions that Melchior Cano called the theological "places." From these, theology draws out testimonies to God's revealed truth about himself and human life. Here the theologian is not primarily introspective, but instead attentive to and receptive of a meaning already given to humankind. Then this phase of ready listening gives way quite naturally, as the pendulum swings, to the more reflective and creative search for further understanding of the testimonies to God's truth and of their significance for human living in the time and place in which theologians carry out their quest.

This fundamental duality in the thought processes of the theologian is not a new discovery, but is traditional and even figures prominently in the classic analysis of theology by the French Dominican Yves Congar (1904–94).[34] Also, the Canadian Jesuit Bernard Lonergan (1904–84) divided theological operations into two basic phases, namely, receptive listening to the tradition and an active construction of patterns of meaning for one's own time.[35] Congar and Lonergan were towering figures in twentieth-century Catholic theology. But our account of theology's basic steps has accents that come from our situation decades after they wrote.

Listening and Explaining in Faith and Theology

Theology is first an attentive listening to the testimonies to the word of God received in faith, especially the faith of the corporate body of the church. Here, following *Optatum totius* of Vatican II, the genesis of belief and teaching is particularly important. But this listening leads to the search for a contemporary explanation that lays hold of the foundations of God's saving work and word and then turns afresh to the issues of living religiously and fostering human well-being in one's own world.

Listening, the first theological act, is in fact the prolongation of a fundamental "hearing the word in faith" (*auditus fidei*), by which one accepts the Christian message and call, because, as St. Paul said, "Faith comes from what is heard, and what is heard comes through the word of Christ" (Rom 10:17). Prior to theology, lived religiosity is, first, the listening of a heart that yearns for a word of grace and redemption, so that a new future may be opened. The Gospel of Christ is in fact a word of meaning and hope graciously given to faith. In one who comes to belief, theology is then a further phase of listening, by which one attends to the full range of testimonies concerning that message in the community of faith.

Theology extends the "hearing of faith" by attending to the genesis of the good news of the Gospel, to its variant forms in history, and to its many implications for the lives of individuals and families. Theology, deeply rooted in the texts of scripture and the living tradition of Christian community, seeks a thoughtful taking to heart of the revelation of God mediated to us by the prophets of Israel, the apostles of Jesus, and those who have come after them in the family of faith. This "positive" moment in theology is the gaining of information, the assembling of meanings and doctrines formulated by the key witnesses, and an encounter with others who have professed their faith and sought to live out its truth.

Then the theological quest shifts to a search for insight into what has been heard. One moves on toward an ordered or systematic account and a pertinent application of what was heard from the privileged witnesses. Avery Dulles calls a theological system "an original construal of the meaning of Christianity," and goes on to describe this phase of theological work: "Faithful to the data of scripture and tradition, as well as to all that is known from other sources, the systematician integrates all these manifold elements by means of certain overarching principles into a complex and unified whole."[36]

Here Christian theology is also a prolongation of faith, namely, of the basic meaning affirmed in the Christian creed. For there is a primordial structure of coherence in confessing God as Creator, as crucified and risen Savior for us and for our salvation, and as the Spirit of sanctification now at work in human lives in our world.

The faith of the church, made one's own at the pivotal moment of "hearing in faith," is not a disjointed mass of particulars, but a complex of good news and doctrines that have their own sense and structure. Theology then prolongs this basic apprehension of meaning in a new, more ordered, and more intense phase. Theology extends the "understanding of the faith" (*intellectus fidei*) already given in the creed by laying bare the foundations of the message, of the act of faith, and of such a profession in one's world. Theology drives on toward the solution of problems that emerge when one reflects critically on the contents accepted in faith. Theology searches out keys of systematic connections found amid the varied testimonies to the faith. Theology, above all, works incessantly to set forth the contributions that the Christian message and its doctrinal implications can make to sane and sanctified living in the world and society.

To do theology, thus, is first to listen attentively to testimony and then to reflect on the word of revelation in a search for further understanding. It is this, because faith is first the hearing of a message of good news and a profession of belief in the work of Father, Son, and Holy Spirit. Faith itself opens upon a work, by God's Spirit, to increase in believers wisdom and insight into God's ways, as we read in Ephesians 1:15–19. The theological quest is a human way to affirm and further that work of grace.[37]

1.4. THE ELEMENTS OF A COMPLETE THEOLOGICAL METHOD

Because the positive, or listening, phase of theological work engages one with the witness of scripture and tradition, where we find considerable variety in the understanding of God's word and of the life of faith, this account of doing theology will explain in some detail the primary theological sources and the steps in a sound methodological use of them. Thus the following chapter will explain in considerable detail the biblical word to which the theologian listens and works to understand (chapter 2). The next chapter will then work out the meaning of the tradition that continually nourishes the theological quest with testimonies and articulated accounts of meaning (chapter 3).

A further section will treat the relation of theological searching to the Catholic community of faith, in which the teaching office or magisterium of the church has a special role (chapter 4). Then we turn to the relation between doing theology and the theologian's personal experience in faith and lived relation with a given environment in the church and the world (chapter 5).

An adequate method of doing theology must take account of numerous sources, norms, and challenges from the theologian's situation. The intellectual task of receptive, attentive listening and then of constructive explanation is not easy, but the ample range and fascinating variety of biblical and traditional testimonies, with their many contributions to sane and holy living, make the effort more than worthwhile.

Review Questions

1. What can be gained by the study of how others did theology in earlier Christian eras?

2. How did Irenaeus and Origen differ in their ways of doing theology?

3. How did Martin Luther and Melchior Cano differ in the ways they proposed for doing theology?

4. What three approaches did Vatican I propose for theology in its search for meaning in God's revealed mysteries?

5. In Pope Pius XII's instruction (1950), what three activities make up doing theology rightly?

6. In 1962, what did Pope John XXIII set before the members of Vatican Council II as their main tasks as teachers of Catholic faith and life?

7. According to Vatican II, how is "tradition" more than a body of fixed teachings?

8. Explain Vatican II's "genetic" order of theological exploration and explanation.

9. What does Vatican II mean by the "hierarchy of truths"?

10. Explain briefly the two fundamental activities in doing theology, bringing out why listening comes first and what kind of explaining then follows.

Projects for Further Study

- Working from the entries on "Gnosis" and "Irenaeus and Revelation" in *Dictionary of Fundamental Theology*, explain the main issues that were argued between Irenaeus and the adversaries whom he branded as heretics.

- Study some works on Luther and by him, as indicated in notes 11–16 of this chapter. Explain three positive contributions that Luther can make to doing theology today.

- Study Pope John XXIII's opening address at Vatican Council II, given in Appendix 1 below. How does his outlook on the modern world differ from that of Vatican Council I (Appendix 4)? Why does Pope John not agree with certain "prophets of gloom" (Address, no. 14)? What follows from the magisterium being "predominantly pastoral in character" (no. 25)? What does the church, in John's vision, offer to human beings (nos. 28–30)?

- From study about Vatican Council II, for example, in Pope Paul VI's addresses in Appendices 2 and 3 below and in works mentioned in note 28 of this chapter, work out an ordered presentation of what the Council contributed to Catholic life and theology.

- Based on study of Vatican II, as in the previous project, name and explain what contributions of the Council you see as having particular relevance in the present day.

Chapter Two

Doing Theology by Listening
to the Biblical Word

A PERSON DOING CHRISTIAN THEOLOGY is first a believer who
shares in the vision and hope transmitted by the church's faith.
This faith brings with it a special relationship to the books of scripture collected in the Bible. Along with other believers, the theologian
looks to the Bible as a source of instruction, spiritual nourishment,
and ever-renewed guidance in life.

The Catholic liturgy expresses well the church's esteem for the
scriptures, for example, when the book of biblical readings is raised
aloft and carried in procession. At solemn mass the book of Gospel
readings is venerated amid clouds of incense, and in every liturgy the
reader bows to kiss the page of the Gospel passage proclaimed to
the people. At Ecumenical Councils, each day of deliberations begins
with placing in plain sight of the members a book of the biblical
Gospels, which is left open during the day's session. When a man is
ordained as a Catholic bishop, the rite includes a prayer said over him
while his head is covered by an open book of the Gospels. The Second
Vatican Council compared the church's veneration of the scriptures
with her veneration of the eucharistic Body of Christ. For the church
regards the Bible as a "supreme norm" of her faith (DV 21).

This esteem for the Bible rests on a fundamental conviction of
faith, namely, that God inspired the biblical books. We believe in
the Holy Spirit, "who spoke through the prophets" (Nicene Creed).
The biblical writers were believers to whom God gave a special gift,
a charism, by which he inspired them as they formulated the narratives, announcements, and instructions of the emissaries who brought
God's word. Scripture sets before its readers the lived and spoken
testimonies of Moses and the prophets, of Jesus and his apostles.

Its "charismatic" origin makes the Bible a wellspring from which believers draw refreshment with confidence. From these convictions, Vatican II drew this conclusion:

> Therefore all preaching of the Church, as indeed the Christian religion itself, should be nourished and ruled by sacred scripture. For in the sacred books the Father in heaven comes lovingly to his children and converses with them. The energy and power of the Word of God is such that it provides the Church with support and vigor, and gives the children of the Church strength of faith, food for their souls, and a pure and lasting source of the spiritual life.[1]

THEOLOGY AND THE BIBLE

For one doing Christian theology scripture is the primary and essential territory for exploration. Scripture conveys a message that contributes daily to the theologian's imagination and reflective consideration. Doing theology, as an activity of clarifying meaning, further explaining, and arguing for what one sees, entails attentive listening to the instruction coming from the prophets and apostles. Through the Bible, the theologian learns from the teachers of Israel, like the Deuteronomist and the author who wrote during the Babylonian exile the "Book of Consolation of Israel" (Isa 40–55), from Jesus as his words and deeds were set down by Matthew, Mark, and Luke, and from the gifted apostolic theologians Paul and John. At times, doing theology revives memories of biblical words and themes fallen into oblivion, doing what the author of 2 Peter laid out as needed instruction to a community in turmoil: "I am trying to arouse your sincere intention by reminding you that you should remember the words spoken in the past by the holy prophets, and the commandment of the Lord and Savior spoken through your apostles" (2 Pet 3:1–2).

The writer of these words, a minister of the word serving a particular church toward the end of the apostolic age, wanted the people to freshen their memory of what the prophets had announced, what Jesus had pronounced as his commandment, and what the apostles had proclaimed and transmitted about Christ the Savior. Here is a perennial model of theological activity.

Also toward the end of the apostolic age, another writer, one standing in the Pauline tradition, addressed a pastor of a local community about the force and power of the biblical word. That pastor, Timothy, had been well formed by Israel's scriptures. Now, to carry out his ministry well, he should be ever again putting down personal roots in the same biblical sources, since they shape a godly life: "You have known the sacred writings that are able to instruct you for salvation through faith in Christ Jesus. All scripture is inspired by God and is useful for teaching, for reproof, for correction, and for training in righteousness, so that everyone who belongs to God may be proficient, equipped for every good work" (2 Tim 3:15–17).

Here the writer of 2 Timothy lays down a rule valid for every Christian age, briefly asserting that the scriptures are inspired sources of wisdom, instruction, and personal formation for life. The rest of this chapter will treat, in three steps, aspects of the Bible that are of particular relevance in doing theology. The Bible is the Christian *canonical,* and so normative, collection of testimonies to realities grasped in faith (section 2.1 below). The Bible is an *inspired* work of true witness, composed under the influence of the Holy Spirit (2.2). But the canonical and inspired Bible requires certain *interpretive operations* to rightly draw out its message for the believer and community of faith (2.3). These elements make up a theological account of the Bible: as a collection of books defined by the canon and having foundational authority; as a source of inspired formulations written under the influence of a special gift of the Holy Spirit; and as conveying a message to be retrieved today by procedures adapted to such a canonical and inspired collection.

2.1. THE CANONICAL SCRIPTURES AND THEOLOGY

St. Paul wrote in large letters in Galatians 6:14–16 about the "rule" (in the original Greek, the *kanon*) of those living under God's peace and mercy: the cross of Christ, freedom from the legal requirement of circumcision, and being a new creation in Christ and his Spirit.

This "canon" comprises what is normative for Christian thinking, discourse, and behavior. Later, as Christian vocabulary developed in patristic times, the term "canon" came to stand for the official list of the books of scripture that give testimony to God's revelation. The books of the biblical canon are, therefore, a normative source for theology in its effort to articulate what has been received in faith by the church.[2] The Greek word *kanon* refers to a stiff rod used by an artisan to make sure he has assembled his building materials in a level or straight manner. In the transferred sense, a canon is a standard by which one judges correct thinking or teaching. For art and literature, Hellenistic scholars around AD 200 were drawing up lists of those ancient works of sculpture, history, oratory, and poetry of such recognized qualities of style that they have "canonical" status as models. In the Christian church, at the same time, the list of its canonical books of scripture was being gradually worked out.

Canon and Canonicity

The term "canon" in reference to the church's scriptures conveys two overlapping meanings. St. Athanasius, bishop of Alexandria (AD 296–373) wrote in 351 that a book called *The Shepherd* by Hermas "is not in the canon."[3] The same writer's Festal Letter of the year 367 to the churches of Egypt catalogues the books of both the Old and New Testaments that the church receives and venerates as being of divine origin. These "canonized" books are a complete and closed set, outside of which are "apocryphal" books lacking official standing.[4] Thus the canon is the complete list of the sacred books constituting the Bible of the church, as is given today in the table of contents of our published translations of the Bible.

However, a different shade of meaning, having deeper relevance for theology, appears when Christians speak of "the canonical scriptures." St. Thomas Aquinas said that theology uses the scriptures as its proper source of data, arguments, and proof. The reason is that "our faith is based on the revelation made to the Apostles and Prophets, who composed the canonical scriptures."[5] Thus the books of the canon are authoritative in theological work, because in them chosen spokesmen for God still address us.

St. Augustine venerated the books now termed "canonical" so much that he firmly believed that none of their authors had ever swerved in the least away from the truth.[6] In Book II of *De doctrina christiana* (*On Christian Doctrine*), written in 428, Augustine listed the canonical scriptures of the churches and then added his judgment that these works provide quite sufficient guidance and nourishment for the whole Christian life of faith, hope, and charity. He then added:

> In all these books those who fear God and are meek in their devotion seek the will of God. The first care of this task and endeavor, as I have said, is to know these books. Although we may not understand them, nevertheless, by reading them we can memorize them or become somewhat acquainted with them. Then, those things which are clearly asserted in them as rules, governing either life or belief, should be studied more intelligently and more attentively. The more anyone learns about these, the more capable of discernment he is. For, among those things which have been clearly expressed in scripture, we discover all those that involve faith and the rules of living, namely, hope and charity.[7]

Therefore the canon of scripture is, first, the complete enumeration of those books that the church officially receives from "the prophets and apostles" as part of its foundation. But as canonical, these books then serve as norm or standard of what is proper and legitimate in communicating revealed truth and in shaping Christian lives.

The fact that a book is canonical is, however, not simply identical with its *inspiration,* which the next section will treat. Faith acknowledges the canonical books as inspired, but this does not exclude the possibility that other writings, not now recognized as canonical, could well have been composed under the Spirit's charismatic assistance.

Furthermore, inclusion in the canon does not determine the literary *authenticity* of a book, that is, its historical composition by the person commonly named in our Bibles as author of the work. The canonicity of a biblical work is quite compatible with the work being *pseudonymous* in origin. For example, the New Testament Epistles to Timothy and Titus are canonical and so are guaranteed to convey valid apostolic traditions of doctrine and church order. But the canonical status of these letters does not rule out the likelihood that they were written, not by the apostle Paul, but by a Christian teacher who reformulated Pauline tradition for a somewhat new situation perhaps a quarter century after St. Paul was martyred in Rome around the year AD 68.

But "canonicity" designates the biblical books as primarily authoritative in the witness they give to God's revelation of himself and of the holy and humane life made possible by the saving work to which the books testify.

The Christian Old Testament Canon

Christian theological work, in listening to the biblical texts, moves from anticipations to fuller realities and from God's promises given to Israel to their fulfillment by the coming of Jesus and of his Spirit. Israel knew God's ways with humankind through the books of the Hebrew scriptures, but these are for Christians an essential pedagogy in faith. In treating biblical themes, theology will repeatedly go back to hear Moses and the prophets, the psalmist and the wisdom writers of Israel. A recent work states this well:

> Faithful interpretation of scripture requires an engagement with the entire narrative: the New Testament cannot be rightly understood apart from the Old, nor can the Old be rightly understood apart from the New.... Our interpretation of Jesus must return repeatedly to the Old Testament to situate him in direct continuity with Israel's hopes and Israel's understanding of God.[8]

Although Jesus and his apostles were deeply formed by the laws, narratives, psalms, and wisdom teaching of Israel's scriptures, a slow development had to unfold before a final list of the Christian Old Testament books was established. But early Christians sensed the canonicity, or authoritative character, of their biblical inheritance from Israel well before the exact limits of that heritage were settled and Christians agreed on a canonical list of the Old Testament books.

The complex history of the Christian reception of Israel's scriptures has been studied and debated from a variety of perspectives by scholars.[9] Here, where our interest is the relevance of the Old Testament for one doing Christian theology, we recall how Jesus' teaching was a striking reinterpretation of the scriptures of Israel. In the Gospel of Luke Jesus begins his teaching, on a Sabbath in the synagogue of Nazareth, with the astounding claim that Isaiah 61:1–2 is being fulfilled by what he is saying and doing (Luke 4:16–21). Coherent with this beginning, in a memorable later scene the risen Jesus begins with Moses and all the prophets to show how his person and work had been foreshadowed by them (Luke 24:27). Jesus' final gift is to open his disciples' minds to understand the scriptures (Luke 24:45).

Christian theology, as it searches the scriptures today, is at one, not only with Jesus and his immediate disciples, but as well with the first Christian theologians of the apostolic church. Much of their instruction, now formulated in the New Testament, grew and took shape as they reread the scriptures of Israel in the light of Christ. For them, Jesus himself was the key to understanding a precious written heritage. Their research was sketched in Acts in Paul's final discourse, made before King Agrippa to refute the charge that his teaching was an illegitimate innovation departing from the faith of Israel:

> [I] declared first to those in Damascus, then in Jerusalem and throughout the countryside of Judea, and also to the Gentiles, that they should repent and turn to God and do deeds consistent with repentance. For this reason the Jews seized me in the temple and tried to kill me. To this day I have had help from God, and so I stand here testifying to both small and great, saying nothing but what the prophets and Moses said would take place: that the Messiah must suffer, and that, by being the first to rise from the dead, he would proclaim light both to our people and to the Gentiles. (Acts 26:20–22)

This text suggests how the earliest Christian theologians worked, namely, by probing every nook and cranny of the books of Moses and the prophets, to find there the foreshadowing of the messianic events and of the grace of the risen Christ offered to Jew and Gentile alike. The first theology of the Christian community is precisely the doctrine of Christ and salvation worked out on the basis of insights into the texts and further implications of the scriptures of Israel. But, sad to say, many in Israel did not accept the apostolic Gospel and earliest Christian rereading of Moses and the prophets.

Within the early church, a development of major significance was the sharp reaction of second-century Christians against the doctrine of Marcion of Sinope in Pontus.[10] Marcion's movement began in the middle third of the second century AD, and continued to spread after Marcion's expulsion from the church of Rome in the year 144. Marcion created a furor by contesting the relevance for Christians of the scriptures of Israel, because they told, not of the merciful Father of Jesus, but of a God of law ever ready to impose punishment upon his disobedient creatures.

In reaction to Marcion, the second- and third-century Christian writers Justin Martyr, Irenaeus, Tertullian, and Origen mounted a major campaign of argument and instruction in defense of the Old Testament as indispensable for Christians.[11] Thus, in postapostolic Christian doctrine, a significant early component was the reaffirmation of the value of the scriptures of Israel. Those books contain a wealth of instruction on the single plan of salvation being carried out by the God who is both Lord of Israel and the Father of Jesus Christ. A perennial characteristic of Christian theology is this anti-Marcionite orientation, by which one step in doing theology is to trace Christian themes and convictions back to their origins in the faith of Israel, God's first covenant people.

The still disputed question about the actual number of books in the Christian Old Testament regards the status of certain books that were contained in the Septuagint Greek translation of Israel's Bible (for Jews living in the Greek-speaking diaspora), but in time were not included in the Jewish canon of sacred books: Tobit, Judith, 1–2 Maccabees, Wisdom, Sirach, Baruch, and parts of Daniel (3:25–90, chapters 13–14). These works are now called *deuterocanonical* in Catholic parlance, but are listed among the *apocrypha*, or noncanonical books, by most Protestants. For Christianity in late antiquity and the Middle Ages, the influence of St. Augustine, combined with that of the church of Rome, assured the inclusion of the deuterocanonical books in the canon of most all churches.

In the sixteenth century, early Protestants contested the authority of the deuterocanonical books as sources of Christian doctrine. But, after Catholic theologians argued for their standing as scripture, the Council of Trent declared, on April 8, 1546, the formal acceptance of the deuterocanonical books as inspired and normative books of the Christian Old Testament.[12]

Thus, Catholic theology works with the more inclusive canon, accepting several books that were in the Septuagint Greek version of Israel's scriptures, but not in the Hebrew version adopted for synagogue use in reconstituted Israel (ca. AD 100–150). Catholics accept the witness given to revelation and Israelite faith even in the first century before Christ when 1–2 Maccabees and the book of Wisdom were composed and included in the Septuagint, the version widely used by New Testament writers, who composed their Epistles and Gospels in Greek.

The New Testament Canon

The official list of Christian apostolic writings, the Gospels and Epistles, was formulated over time through a gradual sifting and selection from a larger body of early Christian books in circulation. Numerous parts of this process remain historically obscure, as do many of the criteria applied in judgments assessing particular books as belonging or not to a body of apostolic writings. By the year AD 200, however, the process was well advanced, but still another century and a half had to pass before the New Testament canon had the exact form that Christians know today.

Two controversies of the later second century stimulated a move toward greater precision concerning a New Testament canon. Marcion's radical notion of salvation by the pure grace of Christ led him to establish a small canon of Christian instruction, consisting of only ten letters of Paul and a version of Luke's Gospel purified of all references to the God of Moses.

But the second-century "gnostic" groups moved in a direction opposed to Marcion.[13] Their teachers, claiming to have instructions transmitted from secret meetings with the Risen Jesus, were prolific in producing new gospels and letters purporting to contain Jesus' teaching and the instruction of his apostles.[14]

But teachers working in major churches, among whom Irenaeus of Lyons stands out, subjected both the Marcionite and gnostic positions to withering criticism and thereby created the basis for a Christian New Testament canon. This would include more than what Marcion admitted, while it stamped as spurious the gospels and other works of the gnostic masters. Striking documentation of Christian canon formation, probably from the late second century, is given by the Muratorian Fragment.[15] The text, in all likelihood, served to introduce the books of the New Testament as used in Rome around AD 200. It presents as normative just four Gospels, the Acts of the Apostles, and thirteen Pauline and three other apostolic letters. John's Apocalypse is canonical, but beside it the Fragment also lists an *Apocalypse of Peter,* which, however, some are said to judge inappropriate for reading in church. But no mention is made of the letter to the Hebrews, nor of 1–2 Peter, James, and 3 John. The Fragment expresses strong convictions about excluding from Christian usage letters infected with Marcion's ideas and certain unnamed works of the gnostic masters.

The author of the Fragment recommends for private reading by individuals *The Shepherd* by Hermas, while he denies it a place in liturgical readings. This document shows that by AD 200, at least in the local church where the Fragment was composed, a strong sense of having an apostolic patrimony of books was present. Here definite criteria were being applied in order to show two things: (1) the canonical standing of Christian works received as fundamental for the life of the whole church, and (2) the rejection of works seen as falsifying the identity of God and the meaning of Jesus.

From centers such as the one that produced the Muratorian listing or canon numerous other churches gradually reached clarity about the set of apostolic books that express the Gospel message and fundamental Christian teaching. The earliest extant New Testament canon conformed to later Christian usage is in St. Athanasius's Festal Letter of 367, which imposed uniformity on the lectionaries of the Egyptian churches and ruled out the reading of gnostic gospels and apocalypses. The Western canons of synods held at Hippo (393) and Carthage (397), along with that of Pope Innocent I (405), agreed with Athanasius in listing twenty-seven books, which together and exclusively make up the New Testament of the Christian churches.

Canon and Church

The canon of scripture serves to identify and delimit for believers, and for those who do theology in the community of faith, a set of works received and read as "word of God," that is, as conveying in written form the witness given by chosen mediators to what God has communicated about himself and his saving work in history. Scripture evolves from what Moses wrote on Sinai (Exod 34:28), what Yahweh's prophets were sent to proclaim (Amos 7:15; Isa 6:9–13), and what the disciples of Jesus heard, saw, remembered, and recounted concerning the Word of life (1 John 1:1–3).

Theological reflection on a closed and normative biblical canon occurs in two ways: first, working out the relationship between canon and church, and, second, clarifying the contribution of the canon to interpreting the biblical books. We take up the first topic now, reserving the second topic for treatment in section 2.3 below.

From a sociological viewpoint, canon formation is a step toward standardizing the church's doctrine and stabilizing community norms. The canon draws a precise borderline around a body of literature expressing the identity that the Christian community has been given in its historical foundation. This restrictive effect, however, is only one side of canon formation. For the canon also serves to identify for believers those works assumed to be truthful and instructive, with power to instill vitality and a lifestyle conformed to the community's vision of itself. The canonical scriptures are, therefore, an indispensable means by which "the Church, in her doctrine, life, and worship, perpetuates and transmits to every generation all that she herself is, all that she believes" (DV 8).

The canon of the New Testament recognizes that certain books faithfully express "the faith that was once for all entrusted to the saints" (Jude 3). Third-century believers articulated with increasing precision the outer limits of this apostolic transmission, as they marked the historical point at which the founding communication to the churches by the apostles and their immediate co-workers came to an end. The Christian Old Testament canon emerged from an analogous process of recognition of those works that fit harmoniously into the life, teaching, and worship deriving from Jesus the Christ and his apostles.[16]

What stands out in this early development is that church-people of the early patristic age, from the second through the fourth centuries, knew well the ways in which their faith and life had taken shape. They consequently took great pains to be in close contact with the events, teachings, and personages of Christianity in its foundational era, *through* the apostolic documents transmitted to them, in which they heard the fundamental witness to Jesus and his work along with reliable instruction on a life worthy of the Gospel.

The biblical books listed in the canon remain canonical for the church in every age, and they set basic parameters for the biblical phase of attentive listening in theological work. The documents of the full canon also link the church with Moses and the prophets, and they contribute to making the church "apostolic," as the creed professes that it is and will remain. Today, because of this canonicity "it follows that all the preaching of the church, as indeed the entire Christian religion, should be nourished and ruled by sacred scripture" (DV 21).

2.2. THE INSPIRED WORD

A fundamental tenet of Christian faith is that the Holy Spirit "spoke through the prophets" (Nicene Creed) and that all the biblical books are "inspired by God" (2 Tim 3:16). For believers, both personally and as they do theology, the books of scripture are like no other books. A conviction of faith is that their texts were set down as the result of a special interaction between the Holy Spirit, giving charismatic guidance, and the authors or author as they or he composed the books. While the biblical books are genuine expressions in human language of preaching and historical interpretation, of poetic prayer and doctrinal instruction, they are as well, by inspiration, authentic vehicles of God's communication to humankind.

Inspiration does not mean that we always find inspiring narratives or heart-warming poetry in the Bible, but instead that it presents us with a trustworthy and convincing record of God's loving-kindness in dealing with his creatures. The Bible itself stems from God's "condescension," in loving adaptation to our human limitations, by which his word has taken form — for us and for our salvation — in ancient

Israel's record of its covenant and in the apostles' varied documentation of their encounter with God's servant and Son, Jesus. God's biblical address does not confront us with the luminous brilliance of divine truth and glory, but in the more accessible, even more earthy, truth of a set of books remarkable for their human multiplicity and variety.[17]

Inspiration as a Charism of Communication

Christian belief in biblical inspiration is one articulation of a more global sense of the sacred character of the Israelite and Christian religious writings.[18] Faith in biblical inspiration was a quite natural part of the life and outlook of the first Christian communities. It was taken for granted as part of the heritage coming from Israel, and so the New Testament books allude to inspiration, rather than demonstrate or explain it, for example, in 2 Peter 1:21 and 2 Timothy 3:15–17.[19] The context that helps us understand this assumption comes out in Paul's vision of a typical community of believers as graced with numerous spiritual gifts or charisms that empower members to serve the common good of all. Here is an obvious setting for the charism of those who write inspired texts.

> There are varieties of gifts, but the same Spirit.... To each is given the manifestation of the Spirit for the common good. To one is given through the Spirit the utterance of wisdom, and to another the utterance of knowledge according to the same Spirit, to another faith by the same Spirit, to another gifts of healing by the one Spirit, to another the working of miracles, to another prophecy, to another the discernment of spirits, to another various kinds of tongues, to another the interpretation of tongues. All these are activated by one and the same Spirit, who allots to each one individually just as the Spirit chooses.
>
> (1 Cor 12:4, 7–11)

By these gifts individuals are marked out and empowered for special service in the church, whether as apostles, prophets, teachers, healers, or leaders (12:28–30). A later apostolic writer, one well schooled in Paul's ideas, also spoke of these gifts of service, seeing them as having been poured out by the exalted Christ upon his ecclesial body. But this writer also made a suggestive addition to the list of ministries.

> But each of us was given grace according to the measure of Christ's gift.... The gifts he gave were that some would be apostles, some prophets, some *evangelists,* some pastors and teachers, to equip the saints for the work of ministry, for building up the body of Christ. (Eph 4:7, 11–12, emphasis added)

The reference to "evangelists" probably indicates the missionary preachers of the late apostolic age. But for us who know well the Gospel writings that were being drawn up at that very time, the term naturally suggests as well the persons who were serving the church by fixing in written form the traditions, up to then handed down orally, about Jesus in the Gospels, that is, documents which relate to their hearers and readers "the Gospel [*euangelion*] of Jesus Christ" (Mark 1:1).

Within the context of the spiritual gifts, described in 1 Corinthians 12, biblical inspiration would be the special charism that enables and animates good communication, given to one serving the community of faith by writing, so that the Gospel preached and a portion of the tradition that is the basis of that community's faith and life might be given fixed and stable form in a written text. This theology of inspiration looks first to the apostolic gift or charism that underlies the work of New Testament letter writers and Gospel composers. By their spiritual gift, the texts that they wrote can serve in every subsequent age as valid instruction, sound nourishment, and authentic guidance of Christian believers. By analogy, a similar work of the Spirit graced the written expressions of Israel's faith and law of life, its prayer and wisdom, all through the life of the first covenant people down to the coming of Jesus.

Inspiration and Patristic Interpretation

Faith in biblical inspiration was in peaceful possession among practically all Christians down to the nineteenth century, and the belief had consequences for their scriptural reading and interpretation. The great patristic interpreters read the Old Testament in line with Paul's certainty that "whatever was written in former days was written for our instruction, so that by steadfastness and by the encouragement of the scriptures we might have hope" (Rom 15:4). The Fathers found in Israel's scriptures much prophecy, in accord with the allusion of 1 Peter to the Spirit of Christ testifying interiorly and in advance "to the sufferings destined for Christ and the subsequent glory" (1 Pet 1:11).

Chapter 1 related how the third-century Alexandrian theologian Origen took inspiration as the basis of his investigation of spiritual meanings lying beneath the surface of narrative in the biblical books. A disciple of Origen in the West was St. Ambrose, the bishop of Milan (340–97), who followed Origen by giving a spiritual, allegorical, interpretation of the story of the Good Samaritan told by Jesus in Luke 10:30–35. The man going down from Jerusalem to Jericho is humankind expelled from paradise, who is beset by evil spirits who strip him of heavenly grace and inflict dire wounds on him. But the Samaritan who came down was Christ the Son of Man, who brought with himself numerous medicines. In the inn of the church the fallen creature will be restored to health until his kindly benefactor returns.[20]

The methods adopted by Fathers like Origen and Ambrose are not models to follow today in interpreting scripture, as will become clear in section 2.3 below. But they do serve to show the early Christian depth of conviction about the inspiration of the biblical books. In their interpretation, many parts of the Bible can well be related to other parts, to underscore Christian teaching. The Bible is fundamentally one book, since the whole collection comes from one and the same inspiring Spirit. Potentially, the overall economy of human salvation can be found expressed in any part of the one Bible. All of it is meant by God's Spirit to be "for us and for our salvation," and so any part can instruct belief and lead to a deeper personal engagement with God's work of our redemption.

Church Affirmations of Biblical Inspiration

The following account of Catholic teaching on biblical inspiration will be a genetic or historical study of the development of doctrine, much as Vatican II's *Optatum totius*, no. 16, recommended more generally for setting forth the results of a theological investigation.[21] This doctrinal development began, in the second half of the nineteenth century, when the work of historical-critical biblical scholars was producing substantial results. In 1883 Julius Wellhausen identified the different source documents that were woven together, long after Moses, to create the first six books of the Old Testament. The prophets were being discovered as the true originators of Israel's monotheism in their polemical preaching aiming to reform abuses in the worship of Israel. Such studies gave little heed to prophetic predictions of Christ. Critical studies of Israel's wisdom literature, like the book of Proverbs, identified what in these books was in fact taken over from earlier works of Egyptian and other ancient pagan literature.

Most Catholics gave little heed to what seemed naturalistic theorizing about the sacred scriptures. But some Catholics did raise questions around 1890 about biblical inspiration, proposing that the Holy Spirit, in inspiring biblical authors, was not concerned with accurate cosmology or history but focused instead on making the Bible the valid and true teaching of the content of belief and moral life. In such a view, much in scripture could be humanly imperfect and even erroneous, while a doctrinal kernel would be inspired and true.

In 1893 Pope Leo XIII issued the first encyclical treating biblical questions.[22] Writing before Catholics became ecumenical, Leo spoke harshly about Protestant scholars who lack the true faith and so never get beneath the outer husk of scripture. Faith in inspiration rules out any and all error in the biblical text rightly understood. Catholic scholars must, according to Leo, devote themselves to showing that further literary analyses, along with historical and archeological studies, can refute charges that scripture is wrong. For it is a basic conviction that the Bible is free of all error, that is, it is "inerrant," which follows from the fact that God by inspiration is the Author of scripture. Thus, inspiration is an influence on the human writers that Pope Leo described as follows:

> By supernatural power, God so moved and impelled them to write — he was so present to them — that the things which he ordered, and those only, they, first, rightly understood, then

willed faithfully to write down, and finally expressed in apt words and with infallible truth. Otherwise it could not be said that God was the author of the entire scripture.[23]

Catholic textbooks throughout the first half of the twentieth century took this text of Leo XIII as the authoritative account of inspiration as a work of the Holy Spirit in the biblical authors. It was cited in 1962 with slight adaptation, along with an account of God as "principal author" using a human organ or instrument in writing scripture, in the first draft of a proposed Vatican II document on the sources of revelation.

But Catholic attitudes toward the Bible changed notably after 1893, especially because of the strong support given to Catholic use of the technical tools of historical-critical biblical interpretation by Pope Pius XII in 1943.[24] This method of interpretation does not of itself undermine faith in inspiration, but the biblical theology resulting from the studies following in the wake of Pius's encyclical did weaken confidence both in Leo XIII's analysis and explanation of inspiration's influence on the faculties of the human author and in the scholastic philosophical theory of the relation between principal and instrumental causes.

Consequently, Vatican II's Constitution on Revelation, which modified notably the 1962 draft on the way to the document promulgated in 1965, makes a forthright affirmation of the work of the Holy Spirit as the one who inspired what is set down in the biblical text. But the Council remains reserved about stating how the Holy Spirit interacts with human authors. To these writers, however, *Dei Verbum* does ascribe the full range of activities characteristic of true authors.

> [The] Church by apostolic faith accepts as sacred and canonical all the books of the Old and New Testaments, with all their parts, because, written under the inspiration of the Holy Spirit (see John 20:31; 2 Tim 3:16; 2 Pet 1:19–21, 3:15–16), they have God as their author and have been handed on as such to the Church. To compose the sacred books, God chose to use the services of individuals who made full use of their faculties and powers, so that, with him acting in them and through them, it

was as true authors that they consigned to writing whatever and only what he wanted written. (DV 11, translated by the author)

The text does not teach that God dictated the words of scripture, but instead indicates that his authority ("authorship") stands behind the text. In a parenthesis the Council lists the New Testament texts grounding its conviction. In the first text, St. John indicated why he wrote his Gospel, suggesting the overall saving purpose of biblical inspiration, namely, "so that you may come to believe that Jesus is the Messiah, the Son of God, and that through believing you may have life in his name" (John 20:31).

Then, *Dei Verbum,* no. 11, reformulates what had been emphasis on the Bible's immunity from error, making a positive statement on the truth of what God, for us and for our salvation, willed to have formulated in the biblical books.

> Since, therefore, all that the inspired writers...declare should be regarded as declared by the Holy Spirit, one must therefore acknowledge that the books of scripture teach — firmly, faithfully and without error — the truth which God, for the sake of our salvation, wished to see composed in the sacred scriptures.

To emphasize even more the positive consequences for believers of the inspiration and truth of the Bible, Vatican II's concise statement then concludes by citing the lines of 2 Timothy (3:16–17), on the spiritual and moral effectiveness of scripture in the work of a pastor and the lives of Christians, as given in the opening pages of this chapter.

The main teaching of Vatican II on inspiration is thus a passage of confident confession of faith about one of the works of the Holy Spirit. By not offering an explanation of just how inspiration has its impact on the biblical writers, the Council respects the mystery of interaction between the Spirit's charism and the activities of these human authors of the texts. The ultimate significance of inspiration is the truth of the Bible, a truth for our salvation. Biblical texts are fully reliable in what they teach about God and his saving work for the human family. The reader of scripture, if he or she is attuned to the inspiring Spirit, will be led by these texts to a greater depth of faith and toward growth in righteousness, being "equipped for every good work," as 2 Timothy asserts.

There is a truth for life and living in the Bible, and so believers come to it with confidence. The shortest path to grasping the nature of the Bible and its truth may well be to see its kinship with the one who claimed, "I *am* the way, and the truth, and the life" (John 14:6). Listening to the Bible, this suggests, informs a person about a "way" to walk, which is a path of living in the light of truth.

But there is more. The listener or reader does not lay hold of the truth offered in the Bible by simply hearing or reading its chapters and verses. This is true for unsophisticated believers as well as for critical scholars and for those trained in doing theology. We lay hold of the saving truth of the Bible's content, message, and way of life by using a set of interpretive operations. An adequate biblical hermeneutic, codifying the procedures of interpretation, has to take account of both the full historical and linguistic humanity of scripture and of its origin in inspiration given by the Holy Spirit. To this we now turn.

2.3. INTERPRETING THE BIBLE

This introduction to interpreting the Bible as a primary step in doing theology has a modest goal. There is no space to survey the numerous interpretive methods applied today in serious study of the Hebrew and Christian scriptures.[25] Here the more limited aim is to state and illustrate the two main efforts that one doing theology has to put into practice in listening methodically to the canonical and inspired scriptures. These are (1) retrieving the distinctive meaning of particular texts, that is, of single books and shorter passages, in their original context of communication between the biblical authors and their initial hearers or readers, and (2) pursuing the potential fruitfulness of the same texts to express a developed meaning in further contexts, as when they become parts of the whole Bible or serve in the life of the church, both of which differ from the original setting in which the authors composed the biblical books.

The aim here is to balance two quite different values that complement each other. Both are necessary, in theory and in practice, for an adequate theological hearing, reading, and study of scripture. Interpretation takes place like a pendulum movement between the exegesis that seeks to recover what the text *originally meant* when first written and an understanding of what the Bible *now means* about what is going on as Father, Son, and Holy Spirit continue to work out the salvation of humans throughout the world.

Underlying this section is the Second Vatican Council's paragraph in *Dei Verbum,* no. 12, on biblical interpretation, which itself begins by subtly pointing toward two controlling principles that should guide a person's theological reading of the books of the Bible.

> Because in holy scripture God has spoken through human beings and in a human manner, it follows that the interpreter of sacred scripture, in order to grasp what God aimed to communicate to us, ought to attentively investigate what the sacred writers meant to convey and God has been pleased to show forth by their words.

This initial orientation points both toward (1) what the authors communicated in the past and (2) what God shows forth now in the text. The text of DV 12 then moves ahead along the lines of the two steps indicated: (1) Interpretation recovers the original meaning of texts in their stylistic peculiarity and historical-cultural setting of the author and his first hearers and readers. (2) Interpretation explores the further meanings attained by "reading in the Spirit," to grasp meaning in a new context of the church with its complete Bible. This distinction legitimates an understanding of the lines cited above as expressing a "both/and" and thereby admitting the possibility that God's communicative intention in a particular case can *both* include *and* go beyond the meaning intended by the biblical writers who served as authors and communicators in Israel and in the apostolic church.

The Retrieval of Original Textual Meanings

Doing theology from the Bible begins with the effort to recover what the author of a text meant to say to the believers for whom the text was originally written. Belief in the inspiration given to the biblical writers strengthens the imperative that the theologian has to regularly devote time to the exegetical study of biblical passages. The same obligation is further confirmed by the church's acceptance of the scriptures, just these texts, as canonical and so of fundamental significance in its own foundation.

Since for Christians these are books like no other books, their original content must be a serious concern in theology. Our listening to and reading of the biblical books entails, first of all, hard work and not inspired intuition. It was the authors' written texts that were inspired by their charism given by the Spirit. To be sure, an interpretation of a biblical book may come in time to have the status of a classic, as in the case of St. Augustine's homiletical treatises on John's Gospel or the exposition of Romans by the Reformed theologian Karl Barth, published in 1922. But even classical commentaries rank below the canonical texts of the church. To the latter we look for nothing less than faithful testimony to God's revelation.

This primacy of exegetical retrieval means that theological work is regularly punctuated by attentive study of *biblical commentaries*. Our primary witnesses to God and his saving economy wrote in ancient languages as people of cultures quite different from our culture today. The strangeness of their idiom and the distance of their setting mean that the theologian of today needs help in grasping what was said in the privileged testimonies to God's revelation.[26]

It is true that by the Christian faith a person has a grasp of the overall plan of the biblical story and of God's revelation, as the creed formulates that plan in its main moments. Systematic theology goes on to further articulate that global structure and may reconfigure its details in fresh ways. But this does not exempt us from attending to the particular texts that underlie the structure of the plan. Abraham's call out of Ur of the Chaldees, the covenant rites at Sinai, the new horizons opened by Isaiah's preaching, and the announcement of God's reign by the words and deeds of Jesus — these particular events and developments have perennial significance in themselves. Consequently theology listens attentively to the particular biblical texts telling of these key moments. And such listening, in theology, involves attending to the detailed exegetical studies that we find in commentaries.

The Bible as a whole is much like a choir that combines many voices. But this image is not completely sufficient, because the canonical collection of texts is not completely homogeneous. Scripture has an abundance of meaning that spills out over our efforts to synthesize it, for example, in a single biblical theology. We need to hear the "soloists," that is, individual voices which the Bible has brought together. The fact that these are many can serve to suggest something of the limitations of present-day theological systems and even of official church teaching. The sheer abundance of biblical testimony suggests that our modern schemes of unifying God's revelation are partial and provisional. Theology gains dynamism and mobility by openness to exegetical results, even at the cost of having at times to dismantle and reconstruct the systematic schemes with which it has long operated.

Sound theological method will thus incorporate the results of scholarly exegesis, for a strong gravitational force draws a person doing theology to particular biblical authors and to specific passages. A fundamental theology of revelation has to treat how God manifested himself in the events listed in the short Israelite creed of Deuteronomy 26:5–11 and in the Gospel passages on the appearances of the risen Christ to his followers. The theologian working out an account of the person and work of Jesus Christ cannot omit an effort to understand the hymn of Philippians 2:6–11, on the humbling and exaltation of Jesus, and to grasp the prologue of John's Gospel, on the Word through whom all things came into being (see John 1:3). A Christian moral theology which does not draw on an exegesis of Jesus' Sermon on the Mount (Matt 5–7) is hardly to be taken seriously.

In key texts like these, individual biblical authors spoke in their own idiom to articulate their faith. Our effort is not guided by the romantic ideal of sharing in some past experience or seeing through the eyes of a past author. The point is not to get inside the skin and head of another believer. The focus instead is on the texts produced by particular authors.

But such key texts are not simply of historical interest as the beginning of a development that reached a provisional end point in a dogma. The texts remain presently relevant as sources on which theology continues to draw. Vatican II said of theology's relation to the biblical text:

> By this word, [theology] is most firmly consolidated and constantly rejuvenated, as it searches in the light of faith to know all the truth stored up in the mystery of Christ. The sacred scriptures contain the word of God and, because they are inspired, are truly that word. So the study of the sacred page should be much like the soul of sacred theology. (DV 24)[27]

Therefore a person doing theology will regularly spend time on issues of biblical vocabulary and the structure of texts, on the ancient genres and their conventions, on the origins of traditions and the interventions during composition by particular biblical authors.[28] The theologian will consult at least some of the best commentaries available and may well study further books or articles treating his or her relevant texts, as such studies are listed in a journal like *New Testament Abstracts*.

But historical-critical analysis of biblical passages is not the only way to grasp the meaning of what Christians believe. Doing theology carries a person beyond original biblical messages to more developed accounts of faith and its meaning. However if the theologian has not listened attentively to individual biblical authors, and if the final results are not coherent with what the texts originally meant, then the theological account must be faulted for not taking seriously the canonical and inspired source of all Christian thinking.

The ideal sketched here is a theology intensely familiar with the foundational literature that served specific purposes in the life of Israel and of the apostolic church. These works of the Bible are privileged witnesses to God's actions at key moments of his economy of human salvation. These works are not organized like our textbooks and they use a language quite different from our own. They are stylized narratives, revelatory preaching, codes of laws and rites, and hymns for use in community worship. But they were written by people who have a deep kinship with believers of today and with those dedicated to the theological search for meaning amid the contents and experiences of belief in God's revelation.

The scriptures were written by people who were attentive to God's presence and call, submissive to his claim over human life, and intent on fostering conversion to the God of Israel and the Father of Jesus Christ. So the inspired and canonical texts of these witnesses have a primary place, and listening to them and studying their literal meaning is a first activity in theology.[29]

Understanding the Bible's Further Meaning

Theology also pursues the potential fruitfulness of biblical texts in expressing more developed meanings in contexts quite different from the original setting of the documents. This way of interpretation complements the first effort to recover what the text originally meant, for it aims in a second step to understand what the Bible means to say now about what continues to unfold as Father, Son, and Holy Spirit work out the salvation of the world. A sound idea of religious texts assumes that they can very well yield a "surplus" meaning beyond what they expressed clearly when they were first written and read. Such further meaning comes to be disclosed when texts are read in a historical context or situation that differs from that of their author and original readers. The potential communication of surplus meaning is a quality of many texts that speak of fundamental human realities.[30] For the Christian theologian, the inspiration of the Bible is a further reason to expect an ongoing textual fruitfulness.

The Second Vatican Council introduced its statement on this further way of considering scripture with a reference to the Holy Spirit's influence on biblical composition and then went on to mention three contexts in which interpretation may well lead to a further understanding of God's revelation.

After speaking of the exegetical effort to retrieve the original meaning of biblical passages, the Council proposed, in a further paragraph of DV 12, another approach that interpretation should take, with "no less attention" than the quest to retrieve the original meaning of the authors, adding this directive:

> However, since sacred scripture must also be read and interpreted in the same Spirit in which it was written, no less attention must be devoted to the content and unity of the whole

of the scripture, along with the living tradition of the whole church, and the analogy of faith.[31]

We follow this text here by first noting two contexts for reading scripture "in the Spirit," namely, (1) the whole canonical collection of both Testaments and (2) the faith of the church.

The following chapters will extend these considerations by speaking of tradition, with special reference to the biblical interpreters of the patristic age (chapter 3, section 2) and by adding another context, namely, the world in which Christians are living and experiencing life (chapter 5). Taking account of each of these further settings can help bring out the communicative potential of biblical texts.

Reading Biblical Passages in the Whole Canon

The canon gives Christians a complete listing of the books given to nourish faith and apply God's word to the circumstances of their lives. The Christian canon has a peculiar shape, first, in linking the books of God's prior covenant with Israel with the apostolic books directly relating to Jesus. This canonical configuration of the Bible is profoundly important for all Christian thinking.

The cross and resurrection of Jesus Christ, together with the universal mission given to his followers, combine to place the earlier experiences of Israel, and the texts of Moses, the prophets, and the psalms, in a new context of fulfillment and of the discovery in them of meanings not seen by earlier readers.

The new framework of understanding and the new inclusiveness do not cut off Christian faith and life from their roots in Israel. In fact, the apostolic generation turned eagerly to the books of Israel's faith and life, precisely to learn more about their new convictions and mission. Integral thinking by Christians, and specifically by theologians, continually draws on the inheritance received from Israel.

Christian teaching moves with a peculiar dynamic from promise to fulfillment and has repeatedly made progress by the recovery and application of forgotten themes of the prior covenant. The two-part Christian canon is relevant for thinking about God's dealings with humankind, while any denigration of the Hebrew scriptures, like Marcion's, is life-threatening for Christian theology and preaching.

The two-part canon opens the way to study of religious and doctrinal development within the Bible. One is invited to be schooled in the biblical pedagogy that carries the mind along various trajectories from promise to fulfillment, from type to antitype, and from limited concerns to universal purposes.[32] One thinks of the new meaning taken on by Isaiah 61:1–2 when it became the leitmotif of Jesus' ministry through its citation in Luke 4:18–19.

The New Testament has its own canonical shape resulting from the juxtaposition of the four Gospels with all the apostolic letters, placing the Acts of the Apostles as a connecting link. Some of the letters, such as 1 Thessalonians, Philippians, Galatians, 1–2 Corinthians, and Romans, were written while the Gospel narratives were still in oral form, while other letters, like 1–2 Timothy and 2 Peter are from the very end of the apostolic age, postdating most of the compositional work of the evangelists.

But the canonical shape of the New Testament expresses something more than chronology, namely, the absolutely foundational role of Jesus presented to us in four versions of the good news of his coming, ministry, passion, death, and resurrection. The apostolic letters then give inspired commentary on Jesus' teaching and work, especially his death and resurrection, as they draw out and apply the meaning of these to believers' lives in the world.

Good theology will often swing like a pendulum between both of these New Testament collections, expecting that they will illuminate each other. To be sure, each of the four evangelists conveys an interpretation of Jesus, as the exegesis of each Gospel brings out. But further significance emerges when we let the two major parts of the New Testament interact and shed light on each other. An example of this is the liturgy of the Good Friday, during which worshipers hear the Epistle to the Hebrews on Jesus the High Priest tested in every way by suffering and so become the source of salvation for all who obey him (Heb 4:14–16, 5:7–9), and then follows the recital of the passion from John 18–19. The passage from the apostolic letter alerts us to deeper meaning in the interrogations of Jesus by Pilate — his testing — and in the moment in which Jesus hands over his spirit (John 19:30).

Reading Biblical Books in the Church

In DV 12, Vatican II stated the interpretive importance of the living tradition of the whole church and the analogy of faith. Our next chapter will treat tradition more at length and will explain the importance of the Eastern and Western Fathers of the Church as commentators who draw out the potentialities of the biblical texts for throwing light on faith and life.

Here we treat a more basic form of biblical interpretation in the church, namely, the reading that relates scripture texts to two central realities of Christian community life. These are the liturgy and the creed's three articles of belief.

When Catholics insist on going beyond "scripture alone" to relate scripture and tradition, the real point is that the Bible should be interpreted in the perspective of faith. Catholic faith includes an explicit commitment to the church's tradition, especially as that is formulated in solemn teaching. But tradition is more than dogma, since it is the living process by which the apostles' message of faith, way of worship, and style of life become present in every age. Thus, tradition is also the community milieu formed by liturgy and spirituality, and to insist that scripture and tradition be held together implies that this lived context has a native congeniality with scripture. The life of the church is a context in which the written biblical text is fruitfully read, understood, and related to life.

The first and most fundamental way one interprets scripture in the church is to relate biblical texts to the structures of the church's worship and profession of belief. Liturgy and creed are settings in which texts become significant in ways going beyond the biblical authors' original interaction with their readers. This does not do violence to the texts, but instead realizes their potential in the ongoing life of later communities that stand in continuity with the communities of the original writing, hearing, and reading.

In liturgy, a basic structure results from the two cycles of the liturgical year that focus on Christmas and Easter. Each year, in the Christmas cycle, the community observes Advent, Christmas, and Epiphany as stages by which "Emmanuel" (God-with-us) entered the world (Matt 1:22) and salvation came near in Jesus as "light of revelation to the Gentiles and glory for your people Israel" (Luke 2:32). The Easter cycle is more ample, stretching from Lent through the commemoration of Jesus' death and resurrection in Holy Week and Easter and then on through the Paschal season to Pentecost, as the church commemorates the great deeds done to free humankind from sin's bondage.

The Christmas and Easter cycles are relevant for biblical interpretation, for they in fact express what faith takes as central in the Bible as a whole. Here, within the elliptical space created by the two focal points of Christ's epiphany and his passover through death to glory, theology can read individual books from the perspective of their center, and see them as a cohesive set of narratives, teaching, and prayers.

The action itself of Christian worship has its own fundamental structures, among which two stand out. Every liturgy has moments of "epiclesis" by which the Spirit is invoked and called down upon believers and the world. This suggests reading the texts with an awareness of the human fragility and sin that have to be overcome by God's healing and renewing Spirit. One way in which the Spirit enters our human space is that of the inspired texts that bear light and solace to a troubled world.

Second, liturgical prayer features the "prayer of blessing," such as Jesus used at meals and the apostles expressed in opening their letters (e.g., 2 Cor 1:3–7; Eph 1:3–10; 1 Pet 1:3–9). Such prayer recites God's gracious deeds, which suggests how the narrative portions of the Bible mean to serve praise and celebration. Further, eucharistic prayer is an ascending movement in which faith gives all honor and glory to the Father, through the Son, in the Spirit. The Bible as sustenance of faith intends ultimately to foster such a movement of the believing heart into communion with the God whom we know as three-personal.

Finally, a reading of scripture in the context of the church takes account of the context given by the three "articles" of the creed. The next chapter on tradition will say more about the three-part baptismal profession of faith. Here we only recall how Christian thinking has its basic order from belief in God the Father, who created heaven and earth, in the only Son, our incarnate Savior, and in their Holy Spirit, sent among us to carry out the saving purposes of Father and Son.

The structure of the creed in three main parts is a basic context of Bible reading, one given to the Christian in the baptismal profession of faith at the moment of his or her entry into the church. The creed provides a framework alerting a reader to main traits in the profile of the God to whom every page of scripture testifies. What faith looks for, as it listens intently to the biblical text, is a more profound sense of this divine identity and a clearer grasp of the path to sharing in his gracious project of saving and sanctifying his creation.

From Meaning to Meaning

Thus, theological work with the Bible, based on its canonical authority and confident about the inspiration of the texts, is an action like the ongoing swing of a pendulum. Theological reading moves from the biblical texts' original sense to the richer meaning they come to have in the perspectives of faith and church life.[33]

The first phase of listening to the canonical and inspired texts is properly exegetical, and this gives a direction to what follows. From the original meaning the quest moves toward hearing and recovering that surplus meaning that texts show forth when they are read in other settings, like the whole canon or the life of the church, which are at some distance from the original actions of the authors' communication to their first hearers and readers. But then the quest also swings back to the original, that is, to the properly inspired meaning expressed when the biblical text was composed as history, instruction, exhortation, and prayer in Israel and the apostolic church.

Review Questions

1. What, briefly, is the biblical canon? What does it mean to say that a biblical book is canonical, having the quality of canonicity?

2. How did Marcion's teaching about the Hebrew scriptures (the Old Testament) have a lasting impact on Christian theology?

3. How was clarifying the biblical canon significant for the early church in its relation to the prophets, Jesus, and the apostles?

4. How does biblical inspiration fit into the variety of spiritual gifts listed by St. Paul?

5. How did belief that scripture is inspired affect the biblical interpretation of Origen, Ambrose, and other Fathers of the Church?

6. How did Pope Leo XIII explain biblical inspiration in 1893, and how then did Vatican Council II differ when it affirmed inspiration?

7. Work out your own definition of biblical inspiration, being sure to connect it with the life of the church.

8. Why does theological interpretation of scripture have to begin with the texts' meaning in the past, that is, with the original author and first readers or hearers?

9. What is meant by reading biblical passages in the whole canon (which joins two Testaments in one Bible and the Gospels and apostles' letters in one New Testament)?

10. How do the principal structures of the liturgical year provide a context for reading biblical texts and finding meaning beyond their original or literal sense?

Projects for Further Study

1. Study the deuterocanonical book of Tobit or the book of Wisdom, chaps. 1–10, and write a report on its special contribution to the overall theological message and teaching of the Bible.

2. Study Jesus' relation to the Old Testament, as found in Matthew 4:1–17 and 5:17–48, in Mark 7, and in Luke 4:16–22 and 24:13–27, and report on it, making use of the notes in the Jerusalem Bible or the New American Bible.

3. In your college library, examine the following works that aid study of the Bible, and write a report briefly describing each, attending to how they can help in doing theology:

   • *The New Jerome Biblical Commentary,* ed. Raymond Brown et al. (1990)

   • A commentary on Mark's Gospel, for example, *The Gospel of Mark* by John R. Donahue and D. J. Harrington, Sacra Pagina series (2002).

- *The Anchor Bible Dictionary,* ed. David N. Freedman, 6 vols. (1992).

- *Dictionary of Biblical Theology,* ed. Xavier Leon-Dufour (1967, 1973).

4. Study Vatican II's chapter on "Sacred Scripture in the Life of the Church" (Appendix 4, pages 184–186 below) and report on the ideal role of the Bible in Christian living, adding a personal account of what Bible reading has done for you or for a relative or acquaintance.

Chapter Three

Doing Theology in the Stream of Catholic Tradition

THE APOSTLE PAUL, in many passages of his letters, is a creative theologian of redemption and new life through Christ and in his Spirit. At times, however, Paul says emphatically that he is not passing on his own teaching, but what he received from others, including the Gospel of salvation itself.

> Now I would remind you, brothers and sisters, of the good news that I proclaimed to you, which you in turn received, in which also you stand, through which also you are being saved, if you hold firmly to the message that I proclaimed to you — unless you have come to believe in vain.
>
> For I handed on to you as of first importance what I in turn had received: that Christ died for our sins in accordance with the scriptures, and that he was buried; and that he was raised on the third day in accordance with the scriptures, and that he appeared to Cephas, then to the twelve. (1 Cor 15:1–5)

Paul received a formulation of this message from others, and he faithfully handed this on when he first announced the Gospel in Corinth.

Earlier as well Paul spoke of himself as a link in a chain of tradition. This regarded the rite of the eucharistic supper, which Jesus began and Paul had learned before he introduced it at Corinth and gave instruction on its regular practice as the way "to proclaim the Lord's death until he comes" (1 Cor 11:23–26).

There were other traditions, both concerning "the form of teaching" (Rom 6:17) and about practices, and Paul singled out the importance of fidelity to them: "I commend you because you remember me in everything and maintain the traditions, just as I handed them on to you" (1 Cor 11:2; also Phil 4:9). To hold fast to orally communicated teachings, rules, and practices was important as well in letters written later in Paul's name: "So then, brothers and sisters, stand firm and hold fast to the traditions that you were taught by us, either by word of mouth or by our letter" (2 Thess 2:15; also 3:6).

These texts from the letters of Paul tell us about an early phase when Christianity was an oral culture with processes of communication by word of mouth and living practice. Much of what was programmatic for the very first Christians came to them by word-of-mouth transmission. In this, the apostolic church was continuing the methods of instruction practiced by the rabbinical teachers of Judaism, from whom Paul learned his vocabulary of "receiving" and "handing on." Paul was first schooled in the traditions by Rabbi Gameliel (Acts 22:3; Gal 1:14; Phil 3:5). The content of early Christian tradition was new, and at times Jesus and his followers sharply opposed particular rabbinical traditions (see Mark 7:1–8), but the apostolic methods of laying the foundations of community life followed forms of Jewish practice.[1]

Today all Christians esteem highly the inspired apostolic letters and Gospels of the New Testament, which set down the initial traditions of the churches founded by the apostles, giving these in the fixed and stable form of texts. But at the same time a more vital form of communication, one akin to apostolic practice, remains centrally important, as Vatican II states:

> The apostolic preaching, which is expressed in a special way in the inspired books, had to be preserved in a continuous succession until the end of time. Thus the apostles, in handing on what they received, urged believers to hold fast to the traditions they had learned, whether by word of mouth or letter [cf. 2 Thess 2:15], and to contend for the faith handed on to them once and for all [cf. Jude 3]. What was passed on by the apostles comprises everything that contributes to the holiness of life of the people of God and to their increase in faith. Thus the church, in her doctrine, life, and worship, perpetuates and passes on to all generations all that she is, all that she believes. (DV 8)

This chapter will treat tradition as the vital context of doing Catholic theology. Tradition is first of all the active process of continually transmitting the apostolic message and teaching, along with the gifts that foster holiness and increase faith. The ample legacy of apostolic tradition became formulated in its doctrinal nucleus in creeds and early dogma (3.1). Section 3.2 will explain how doing theology can be nourished by the witness to tradition expressed by the Fathers of the Church, the liturgy, and the lives of holy people. Finally, section 3.3 will show the relation between the multiple traditions and the global tradition by which the church of today extends in time "all that she is" as a community of faith, prayer, and witness. At the end we will attend to a peculiar dialectic in church and theology between growth of the tradition and ongoing critical adaptation through reform of traditions.[2]

3.1. FROM THE APOSTOLIC "DEPOSIT" TO CREEDS AND DOGMA

A genetic line of development links the founding work of the apostles in the earliest churches to the first creeds and the first dogmatic definition by the Council of Nicea in AD 325. Dogmatic teaching has to be a major concern to one doing Catholic theology, both in grasping the genesis and original content of such teaching of God's revealed truth and then moving on to discover the relevance of dogmas for Christian living in our own time. Here we will trace the steps that led from the apostolic tradition and "deposit" through the "rule of faith" to baptismal creeds and then to a creed expressing a dogma, that is, a formal church definition calling for faith in a particular truth derived from what the apostles handed on.

Creeds and dogma, through which tradition gives the theologian fundamental points of reference, do not, however, exhaustively express the Christian tradition. Tertullian, writing in North Africa about AD 215, gave a short list of Christian practices not set down in scripture that are nonetheless observed in the churches. The morning Eucharist, offerings for the deceased, always standing for prayer during the paschal season, frequently making the sign of the cross — these are not biblical, but still are respectfully observed as strands by which a communal life is woven together, with some of these practices coming from the apostles themselves.[3]

But the main reality of early tradition was not so much the complex of such customs as the central apostolic legacy, namely, the "deposit" of teaching and practices that pastors and teachers handed on as those charged with guarding the integrity of the apostolic faith and lifestyle in the churches.

A late letter of the apostolic age encouraged its readers to continue contending "for the faith delivered once for all to the saints" (Jude 3). "Deposit" is the inclusive term for the faith and ways of worship and life bequeathed by the apostles and their co-workers to the churches they founded. The apostles left as their legacy a coherent pattern of faith, of teaching and modes of biblical interpretation, of worship and community structures of service, and of life in the world according to the word and example of Christ. The foundation of Christian teaching and life in every age remains the "deposit" of tradition left by those whom Jesus sent out to communicate his revelation and saving gifts. The church lives from this deposit of apostolic tradition in its full form.[4]

The Apostolic "Deposit"

The Old Testament contains laws outlining a trustee's obligation before God of conscientious safekeeping of valuables entrusted to him (Exod 22:6–12; Lev 5:20–26, NAB). Against this background, the New Testament letters to Timothy see the tradition coming from Paul as a precious legacy that has to be maintained intact and guarded against falsification (1 Tim 6:20; 2 Tim 1:14).[5] The Pastoral Epistles, written late in the first Christian century, see in the "deposit" the complex outcome of Paul's many-sided ministry. They do not give a complete catalogue of its content, but they do insist on its continuing importance as a norm of community life well after Paul's death. The pastors are trustees obliged to protect the apostle's legacy by faithfully announcing his Gospel, giving sound instruction, regulating community prayer, carefully selecting other ministers, and withstanding alien and subversive doctrines. The New Testament "deposit" is the seedbed of all Christian theology, for it is apostolic tradition in its ample and complex form, in communities for which it was the norm of faith and source of life. Maintaining the identity once given these communities depended on fidelity to what was received. For such a work, human effort does not suffice and so one must look to an enabling power given to the communities and their pastors: "Guard the good treasure entrusted to you, with the help of the Holy Spirit living in us" (2 Tim 1:14).[6]

The Rule of Faith

Christian writers of the late second century speak of a second notable form of apostolic tradition. What they call the "rule of faith" is less comprehensive than the full deposit left by the apostles, but it is more pointed in expressing the main lines of the beliefs and doctrines belonging to the deposit.[7] Writers of the late second century like Irenaeus of Lyons mention with some frequency that their churches have a known "canon of truth," that is, a set framework and content of teaching, or more simply a "rule of faith" (*regula fidei*). Some of these writers give summaries of the main points, expressed in variable terms but with the same outline. The rule is to believe in God, the Father Almighty, who created all that is; to believe in Jesus Christ, the Son who became incarnate for our salvation; and to believe in the Holy Spirit, who spoke through the prophets about Christ's birth, passion, resurrection, and ascension, of the future resurrection, of the coming manifestation of Christ in glory as just judge of all.[8]

The late second-century rule of faith was not a creed or confession of faith in a verbally fixed form, although concise confessions, for use at baptism, were then evolving in conformity with the rule. The rule expressed the central contents that faith embraces as coming from Christ through his apostles and the church. Faith then becomes a rule and by it new formulations of teaching can be tested for their coherence with basic beliefs about God and his work.

For one doing theology, the traditional rule of faith shows the unity of God's revelation of himself and of his saving work. The rule shows that the minds of postapostolic believers were not stretched this way and that way by scattered fragments of belief, but had instead a coherent vision of God, creation, and human life in the world.

A basic moment in Christian theology is to envisage and express a coherent account of God and his intended project for humankind.

Theology aims at further penetration into the meaning of beliefs and into their many correlations with each other and with human life in the world. Theology strives as well for fresh syntheses. But a given framework and order arises from faith itself, whose basic act lays hold of a primordial Christian synthesis given in the apostolic rule of faith.

The Early Creeds

By the fourth century, it was common for Christians who came under suspicion of teaching error to lay before others the creed they professed and taught to others.[9] Such confessional acts and formulas have deep roots in the New Testament, as in the declaration of faith "Jesus is Lord" (1 Cor 12:3) and in the saving act to "confess with your lips that Jesus is Lord and believe in your heart that God raised him from the dead" (Rom 10:9; see also Phil 2:10; Acts 2:36).

The earliest known creed for professing the Christian faith had the structure of a dialogue. Faith took the form of responding "I believe" to the questions about God and his structured work of salvation asked by a church minister at the central moment of one's incorporation into the community by baptism.[10]

Many fourth-century creeds functioned in the catechumenate. While the question-and-answer format remained central in baptism itself, the handing over of the church's creed (*traditio symboli*) to the catechumens marked their passage into an advanced stage of preparation for baptism. They were told the formula of profession of faith used in the church they were entering, required to learn it by heart, and then heard instructions, usually by the bishop, on the meaning of each part of the text.

Shortly before being baptized, the candidates marked the end of their prebaptismal instruction by professing the transmitted faith at the rite of "giving back" the creed (*redditio symboli*) by reciting it. In the creed the candidates make a declaration of the church's faith, that is, of a content that expands somewhat the dialogue creeds of baptism itself, in accord with the rule of faith of the different local churches. With the creed, the believer gives compendious expression to the faith of the community into which he or she is being initiated.

The Apostles' Creed is one such formula for expressing the evangelical core of God's revelation of himself and his work of salvation in Christ.

To do theology is to deal regularly with doctrines, and as an intellectual exploration theology at times works out complex theories about what is believed. But the very first role of creedal doctrines is to express the believer's adherence to Christ as Son of God, risen, and Lord. The "three-article," trinitarian structure of creeds makes them apt means in consigning one's life over to the saving purposes of the Triune God.

The creed is one element in the liturgical and ecclesial expression of conversion, as a passage from sin and alienation into the community of the "household of God" (Eph 2:19), where one joins a community of witnesses and believers who share life with each other, and with God (see 1 John 1:1–3). An important work of theology is to relate doctrines, studied first in their development and particular historical circumstances, to the personal profession of faith first made at baptism and then renewed along with others in the corporate expression of the church's faith.

A Dogmatic Creed: Nicea, AD 325

The Council of Nicea in 325 signaled a change when bishops gathered in council promulgated a declarative creed for the whole church, that is, a formal statement that expresses a part of the common rule of faith in new terms to exclude a specific error.[11] This new, revised creed was initially less for use by individual believers as their personal profession and more to serve as a norm of orthodoxy by which legitimate bishops might be known and other bishops might maintain the bond of ecclesial communion with them.

The Nicene Creed rules out tenets promoted by Arius, a deacon of Alexandria, especially by specifying that the Son of God is generated eternally from the Father's being or substance (*ousia*) and is as a consequence "one in being [consubstantial, *homoousios*] with the Father." The intention here was not to raise a philosophical technicality to the level of faith, but instead to counteract and rule out what Arius had been teaching about the beginning of the Son as "created . . . at the beginning of his work" (Prov 8:22).[12]

Arius interpreted the New Testament from the viewpoint of texts like John 14:28, where Jesus says, "The Father is greater than I." Arius also stressed that if Jesus is to give us an example to follow, he must not be radically different but instead wholly one of us and then merit his exaltation by good deeds before God. But Nicea declares instead that God himself is present in Jesus of Nazareth. The Council did not elaborate the meaning of "consubstantial" and "one in being." But the intent of the teaching is clear from the addition to the creed of a short list of Arian formulations that deny the Son's divinity, for example, "There was a time when he was not," which are now forbidden, in preaching and catechesis, under pain of excommunication.[13]

The Nicene Creed is in fact a model of all future dogmatic declarations. From it theology gains an initial, functional notion of a dogmatic definition in clarification of the faith. First, the creed regulates the language of instruction in the church, for example, by ruling out the Arian slogans. Second, it lays down a guideline to follow in laying hold of the meaning of scripture. Priority should be given, for example, not to John 14:28, but to a text like John 10:30, "The Father and I are one." The Nicene Creed thus excludes both an unacceptable rule of belief and principle of biblical interpretation. Third, the dogma establishes a criterion of communion, a way of expressing oneness in faith, between bishops and their churches.

Throughout the work of theology, solemn church teachings have to be related to the life of the church, as done here for the Nicene dogma, through which a component of apostolic tradition came to precise formulation. That new formulation was then communicated from the Council to the other bishops of the world, for whom it gradually became a standard of common profession and norm of the ecclesial communion of faith.

St. Thomas on "Articles of Faith"

A final point about the creed, one that has ramifications for everyone doing theology, was articulated by St. Thomas Aquinas.[14] Concerning the multiplicity of distinct "articles" of creedal content, he says that all the articles that we believe should be seen as implicitly contained in just two primordial or fundamental tenets, namely, that God exists and that he has a providential care for our salvation. The number of articles has increased over time, as the biblical depth of the basic truths has been more fully grasped, but this has brought a series of explicitations of what is present in the most fundamental conviction of faith.[15]

Also illuminating is what St. Thomas says about the dynamic movement of the believing heart and mind when it affirms articles of faith. For him the ultimate object of faith is not the set of articles that we confess. We need such formulations of God's revelation because we lay hold of reality by assenting to true affirmations. The creed and articles of faith offer such affirmations of the truth of God and his saving work. But faith is also a spiritual movement born along by grace toward union with God our Savior, who in his utter simplicity is the First Truth (*prima Veritas*) toward whom we are being led by faith.[16]

From the viewpoint of faith itself, Thomas enunciates a principle that theology can apply to each article of faith and to the creed as a whole: "The movement of the believing heart does not reach its goal in the formula of faith but in the reality itself that is believed and formulated."[17] Faith, for Thomas, is a movement of the graced human spirit that affirms the creedal article in the act of faith, but the spiritual dynamic of belief carries one beyond the article or doctrine to the reality that the doctrine describes. An article or solemn teaching formulates a truth of God's revelation, but the article is not the final object of faith. "The article of faith is how we lay hold of divine truth as one moment in tending toward union with that truth itself."[18]

Thus, theology, as it treats the formulated beliefs that emerge in the church's tradition, has to withstand the temptation to lose itself in the historical details or to be satisfied with no more than a precise account of the doctrinal vocabulary used in teaching. Doctrines are "for us and for our salvation," and the articles of faith are ways by which Christian believers come together and in or by their faith relate to God as sharers in the truth that he ultimately is.

Faith in a particular truth involves a movement that transcends the formulated content of faith. Faith brings the person into union with God, the *prima Veritas* (First Truth), who even now, by revealing himself, shines the light of his presence into human hearts. Theology, while probing the meaning of formulations of traditions, creeds, and dogmas, intends to show the way to life in this light, God's light, radiating into our world.

3.2. TRADITION IN THE FATHERS, THE LITURGY, AND THE SAINTS

The person doing theology studies the past especially in order to understand the *genetic development* of Christian faith down to today. Scripture and dogma are decisive moments in a larger process. The Word of God, entering human history first in Israel and then climactically in Jesus, set in motion a process, and God's Spirit has kept the process going as a lived history in which we are now protagonists. This is the "development of doctrine" in the specific sense, on which Cardinal Newman has offered a perceptive analysis.[19]

The previous chapter dealt with the biblical phase of revelation, expressed in salvation history and in Jesus, to which the prophets and apostles have given witness in writing. Now we treat the contributions of three influences on further doctrinal development, influences still present for a theologian to draw on for understanding scripture, namely, the Fathers, the liturgy, and the witness of lives marked by holiness. These are major resources to enrich one's theological perception of God's Word as it makes its impact on believers' lives.

Our "Fathers in the Faith"

The Fathers of the Church are major teachers who worked and wrote during the first six centuries of the postapostolic church (AD 100–700), many of whom contributed decisively to the church's reception of the Bible's message as a coherent pattern and content of faith.[20]

The Fathers taught before the transformation that occurred in medieval Western Europe when theology became a principal subject taught and studied in the universities, where theologian-professors developed a philosophically based standard vocabulary and refined techniques of analysis and debate. Before this, many of the Fathers, in contrast, were bishops, and their teaching bears the marks of their pastoral engagement with the people of their churches. Many of the works of the Fathers that we now read in printed texts were first given orally to communicate the biblical word and the central doctrines of God's revelation, always with a sense that these are vital, saving truths for persons and communities to assimilate as basic convictions by which they relate to God and shape their lives in this world.[21]

At Vatican Council II (1962–65), study of the Fathers was a source of decisive impulses through influential Vatican II theological experts, like Henri de Lubac, Yves Congar, Jean Daniélou, and Joseph Ratzinger.[22] They had been formed by having studied the Fathers of the Church, and so could propose elements of a fresh theology more closely related to preaching, prayer, and the struggle of faithful living in the world. Appendix 5 of this book recounts the roles played by theologian-experts at Vatican II.

According to Vatican II, the life-giving apostolic tradition comes to expression in the teachings of the Fathers, as the riches of that tradition spill over into the prayer and life of the church (DV 8). The Fathers express the ongoing tradition of understanding scripture ever more deeply for the nourishment of faith (DV 23).[23] In the genetic treatment of doctrines recommended by the Council (OT 16), the contribution of the Fathers follows scripture in the account of the truths of revelation.

Some have pointed out obstacles that make it hard to understand the Fathers and give them much importance in theological work.[24] But serious work in theology cannot neglect the Fathers of the Church. There are three main reasons for their theological importance.

First, the Fathers' homilies and explanatory treatises on scripture show us the biblical word in the form of an accepted and understood word of life. The Fathers are part of the vital history of the inspired scriptures, a history of the word at work to bring out a further and more developed understanding of its meaning. This is the history of the impact of scripture, in which the texts of the books have left the situation of their origin in communication between a particular author and his first hearers or readers to be heard later as they are read in new situations by further generations. This early biblical understanding shown in the Fathers, we realize today, is truly a part of the full meaning of the Bible as scripture exerts its influence on believing and thinking Christians.

Second, the Fathers are exponents of a unified vision of God's revelation of himself and of the economy of salvation. Imbued by the early rule of faith and shaped by the creeds, they rarely teach detached items or fragments of doctrine. They are models of coherent teaching, notwithstanding the variety of the ways they think of doctrine in ways conditioned by their different cultures. The Fathers' abilities in making the connections between different testimonies to God can school theologians in coherent teaching around a central focus of unity, one always alert to the meaning of God's word "for us and for our salvation."

Third, the Fathers are engaged thinkers, whether this be a more pastoral or a more doctrinal commitment. Much patristic literature is homiletic in nature, serving the "spilling over" of apostolic teaching and ideals into "the practice and life of the believing and praying church" (DV 8). The Fathers regularly connect the content of God's revelation with liturgical worship of praise and repentance and with their hearers' daily life in the world.

The Fathers also created memorable works of doctrinal controversy in defense of God's word, such as Irenaeus's *Against the Heresies* against gnosticism, Athanasius's defenses of the Nicene dogma, and Augustine's arguments from Paul against the Pelagians' neglect of God's helping and healing grace as they exalted human striving to gain salvation. In these cases, the Fathers show how the circulation of erroneous ideas about God, Christ, and the Christian life exert pressure on the Christian mind to grasp God's revelation more fully, even moving it to see new aspects of God's truth. These three examples are works that contribute much to well-grounded theological accounts of God's revelation (Irenaeus), to the doctrine of the Tri-personal God and of Christ (Athanasius), and to the Christian vision of being fully human (Augustine).[25]

The Fathers exemplify theology in an encounter with culture, since their cultural surroundings often generated attitudes and arguments hostile to the Christian way and Christian belief. Numerous works of the second-century patristic "apologists" are the earliest models of Christian thinkers giving a rational accounting of the Gospel and of fundamental teaching before a nonbelieving audience. The discipline of *fundamental theology* begins with these early Fathers.[26]

We know in the early twenty-first century that an adequate Christian theology must respond critically to its cultural context. The Fathers were creative in responding to their situations and contexts shaped mainly by their Greek and Latin cultures, but they also remained doggedly faithful to what they received from the apostles as the meaning of God's revelation. Their creative fidelity can instruct us all.

Liturgy as a Theological Source

Our previous chapter on scripture included an account of the role of the church's liturgy in interpreting scripture. The life and worship of the church have a basic congeniality with the Bible and serve to bring out the surplus meaning of which the biblical texts are a fertile source. The calendar of the liturgical year expresses the unity of biblical history, by passing from God's epiphany in Jesus (the Advent–Christmas cycle) to his saving passover of death, resurrection, and sending of the Spirit (Lent–Easter–Pentecost).

Systematic theology can take much from the liturgy, acting on the conviction that the worshiping church is transmitting "all that she herself is, all that she believes" (DV 8). Theological reflection on human existence and the human calling, for example, can draw on the simple fact that every celebration of the Eucharist begins with the community's confession of sin and appeal to God for forgiveness. The liturgy thus gives backing to those who, with Luther, want to say that in this life the believer is "righteous and a sinner at the same time" (*simul iustus et peccator*). Near its center, every liturgy also has moments of *epiclesis* by which the Spirit is invoked upon believers, on the world, and on our offerings of bread and wine. This suggests perception of the full range of human fragility and sin that are overcome by God's healing and renewing Spirit.

Beyond the basic structures of liturgical action, there are the texts themselves of the church's prayer. Some of these serve to draw out the meaning of doctrines and indicate their impact on the lives of believers.

Liturgical prayer, for example, often expresses the Christian doctrine of the Triune God by directing itself "to the Father, through the

Son, in the Holy Spirit." An ancient rule, formulated at a late fourth-century regional council, laid down as binding the practice that "at the altar, prayer is always directed to the Father."[27] In such prayer the risen Christ mediates for his people as their high priest before the Father, both in the "ascending" direction of presenting their praise and petition to the Father and in the "descending" direction of his communicating to church and world the blessings that come from the Father in response to prayer.

In its creed, the church confesses the Son to be "one in being with the Father," as Nicea laid this down, but liturgical prayer expresses the complementary truth of the Son's role as mediator for our human family with which he is one by his human nature. An essential topic of theological investigation of the person and work of Christ has to be the ongoing mediation of Christ risen and exalted, as especially the liturgy expresses this.

Liturgy, of course, is more than the structured formulae of its standard texts. Liturgy says much to the theologian of creation by its incorporation of material things into rites and sacraments. Theological anthropology is also instructed by liturgical gestures, the most fundamental of which is the laying on of hands. In Acts, Philip's preaching of Christ led to Samaria receiving the word of God. At this the apostles sent Peter and John down from Jerusalem to complete what Philip's word had begun: "Then Peter and John laid their hands on them, and they received the Holy Spirit" (Acts 8:17). Today, sacramental confirmation is imparted by anointing on the forehead with the imposition of hands by the minister. As well, sacramental ordination to the diaconate, priesthood, and episcopate is by the laying on of hands with prayer. Here a gesture of touch, distinctively felt by minister and recipient, signifies and effects the giving of God's Spirit and grace. Thus, the liturgy speaks about the human body in its basic dignity and about bodily existence and action in the unfolding of God's saving purposes. Theology is enriched here by what the liturgy expresses in action and word.

Holy Lives as a Theological Source

Martin Luther, at one point in his debate in 1525 with Erasmus over God's grace and the power of human free choice, showed a good sense of the relative value of theological sources. Erasmus had referred to writings of St. Augustine and St. Bernard of Clairvaux in which these theologians explained how grace and free choice must go together in some kind of interrelation as we work out our salvation. But against this appeal to books by these saints, Luther made a telling riposte:

> I can easily show you, on the contrary, that the holy men such as you boast about, whenever they came to pray or plead with God, approach him in utter forgetfulness of their own free choice, despairing of themselves and imploring nothing but pure grace alone.

When they write and dispute, the saints may move by reasoning and argument to say one thing, but their deeper feelings, where they sense their total need of grace, are different and serve better as indices of the truth. "Men are to be measured by their feelings rather than their talk."[28]

Thus, the actual living of God's word by a holy person can be a telling indication of what that word means. In the saints this meaning, assimilated into their very flesh and blood, is writ large. Luther could have very well cited specific passages of Augustine's *Confessions*, especially Book X, where, after recounting his past life, Augustine tells of his present imperfect condition and makes a poignant appeal to God, the physician of his soul:

> My life is not yet filled by you and I am a burden to myself. The pleasures I find in the world, which should be cause for tears, are at strife with its sorrows, in which I should rejoice, and I cannot tell to which the victory will fall. Have pity on me, Lord, in my misery! . . . I do not hide my wounds from you. I am sick and you are the physician. You are merciful; I have need of your mercy.[29]

In the same vein, we can cite St. Thérèse of Lisieux's striking sense of her own sinfulness and need of grace, as this came out in a conversation just before her death.[30]

Of course theology cannot build on just one theme expressing holiness of life. The word of God is renewing and takes hold of individuals for serving God's purposes in this world. This side of

Christian existence was expressed in a direct manner in a work that was composed at the very time Luther was contending against Erasmus, namely, the *Spiritual Exercises* of St. Ignatius Loyola.

The *Exercises* are a set of meditations to bring one, under the guidance of a director, to a personal sense of God's will and call and then to respond with selfless dedication in carrying out a vocation in the church or the world. Based on Ignatius and on the thousands of lives shaped by the *Exercises,* one goes beyond Luther's perception of our bondage to know how God can and in fact has freed many for zealous engagement in this world.[31]

Holy lives, in which God's word comes to expression, are not found only in the past. Vatican II's main paragraph on the tradition of what the church is and what she believes ends on an actual note, concerning the present. Living transmission makes the biblical word constantly operative.

> And thus God, who spoke in the past, converses without inter-
> ruption with the beloved spouse of his Son, and the Holy Spirit,
> through whom the living word of the Gospel (*viva vox Evan-
> gelii*) resounds in the church and through the church in the
> world, leads believers into all truth and makes the word of Christ
> dwell in them more abundantly. (DV 8)

Holy people of today, whom we meet and hear about, are those in whom the Gospel is finding hearts in which to dwell, to become there formative of generous living and serving. The thoughtful consideration of such lives can be theologically most fruitful.

3.3. TRADITIONS IN THEOLOGY – THEOLOGY IN TRADITION

So far this chapter has treated distinct types of traditions that, along with scripture, contribute to theology. These testimonies to God's revelation received in faith, transmitted from generation to genera-tion, include the creed and dogmas, teachings of the Fathers, liturgy, and holy lives, which are each in their own way sources for a theo-logical account of God's word to us and of what his word and grace bring into our lives.

A central Catholic conviction holds with Melchior Cano that the theological sources are multiple and diverse. But Catholic thought also takes seriously a single, global tradition beginning with the apostles and perpetuated in the church. There are many and varied traditions that express God's word and authentic human responses, but there is also the single culture and environment that endures over time, which is also tradition, with a central evangelical content that forms community and gives to the members a characteristic spirit and ethos.

The Council of Trent, in 1546, spoke of multiple "traditions." On the global tradition, we will hear Cardinal Newman, before returning to Vatican II to reflect on the ramifications for theology that emerge from the fruitful tension inherent in tradition in the church. These voices combine to speak pointedly both about multiple traditions as theological sources and about a single, living tradition as the habitat of the Catholic theologian.

Trent's Reception of Unwritten Traditions

The Council of Trent, which began in 1545 and, after two interruptions, ended in 1563, created a body of doctrine, in teachings on God's grace and the human response, on the Eucharist and other sacraments, while also laying down numerous practical regulations to reform the church in a way that shaped the identity of Roman Catholicism in the modern era.[32]

For doing theology, Trent's most important teachings concern the Gospel and its communication in the biblical books and apostolic traditions, which therefore are normative sources of Christian doctrine. Before the Council, numerous Catholic writers had already advanced arguments against Luther's use of scripture as the sole norm of doctrine and life, especially contesting the Reformation claim that scripture has in itself a self-interpreting capacity (*sacra scriptura sui ipsius interpres*, according to Luther). St. John Fisher (Bishop of Rochester, England, martyred in 1535) drew together most of the main points of the Catholic case. (1) Much in the Bible is hard to understand, as 2 Peter 3:16 indicates regarding the letters of St. Paul. The Bible taken alone, instead of resolving controversies, actually leads to errors and divisions. In fact, practically every Christian heretic known from history appealed to scripture and interpreted it as justifying teachings that distorted the faith. (2) There has developed in the church, under the lead of the Holy Spirit, a normative tradition of how the Bible should be interpreted, namely, the teaching of the orthodox Fathers and of the Ecumenical Councils. (3) Further, the church has in the successor of St. Peter a "judge of controversies" to whom recourse must be had for an answer when disputes break out over doctrine, forms of worship, and the norms of Christian life. (4) Then too the apostolic writings themselves, for example 2 Thessalonians 2:15; John 20:30, 21:25, show the existence of an oral communication of doctrine and rules beyond what is set down in the writings collected in the Bible, and some practices of the universal church derive from this nonwritten source.[33]

Following the orientations of Fisher and other Catholic writers against the Reformation, Trent framed its teaching on the transmission of God's revelation in decrees approved April 8, 1546. A first document is the Council's formal reception of both the biblical books and apostolic traditions relevant to faith and church practice.[34]

The Council states three principles. (1) The starting point of faith is the Gospel of Christ, which Trent intends by its decrees to preserve in its purity as the one source of all saving truth and Christian practice. (2) The whole corpus of doctrine and norms for life arising from the Gospel was not given in written books alone, and so certain unwritten communications and practices ("traditions") must be taken into serious consideration, namely, those that come either from Jesus' oral teaching, not recorded in the New Testament, or from the Holy Spirit's interior teaching of the apostles. But the decree does *not* say that the doctrines and practices of the Gospel are given partly in writing and in another part in traditions coming to the church. They are in both, however one wants to construe the content of each.[35] (3) However, not all traditions are definitive and normative for the church. Trent circumscribes considerably their ambit by receiving only the transmitted doctrines and practices that (a) originated with Christ's apostles, and (b) are transmitted in unbroken succession to the living, teaching, and worshiping church of today. Examples of such traditions would be the keeping holy of the first day of the week, a change from observing the Jewish Sabbath, and the linking of the Lord's Supper with a liturgy of the word. Usages of strictly human origin, such as ecclesiastical laws on celibacy and fasting, are not considered here, since the Council intended to lay down reform directives which in given cases could conceivably change some of these.

A second step of long-term importance was Trent's insistence on a normative ecclesial interpretation of the Bible.[36] Here Trent is expressing the church's sense of possessing — and being possessed by — the overall meaning of the biblical message. It specifies that this understanding is an ongoing part of the very being of the church. The text mentions the Fathers of the Church, echoing John Fisher's statement that there is a normative patristic and conciliar tradition that interprets God's word. Because the church has a connatural relation with the meaning of the Bible, Trent specifies that "it belongs to the church to judge the true meaning and interpretation of holy scripture." At that time, the term "magisterium" was not yet in use to designate the teaching office, but the reality is present here, where Trent appropriates what the controversialists had proposed about the existence of a "judge of controversies" in the church.

The main conclusion, however, from the two decrees is that for formulating Christian doctrine and guiding Christian life, while an appeal to what one hears from the Bible must be made, this however does not suffice. One must consult other theological sources, or *loci,* as Melchior Cano called them. The Bible has made the meaning of God's word resound in the church, and so its interpretation is to be heard, along with its received ways of expressing the apostolic faith in life and worship.

The Council of Trent pointed out the importance of certain apostolic traditions passed on by ways other than writing. Thus, we are alerted to a span of traditions that communicate the faith and foster Christian living. But reflection on the theological sources has taken a new turn more recently regarding the traditions, now emphasizing not their multiplicity but their coherent unity.

Newman on Tradition's Coherence and Fecundity

As an Anglican, John Henry Newman (1801–90, became a Catholic in 1845) opposed the notion that scripture was by itself a sufficient guide to faith and life. Against the fragmentation arising from the modern Protestant principle of private judgment on the meaning of the biblical text, Newman appealed to the tradition and rule of faith from the apostles, by which the church grasps unerringly the "one direct and definite sense" of revealed biblical teaching.

Writing on apostolic tradition in 1836, Newman cited 1 Timothy 6:20 to show that the apostles delivered over to their successors the "deposit" that was meant to be further transmitted. Newman added a characteristic description to make clear that the apostolic legacy cannot be expressed sufficiently in written documents:

> Such teaching... was too vast, too minute, too complicated, too implicit, too fertile, to be put in writing, at least in times of persecution; it was for the most part conveyed orally, and the safeguard against its corruption was the number and unanimity of its witnesses. The canon of scripture was an additional safeguard — not, however, as limiting it, but as verifying it. Also it was kept in position, and from drifting, by the creed: that is, by a fixed form of words.... It followed from the very Catholicity of the Church that its tradition... was manifold, various, and independent in its local manifestation.[37]

For Newman, the Christian tradition moved from person to person by living contact, not just indoctrination, and this resulted in the body of truth that penetrates the church like its very atmosphere.

When Newman became a Catholic, the amplitude and fruitfulness of the apostolic deposit continued to have a central place in his reflections. His studies of the Arian crisis of the fourth century and of the Council of Chalcedon (AD 451) convinced him that revealed truth was meant to develop under the guidance of an "oracle" able to exercise inerrant teaching authority. As he explained in *An Essay on the Development of Christian Doctrine* (1845), Christianity is a fact that impresses itself upon the believing mind in a way that leads to a multitude of repercussions. It is dogmatic, devotional, social, and practical all at once, and no single expression serves to define it.

Scripture, in Newman's view, introduces us to a vast territory that we cannot map out or describe in a single account. In the time of the church, exploration of the many parts of revelation is a work of inquiry, contemplation, and the resolution of controversy. New dogmas have to be declared at times, but fundamentally they only manifest the church's newly achieved awareness and understanding of what was implicit in the deposit handed on by the apostles at the beginning. Newman stresses how one insight leads in time to another, but this rests on the original deposit having its own unity and cohesion. Great ideas, Newman notes, are not taken in by our minds all at once, but they have to grow in us toward perfect comprehension in the course of time. Devout and enlightened minds open themselves to give space to the word of God, and it generates further knowledge of itself in its diverse parts and multiform relations to the different spheres of life. Answers to questions come by gradual and homogeneous developments of the one comprehensive deposit. Much like the Word made flesh, so also God's revealing word has resolutely entered into human history.

Clearly, the working of human minds can result in the twisting or deformation of revealed truth, for example, by incautiously asserting just one doctrine to the detriment or exclusion of other truths of faith. And so Newman set forth his famous criteria or tests for sifting the doctrinal wheat from the chaff, that is, discerning true developments of the original deposit from corruptions of it. Newman's tests are ways of discovering expressions of the original tradition in the midst of multiple traditions of teaching and practice.[38]

Newman's theology rests on his awareness of the potential of original tradition for growth over time. His engaging reflections carry us from the multiple to the single, from the many later traditions to the one original apostolic tradition. In this way, Newman was, with others like J. A. Möhler and Maurice Blondel, a notable precursor of the Second Vatican Council.[39]

Vatican II on the Living Tradition

At Vatican Council II the main statement on tradition occurs in chapter 2 of the Constitution on Divine Revelation (DV 7–10).[40] Here we draw out three points of this declaration on the apostolic tradition and its presence in the church. First, the apostolic patrimony given to the church is more than a body of doctrine expressing God's revelation and its immediate consequences. To be sure, Jesus did teach his disciples in striking ways in his parables, his fresh interpretations of Israel's scripture, and his discourses and declarations about his own coming and role in God's plan. Some of Jesus' disciples were sent as apostles to announce his Gospel, and they then carried out their own ministry of teaching in the churches they founded. But Jesus' companions were formed as well, or even more, by the deeds of Jesus that they witnessed and their sharing of life with him. Then in the communities the apostles communicated God's gifts by what they said as teachers and interpreters of Israel's scriptures in the light of Christ, but also by how they lived and the structures of ministry and worship that they instituted (DV 7).

The apostles' many-sided influence created the global tradition that forms both belief and behavior: "What was passed on by the apostles comprises everything that contributes to the holiness of life of the People of God and to their increase in faith." After the apostolic age, this continues as a global form of faith and community life: "Thus the church, in her doctrine, life, and worship, perpetuates and passes on to all generations all that she is, all that she believes" (DV 8). Tradition communicates what the church *is,* while creating an environment or milieu of life in communion, with many different concrete forms of worship and mutual service and practices that are all ordered to personal formation in wisdom and holiness.

Second, while God's founding revelation is complete with Jesus and his apostles (DV 4), what was given once-for-all is meant to grow and develop. The apostles were led by the Holy Spirit to a fuller understanding of salvation in Christ that is now expressed in the New Testament writings (DV 7). In the church, the meaning of the apostolic deposit emerges gradually and comes to fuller expression. Over time, numerous factors influence a vital process of development, not the least of which is the ongoing influence of the Holy Spirit:

> This tradition coming from the apostles develops in the church under the influence of the Holy Spirit. There is growth in insight into the realities and words being passed on. This comes about through the contemplation and study of believers who ponder these things in their hearts (see Luke 2:19 and 51). It comes

about by understanding the spiritual realities that believers experience. And it comes about through the preaching of those who stand in the line of episcopal succession, endowed with a sure charism of truth.[41]

The tradition of doctrine, worship, and life leads to participation in life with God, as 1 John 1:1–3, cited in DV 1, indicates. God's gifts impinge on feelings and perceptions. From this a familiar understanding can arise, which is a personal knowledge, open to growth, of Father, Son, and Holy Spirit, and of their ways of dealing with human beings.

Vatican Council II, when it made this affirmation about the development of tradition, did not fall victim to unreal optimism about progress in the church, for the same Council stated as well the need of ever recurrent interventions to reform church practice and teaching (UR 6). Here, historical modes of thought are prevailing, as Vatican II treats the presence of the apostolic deposit in the church.

Third, this passage sees the importance of reflection on lived experience, rooted in the interior "sense of the faith" (*sensus fidei*) of the whole people of God (LG 12).[42] This manifests a notable change from the teaching of Pius XII in his encyclical *Humani Generis* (1950). The deposit of scripture and living tradition, Vatican II declares, is delivered over to the whole church, not simply to the magisterium. Tradition is the basis and inspiration of life in the image of the ideal apostolic community of Acts 2:42:

> Sacred tradition and sacred scripture form a single sacred deposit of the word of God entrusted to the church. By adhering to it, the entire holy people, united with its pastors, continue in the teaching of the apostles, in communion of life, in the breaking of bread, and in prayer. (DV 10)

Christian believers have thus received a precious legacy. The scriptures and the more ample and articulated testimony to revelation emerging from the milieu of tradition combine to endow believers and their communities with abundant instruction and guidance, with inspiration and encouragement.

Theology in the Tradition

Doing theology is a pursuit of the meaning of God's word and of life in faith, by one trained for the kingdom of God, "like the master of a household who brings out of his treasure what is new and what is old" (Matt 13:52). But to do theology is more than just restating traditional lore, since the stream of tradition continues to flow in the communities of God's people.

Theology is also like the work of a prospector searching for precious ore. The ample number of the "places," the *loci* of M. Cano, and the global inclusiveness of tradition as transmitted life means that there is need of constant sifting by discernment and evaluation. Here the results of biblical interpretation and of investigating the tradition have to be brought ever anew into contemporary application. Present-day teaching and living of the faith have to be tested, lest they become encrusted with forms too beholden to an era now passing. Here, the biblical expression of the Gospel, as cited at the beginning of this chapter, has a critical role. The full range of Jesus' own teaching and actions are supremely normative. What we claim to draw from scripture and tradition has to enliven and deepen faith in the Gospel and life in the image of Jesus.

Theology thus tries to separate what is chaff to be burned from the wheat with which the theologian and others can nourish themselves today and tomorrow. But theology is not the only activity oriented to the meaning of God's word in the community of faith. Our next chapter will treat theology's relation to what is set forth for Catholic believers by the church's pastoral teaching office, the magisterium.

Review Questions

1. What are the contents when St. Paul speaks of his "receiving" and "handing on what he received" to the churches? What does this tell us about the apostolic church?

2. Explain the different contexts in which Catholic theology refers to the "deposit" of faith or revelation.

3. What was the "rule of faith" for the late second-century Fathers cited in note 8 of this chapter?

4. How did the early creeds of the third and fourth centuries function in the life of the churches?

5. What did the creed of the Council of Nicea (AD 325) define, and how did this creed then impinge on the life of the churches?

6. How does St. Thomas relate "articles of faith" to the act of believing? How can his explanation contribute to doing theology today?

7. Why are the Church Fathers of AD 100–700 major resources for those doing theology? (See note 20 on page 253.)

8. Indicate with examples how the church's liturgy can be a major resource in theology.

9. What did the Council of Trent contribute to the understanding of tradition and church traditions in relation to the Gospel?

10. In what ways did Vatican II's account of tradition present new accents going beyond Trent and Pius XII's teaching in 1950?

Projects for Further Study

1. Study the entries in *Dictionary of Fundamental Theology* on "Deposit of Faith" and "Tradition" in order to work out an ordered presentation of the relations between revelation and tradition.

2. Study Cardinal Newman's *Essay on the Development of Doctrine* and from it develop an account of how Christian doctrine develops and why it must do so.

3. From study of the Councils of Trent and Vatican II on tradition, for example, in the works of Joseph Ratzinger indicated in notes 34 and 40 of this chapter (pages 255 and 256), present how one should understand the relations between scripture and tradition.

4. From the main contents of the chapter, work out an argument showing how tradition helps theology to be vital. Can one say that for theology to move ahead it must keep going back to earlier witnesses and their testimonies?

Chapter Four

Doing Theology in the Light of Church Teaching

THIS INTRODUCTION has repeatedly made a point of connecting theological listening and the theological search for meaning with the life of the church. Specifying this connection more closely, we now take up the role that past and present church teaching plays in doing theology in the Catholic community. For Catholics, their theological investigation takes seriously the teaching of those who today have the role foreshadowed by the New Testament "overseers" (*episkopoi*), with their characteristic service of the community, who according to St. Paul in Acts are placed in the church as its pastors (Acts 20:28).

In this chapter, we set theological method in relation to church teaching, with extended attention to the contemporary formulations of God's word and of its consequences, as these are expressed by those who hold pastoral office. This is the work of the church's "magisterium" of the councils, bishops, and the pope, who carry out for Catholics the mandate of Jesus to teach his doctrine to those who become his disciples by baptism (Matt 28:18–20).

An example of such official church teaching lies close at hand in the sixteen documents of doctrinal teaching and doctrinally based reform decrees of Vatican Council II (1962–65). Because of the Council's importance as relevant magisterial teaching, the Appendices of this book give six texts immediately connected with the Council, that is, the guidance it received from Popes John XXIII and Paul VI, its account of revelation and faith, the contributions made to Vatican II by its theological experts, and the way it is best interpreted in its overall meaning today. Vatican II exemplifies in striking ways the work of the church's teaching office, the "magisterium," and its documents remain touchstones for constant reference as a person does theology today in and for the Catholic community.

To account for this office of church teaching and show its importance, this chapter begins with the New Testament texts that speak of the persons whom the apostles designated for an ongoing teaching ministry (section 4.1). Then comes a historical review of some exemplary cases of the work of the teaching office, especially in its connection with doing theology. This review concludes by describing the features that link together magisterial teaching and theological work and that distinguish them as activities in the church (4.2). Then a final section will sketch the work of theology in interaction with teachings issued by the magisterium of the church's chief pastors (4.3). Others have presented the teaching office more amply, but here the focus is on its relation to theology.[1]

4.1. THE TEACHING OFFICE IN THE NEW TESTAMENT

An obvious concern pervading the New Testament is the communication of true teaching to the members of the first Christian communities and the fostering of their perseverance in the truth that they have received. For God our Savior "desires everyone to be saved and to come to the knowledge of the truth" (1 Tim 2:4).

Jesus himself had been hailed as one who taught the crowds "as one having authority, and not as their scribes" (Matt 7:29). He communicated the truth that he heard from God (John 8:40) and told Pontius Pilate, "For this I came into the world, to testify to the truth" (John 18:37). Making his final promises to his followers, he said he would send upon them an interior teacher of the truth: "When the Spirit of truth comes, he will guide you into all truth" (John 16:13).

A remarkable apostolic letter from late in the first age of Christianity, the First Epistle of John, urges believers to hold fast in their hearts to what Jesus' apostles had testified, for such constancy is the sure way to "abide in the Son and in the Father" (1 John 2:24). The witness of the apostles was about "the word of life," that is, Jesus himself, whom the apostles had known by living close to him (1:1–3). However, holding fast to the apostolic word of life is not a matter of unaided human exertions of willpower or of the insistent pedagogy of other believers. First John addresses believers in the assurance that they are persons anointed by God's own Spirit, who plants the truth in their hearts:

> You have been anointed by the Holy One, and all of you have knowledge.... The anointing that you received from him abides in you, and so you do not need anyone to teach you. But as his anointing teaches you about all things, and is true and is not a lie, and just as it has taught you, abide in him. (1 John 2:20, 27)

Maintaining believers in the truth is a principal work of the life-giving Spirit poured out on the community of the disciples. But the Spirit does not only teach and guide individuals directly and from above, for there are the apostles and teachers whom the Spirit takes into this work of teaching. The concern here is with the service given to the Holy Spirit by the church's qualified teachers, especially by those designated for this by ordination and by the office of pastoral leadership. Under the Spirit, these individuals work together with many others, some of whom have become qualified as "doctors of theology" and so professionally prepared to serve the truth by their intellectual expertise and scholarly mastery of the Christian sources.[2] But teaching enters the lives of all serious believers, some of whom take up the theological quest by probing the sources of teaching and exploring its meaning for their own lives and for others.

Apostles and Elders/Bishops as Teachers

There is no need to dwell on the unique role of the apostles of Jesus Christ in the early Christian communities between Pentecost and ca. AD 70. The New Testament is full of references to them, and they continue to teach its readers through their letters and through the Gospels collected as Christian scripture in the New Testament. One summary description of the earliest Jerusalem community says that the newly evangelized and baptized members were holding to "the apostles' teaching" as a primary component of their life in common (Acts 2:42).

Early Christians clearly valued what the apostles handed on from Jesus and what they taught about him when they instructed the churches. No little energy was devoted to collecting the apostles' instructions about Jesus and giving to these a fixed and lasting form in the four canonical Gospels. Apostolic letters were also cherished, and we read about a collection of Paul's letters being studied — not without difficulty — along with "the other scriptures" (2 Pet 3:16).

What does need attentive study is not so much the apostles' activity of teaching as the scattered New Testament references to other teachers in the churches who continued a pastoral ministry of teaching after the demise of the initial apostolic generation. The apostles conveyed a body of teaching to the churches, but we have to ask, who maintained the churches in that teaching, in that truth about God in Christ, when the apostles were no longer present? How did later generations receive the true teaching originating with the apostles who spoke and wrote with the unction given by the Holy Spirit at Pentecost?[3]

In the previous chapter, section 3.1 indicated how one first-century author in the tradition of Paul valued the apostolic legacy or "deposit" of a coherent set of doctrines, interpretations of Israel's scriptures, community norms, and ideals of living that came ultimately from contact with Jesus. The letters to Timothy give the mandate to their recipient to maintain, protect, and further communicate what the apostle Paul had passed on and entrusted to him: "Guard the good treasure entrusted to you, with the help of the Holy Spirit living in us" (2 Tim 1:14; also 1 Tim 6:20). Timothy was a younger co-worker whom Paul left in Ephesus with numerous pastoral duties, among which teaching had a clear priority (see 1 Tim 1:3–5, 4:11–16, 6:2–3), which was also the mandate given to Titus, who should be in Crete unflagging in insisting on sound doctrine (Titus 2:1, 15; 3:8).

But Timothy and Titus were not end points in serving the apostolic tradition and teaching. Titus is to appoint elders or overseers/bishops (*presbuteroi, episkopoi*) in every community. In each case, Paul's collaborator Titus should choose a capable and dedicated believer who holds firmly to the true message as taught, "so that he may be able both to preach with sound doctrine and to refute those who contradict it" (Titus 1:9).

Timothy becomes a link in a chain of teachers in a line from the apostle: "what you have heard from me through many witnesses

entrust to faithful people who will be able to teach others as well"
(2 Tim 2:2). Clearly, the "faithful people" in this series are not
apostles with firsthand experience of Jesus before or after his resurrection. Neither are they the apostles' younger but immediate
co-workers, as were Timothy and Titus. Instead they are "elders,"
"overseers," or "bishops" who have the serious obligation of further
communicating and protecting the apostolic legacy, with its central
doctrinal element, which had been given over to the churches.[4]

The letters to Timothy and Titus envisage an ongoing service of
teaching and supervision, which will of course be made effective only
by the presence and action of the Holy Spirit who gives unction and
depth to what these postapostolic pastoral teachers say and do.

Beyond the references in the letters to Timothy and Titus, elders,
overseers, and bishops are also mentioned in the New Testament in
Acts 11:30, 14:23, 15:2, 6, 22–23, 16:4, 20:17, 28; Phil 1:1; 1 Pet
5:1–5; Jas 5:14; and in the opening salutations of 2 and 3 John.

Paul's Mandate to the Elders of Ephesus (Acts 20)

In the Acts of the Apostles, the discourses of Peter and Paul regularly
punctuate the narrative of the spread of the Gospel, giving to us and
to our theology numerous remarkable formulations of the good news
of Christ. Acts tells of the apostles fulfilling Jesus' word that, once you
are empowered by the Holy Spirit, "you will be my witnesses in Jerusalem, in all Judea and Samaria, and to the ends of the earth" (Acts
1:8). In the discourses of Acts, we hear Paul's missionary preaching
first in the synagogue of Antioch in Pisidia (Acts 13:16–41) and then
before cultured gentiles at the Areopagus of Athens (17:22–31). In
later discourses in Jerusalem, in chapters 22, 24, and 26, Paul mounts
a defense of his call and ministry after he was arrested and accused
of preaching doctrines subversive of Judaism.

But before Paul went to Jerusalem, he gave a concluding missionary
discourse, saying farewell to the church that he had founded and
formed at Ephesus, addressing the elders of that church who came to
see him at Miletus (Acts 20:18–35).

Paul says clearly that his ministry in that area is finished (20:24),
and he sums up for the elders his characteristic insistence on the Gospel of God's grace, on repentance, and on faith in our Lord Jesus

Christ (20:20–21, 24). From Paul the elders have learned of the entire plan and saving work of God (20:27), and they are from now on to maintain and defend this doctrinal legacy for the benefit of the whole community: "Keep watch over yourselves and over all the flock, of which the holy Spirit has made you overseers (*episkopoi*), to shepherd the church of God that he obtained with the blood of his own Son" (20:28). This commission is urgent, because the Gospel and doctrine concerning God's saving work, taught by Paul, is endangered by some who try to pervert the truth, and so the elders have to exercise constant vigilance and careful discernment of new teaching (20:29–31).[5]

These New Testament texts introduce us to a group of pastoral teachers, working after the apostles in the last quarter century of the first Christian century, a time of turmoil in many of the churches founded by the apostles. The elders, overseers, and bishops were mandated to deal with the danger that amid this turmoil these churches might lose the identity given them by the Gospel and the apostles' instruction.[6]

We find a concise summary of the central point of these New Testament texts on the postapostolic teachers mandated to protect, defend, and pass on the apostles' life-giving "deposit" in Vatican II:

> In order that the Gospel might always be preserved integrally and vitally in the church, the apostles left bishops as their successors, "handing on to them their own teaching role."[7]

The Magisterium of the Church
Seen from the New Testament

These New Testament texts that present the pastoral teachers commissioned to serve and teach after the apostles allow us to speak of the church's episcopal and pastoral teaching office, the magisterium, in a fresh way. The sources show that it is not simply a governing authority to rule over the work of teaching. As well, it is less a creative function for issuing new teaching than a protective role, since the central responsibility is to preserve in its fullness and genuine character what the apostles had first given to the churches about Jesus' life, teaching, and saving work. Official teaching has to be related to the original message of salvation, which the teachers themselves had heard and taken to heart in faith, and then have to further communicate as the "good news of God's grace" to which an apostle like Paul gave witness (Acts 20:24). Pastoral teachers are to work (1) after the apostles have proclaimed the saving message of Jesus' cross and resurrection and (2) during the time in which the texts were taking shape that enshrine accounts of Jesus' works and teaching, that is, the Gospels, while apostolic letters or Epistles were serving to focus the meaning of his coming, death, and resurrection. The pastoral teachers had an ample basis for their teaching and guidance of believers.

The teaching office serves the communication of an instruction aiming at "love that comes from a pure heart, a good conscience, and sincere faith" (1 Tim 1:5). The original message should be a renewing force for humane and holy living, as Pope John XXIII insisted as he set forth the goal for the bishops to promote at Vatican II, especially in his opening address (Appendix 1 below). The magisterium stands in the service of the apostolic Gospel to ensure its integrity and foster its vitality so that the Gospel might reach ever anew believers and the world.

The pastoral teaching office of elders, overseers, and bishops has therefore a key role in the church, one that makes it relevant for anyone doing theology in the Catholic community. But the theological life is more than just listening to official teaching by pope and bishops. It is also clear that the New Testament foreshadowed an active role for other teachers (*didaskaloi*), who have a charism of knowledge (so in 1 Cor 12:28). Even more important was and still is the interior teacher of all believers, the Spirit of truth (John 15:26), given to anoint hearts (1 John 2:27) and guide believers into all truth (John 16:13).

4.2. THE TEACHING OFFICE AND THEOLOGY INTERACTING IN HISTORY

Beyond scattered New Testament indications, the relation between the pastoral magisterium and theology came to be shaped in notably different ways in Christian history. Here we present some selected examples.

The Patristic Episcopal Magisterium

In the whole first millennium of Christianity, the church's teaching office and theologians were not really distinct, since most of the major early teachers, the Fathers of the Church, combined the two roles in their own persons, being bishops who actively promoted, in discourses and writing, a deepened understanding of the meaning of the content of faith. In the patristic "golden age" of AD 350–450, of the twelve major Fathers of East and West, only Ephrem and Jerome were not bishops.[8]

In the first major epoch of Christian teaching, bishops not only treated doctrine in Councils but also produced works of theological depth to instruct in the faith, to expound the meaning of scripture for their communities, and to refute erroneous views on Christ, the Trinity, and God's saving influence on human beings by grace and the sacraments.

In the early church, episcopal teachers played a role in the determination of the biblical canon, when they issued lists of the books received in their churches for public reading as foundational testimonies to Christ. Bishop Athanasius of Alexandria intervened in Egypt against gnostic writings, and North African bishops, in synods at Hippo in 393 and Carthage in 397, gave the deuterocanonical books an official place for public use.[9] Here was a fundamental magisterial activity that identified for believers the foundational books of the Israelite and apostolic heritage.

The most striking early magisterial actions were the collegial deliberations and decisions of bishops gathered at the Councils of Nicea (325), Constantinople (381), Ephesus (431), and Chalcedon (451). These were milestones in the encounter between the apostolic message and instruction and the intellectual culture of Hellenism, especially Stoic and Neoplatonic thought, in the late Roman Empire. At each Council the bishops formally received the transmitted faith coming from previous teachers but ultimately from Jesus and his apostles.[10] We recall the paintings of these early Councils in the Sistine Hall of the Vatican Museum, with the bishops gathered before a chair holding the open book of the Gospels, through which Christ teaches the faith that the Council had to defend against error and further formulate for the church of its day. The bishops in Council issued for the church formulations of what was to be taught publicly — and not to be taught — as a present-day communication of the biblical witness to God and Christ in the work of salvation.

History thus shows that an essential concern of the episcopal magisterium is the canonical scripture, the books that daily nourish faith and serve as the basis of catechetical instruction. As a short expression of the main contents of scripture, the creed was revised and renewed in the early Councils, to give pastors and believers their language of confession, in formulated "articles of faith," which according to St. Thomas open the passage for faith to move on beyond the words to union with God so revealed.[11]

The Early "Petrine" Magisterium

In the fifth century it became increasingly evident that the one particular bishop, the successor of Peter in Rome, had a special role to play among the episcopal teachers of the churches. This emerged clearly in the response of Pope Innocent I in AD 417 to the bishops of North Africa, who had sent to him the decrees of their recent provincial council held at Carthage. To settle disputes over the teaching of the monk Pelagius, the bishops had formulated doctrines that stressed the human need of divine help to live morally and devoutly, that is, on original sin, baptism of infants, and God's helping grace. From Rome, Innocent expressed his satisfaction both with the content of the African synodal decrees and with the step taken to send them to Rome for ratification. Innocent convalidated the decrees and indicated that he would circulate them further. Other churches would thus learn what teachings they should avoid and what to insist on, through the doctrinal formulations originating not in Rome but in North Africa.[12]

History shows that a special role for the Roman "Petrine" magisterium emerged out of the conciliar or synodal teaching activity of bishops. The two functions are closely connected, however, as is clear in Innocent's interaction with the North African council of Carthage and with bishops of the other regions of the West who were then informed of the African decrees and of their Roman convalidation.[13]

Another form of interaction between pope and bishops appeared in the year 451, when Pope Leo I sent his doctrinal *Tome* on Jesus as truly God and truly man to the bishops assembled in council at Chalcedon in Asia Minor. The Council accepted Leo's doctrine enthusiastically with the acclamation, "Peter speaks through Leo!" and their dogmatic decree on the true human nature of Christ was then a concise expression of what Leo had set forth at greater length.[14]

Magisterium and Theology in St. Thomas and Gratian

In the Middle Ages, St. Thomas Aquinas (1225–74) gave a notable account of the magisterium of the pope in his treatment of how in a time of crisis the church's creed can come to be revised and newly formulated. While it is clear from history that a general Council representing the whole church can do this, Thomas points out reasons for holding that the pope as well, in certain circumstances, can act on his own to update the creed.

Two aspects of church law point toward Thomas's conclusion about the pope: (1) The canons ascribe to the pope the power of convoking a general Council, which shows that his authority is on the conciliar level. (2) The same laws give him as well the power of resolving major issues (*maiores et difficiliores quaestiones*) affecting the life of the church. Furthermore, our Lord prayed for Peter that his faith may not fail, so that in time he might "strengthen your brothers" in faith (Luke 22:32). From this Thomas concludes that in a time of confusion and uncertainty, the holder of Peter's office can issue an updated creed, making more precise a point of the church's faith, because this is one way to settle questions expeditiously and so give the whole church a way to profess and teach the same faith.[15]

The medieval centuries also saw some notable expressions of the distinctive role in the church of theological scholars and interpreters of scripture. The same Thomas Aquinas juxtaposed two "chairs" (*cathedrae*) of teaching: (1) the chair of the bishop in his cathedral church or of the pope's "chair of Peter," and (2) the chair of the professor, a doctor of theology, appointed to teach in a university faculty.

From the episcopal or pontifical chair, a bishop or pope speaks with pastoral authority and out of love for the believing community.

Threats to unity and to the purity of faith have to be warded off by decisions from this chair, which call for obedience. The other chair, that of the teacher (*magister*), Thomas calls the "magisterial" chair.[16] To the latter a person is appointed by reason of demonstrated competence and eminent learning, so that benefits coming from theological study and reflection may be communicated to others. The second chair is a platform from which to spread understanding of God's word in the church and in the world. But when the church's faith is in question, naturally the holder of the scholarly chair is subject to those holding the episcopal or pontifical chair, without however being absorbed into it.[17]

Medieval church law also knew that those holding pastoral authority or jurisdiction are not alone in contributing to the church's doctrinal life and well-being. Master Gratian of Bologna, whose *Decretum* (written around 1140) was the church's basic codification of earlier laws and norms, made the distinction between those empowered to resolve cases in an authoritative manner and those competent to interpret scripture.

Gratian wrote that in a doctrinal dispute those holding pastoral office in the episcopate or papacy can intervene to declare authoritatively what must be held. But Gratian added that interpretations of scripture by those with scholarly competence also have authority when their contribution to understanding God's word rests upon spiritual gifts, diligent attention to the sacred text, and sound reasoning.[18]

This dual conception of Christian teaching, held by St. Thomas and Gratian, was evident at the Council of Constance (1414–18) where those holding doctorates in theology or canon law were voting members of the Council along with the bishops in attendance. Before Constance and for a century after, the role of the theological chair was assumed by the professors of theology of the University of Paris, who regularly examined the positions held by other teachers all over Europe and at times subjected them to censure and condemnation as erroneous or heretical.[19]

Magisterium and Theology: Modern Developments

In the sixteenth century, in answer to early Protestant claims and doctrines, several Catholic theologians worked in the front lines of

controversy, giving both arguments against the reformers and positive formulations of Catholic positions. We see this in the works of
Johann Eck, professor in Ingolstadt, Cardinal Cajetan (Tommaso de
Vio, OP), St. Thomas More, Jacob Latomus of Louvain, and St. John
Fisher, bishop of Rochester in England, whom King Henry VIII had
executed in 1535.[20] But the official and comprehensive Catholic
answer to the Reformation came in the Council of Trent (1545–
63), which then shaped Catholic identity for nearly four centuries.
At Trent, the theologians were clearly subordinated to the bishops,
who alone were voting members of the Council.[21]

Theologians at the Council of Trent held regular meetings on the
doctrinal questions, such as (1) original sin and how it is neutralized
by baptism, (2) God's grace and human freedom, (3) the nature of
sacraments, (4) the eucharistic real presence and sacrifice, and (5) the
particular sacraments, especially penance and holy orders. Often the
deliberations began with a list of positions taken from Lutheran writings, leading to a discussion of why positions of these adversaries
were wrong and on what basis and at what level the Council should
condemn them. Some theologians at Trent examined the decrees of
earlier Councils, texts of the Church Fathers, and works of classic
medieval theologians to amass data that could show that the Protestants were deviating from the perennial teaching of the Catholic
tradition.

But the theologians at Trent did only preparatory and provisional
work. Their conclusions were then discussed by the bishops, the
voting members of the Council, and the positions taken by the bishops then determined what was said in the eventual doctrinal texts.
Emending the draft decrees and voting to issue them as conciliar
teaching was exclusively the role of the bishops.

While the Council worked at Trent, the popes remained in Rome,
but they sent directives to their legates who presided over the Council's deliberations. The cardinal-legates, usually three, set the agenda
of topics, but had no veto power over outcomes of the deliberations.
Once the Council ended, its fourteen doctrinal texts and thirteen
decrees on reform gained their full binding power in the Catholic
Church by being confirmed by Pope Pius IV in 1564.

To assure that Trent's conciliar teaching and reforms would shape everyday instruction of the faithful, a group of four theologians worked in Rome after the Council under Cardinal Charles Borromeo to complete the *Roman Catechism,* which Pope Pius V formally issued in 1566 as the normative expression of Catholic doctrine, now made precise on many points by the Council of Trent. Existing catechisms in different countries had to be revised so that early modern Catholic teaching would follow what Trent had laid down, as presented in an ordered fashion in the new handbook, popularly known as *The Catechism of the Council of Trent.*[22]

Trent thus began an era of subordinate service by theologians in aid of the official teaching office of bishops and the pope. The nineteenth century saw this accentuated when the central magisterium and many leading Catholic thinkers urged a strong assertion in the church of the principle of authority against the egalitarian ideas stemming from the French Revolution.

Pope Gregory XVI, with the encyclical *Mirari vos* (1832), initiated the most characteristic modern form of papal teaching through encyclical letters addressed to all the Catholic bishops of the world. The encyclicals treat many issues of religious practice and devotion, but they also communicate papal pronouncements on the content of faith and doctrine, which was to be immediately absorbed into the teaching of theologians as theses having the backing of papal teaching authority.[23] In the modern phase the popes came to the forefront of teaching, but in fact a group of theologians who taught in the ecclesiastical universities in Rome had considerable anonymous influence through their work preparing draft texts of encyclicals. In these cases, the two chairs were in effect fused into one.

The practice of the Council of Trent and its aftermath set the form of the relationship between the papal-episcopal magisterium as it lasted down to Vatican Council II. Pope Pius XII formulated the relation in the encyclical *Humani generis* (1950), when he said (1) that the magisterium is to be the theologian's "proximate and universal norm of truth" and (2) that the task of theologians is to show how present-day magisterial teaching has developed organically and homogenously from the original sources, leading to what today's official teaching makes explicit and clear in conclusions from the suggestions and implications of the original biblical and traditional texts.[24]

It is not too much to say that in the 1950s, just before Vatican Council II, the papal magisterium became the primary *locus* of Catholic doctrinal teaching, as the official and authoritative interpreter of what was given and meant in the original witnesses to God's revelation. The pope was a living and active oracular presence whose teachings were contemporary and relevant. Behind his authority stood the declaration by Vatican Council I (1870) that the pope was protected from error and so infallible in certain actions of declaring a dogma of the faith. The modern popes have made only two such solemn declarations, first, of Mary's Immaculate Conception (Pius IX, 1854), and, second, of her bodily assumption into heaven (Pius XII, 1950). But these exercises of official teaching authority at its highest level had a broader effect of orienting all Catholic theological work to the teachings of the papal magisterium at its various levels of doctrinal activity.

With Vatican Council II, a New Relationship

Regarding the relationship between the papal-episcopal magisterium of the Catholic Church and those who do theology, Vatican II signaled the end of one era and the beginning of a transition to another way of relating. The bishops who were the voting members at Vatican II became aware of an immense contribution made by the theological experts who served the Council by offering insights and formulations based on biblical theology, the history of doctrine, ecumenical experience, and reflection on the relation between Christianity and the secular world. The theologians helped in preparing many oral and written interventions by the bishops on Council topics, and the Council's commissions called many of these experts into service during the Council to help compose and revise the texts to be evaluated and voted upon by the Council members. Appendix 5 below relates the many-sided role of theologians at Vatican II.

In the immediate aftermath of Vatican II, many theologians provided an essential mediation between what the Council had formulated and the wider public of the church, especially in their introductions to and commentaries on the sixteen Vatican II documents. The ecumenical opening sanctioned and promoted by the Council then led to many Catholic theologians having an intense service of the church, continuing today, on ecumenical commissions for dialogue with their opposite numbers who represented the Orthodox, Anglican, Lutheran, Methodist, and other Christian traditions.

The years following Vatican II were also marked by theological controversy, as some Catholic theologians tested the limits of acceptable reformulation of the received doctrinal heritage. Under Pope John Paul II, the magisterium, speaking through the Vatican Congregation for the Doctrine of the Faith, responded with critical censures that pointed out untenable positions in works by theological writers such as Hans Küng, Charles Curran, and Leonardo Boff. The same Congregation, often with explicit approval of the pope, has continued to propose doctrines, as in its "Considerations" on the pope's ministry of unity (1998) and in the much-discussed declaration *Dominus Iesus* (2000), which addresses the religious pluralism of our world with a firm statement of the singular role of Jesus Christ as Lord and Savior of all peoples.[25]

But in the last decades of the twentieth century, many theologians were contributing constructively to the Catholic community, for example, by their entries, inspired largely by Vatican II, in new theological reference works in dictionary style.[26] Also, a group of thirty Catholic theologians continues to work on the International Theological Commission, serving as a Catholic theological "brain trust" with a degree of official recognition of their complementary role alongside the official teaching office of the pope and bishops.[27]

The Magisterium and Theology Today: Related but Different

In the new relationship that has emerged between the church's official teaching and Catholic theology, the central fact is that they make up a joint activity in understanding and communicating the meaning of the word of God. The magisterium acts as an institutional component of the church, endowed sacramentally by episcopal ordination for a public ministry of both promoting and critically overseeing teaching of the Catholic doctrinal heritage. Theologians work on the basis of their scholarly competence, both alone and collaboratively in associations, conferences, and academic groupings, to gain and propose insights into the meaning communicated by the different testimonies to God's word about himself and human life in his grace. From both sides, enrichment comes to the life of faith for the good of individuals and the world.

God's truth is present in the world in different forms, as in the texts of scripture, the expressions of the church's living tradition, and in the faith and life of believers. The magisterium communicates formulations of this truth, aiming at an integral presentation that can form believers in a deeper faith and greater holiness of life. Theology relates to the same *loci* ("places") of truth, both by analytical and scholarly investigation of texts of faith and by reflectively working out systematic accounts of the Christian message and its implications for life.

A popular notion of the magisterium as watchdog of orthodoxy may place it in constant tension with creative works of theology, but this impression should not obscure the fundamentally convergent character of the goals and operations of the two activities. Both aim at helping faith to flourish. Both have instrumental roles under the Spirit of truth, who is the interior teacher of the Gospel and of its ramifications for enhancing human life in this world.

Two Situations and Manners of Service

The difference, and connection, between magisterial teaching and theological research and its communication can appear more sharply through a reflection on where they work and how they communicate their message and teaching.

The ecclesial magisterium works in proximity to the genesis and development of believers' graced life in Christ. Bishops who hold the teaching office work regularly, even daily, together with pastors, in making the Gospel actual and better known through liturgical worship, administering the sacraments, and catechesis. Bishops follow closely the public witness given by believers and their communities. Diocesan and parish pastors stand in the midst of the churches in which they speak and act as those entrusted with bringing the apostolic heritage to bear on lives of believers so that they may grow in faith and holiness. The fundamental teaching responsibility of the pope and other bishops is thus not so much for creative input as for the complete expression and faithful communication of what the church already is and believes.

A characteristic action of the magisterium is the overseeing of cate-chetics. The church's pastors bear responsibility for recognizing and affirming what truly tells of the meaning of Christ and builds up his people in faith, hope, and love. They do this from a lived proximity to the sacramental life of the church, especially eucharistic celebra-tion, where by regular presiding and participation they will in the best case develop an instinct for what fits well with the original apostolic tradition and so really promotes a deeper faith and greater holiness.

Vatican II adopted a phrase from Irenaeus of Lyons and applied it to the members of the episcopate, namely, that they receive a "sure charism of truth" (*carisma veritatis certum*), but this came in DV 8 just after the Council gave its holistic notion of the apostolic deposit, of "everything that helps the people of God live a holy life and grow in faith" (DV 8). The magisterial charism is for discerning and acknowl-edging, as by a developed instinct, what expresses and advances what the church has received from the apostles.

Regarding biblical interpretation, the magisterium's concern is with contemporary interpretations and their coherence with the sense of scripture that lives in the church. Church documents do not pro-nounce on the original meaning of the biblical texts in the initial expression and meaning given by the authors. When Councils deal with scripture, as when the Council of Trent spoke on Jesus' words of eucharistic institution and on the basis of sacramental anointing of the sick (Jas 5:14), they are not doing historical-critical exegesis, but instead are affirming the coherence and legitimacy of the develop-ment that led from the texts themselves to their common application in the church. Retrieval of the precise intent of the authors, in their original formulation, is left to experts in biblical languages and forms of composition.[28]

In contrast with magisterial discernment in the midst of the church, good theology bases itself on a broad intellectual and spiritual cul-ture. The able theologian works in very different "places" (*loci*), drawing on numerous sources of understanding. God has in fact spoken "in many and various ways" through the prophets, his Son, and the apostles (see Heb 1:1–2), and their witness permits our human family to share in the inscrutable riches of Christ. Profound theological meaning, thus, cannot be found in a single source nor can it be conveyed one-dimensionally.

The testimonies of faith and life in the Lord are manifold and varied, as they arise from God's word and gifts of grace making themselves present and active in believers' lives. This has gone on in every Christian century and continues today. Theologians sometimes search for documentation of truth and the graced life in what might seem to be obscure corners of Christian tradition and human experience. They are right to do so, for at no time does the most recent tradition of doctrine express exhaustively God the savior and our graced human life. Topics and schemes of understanding, found under the dust of the past or in the far reaches of the present, can prove renewing when taken hold of, penetrated for their meaning, and freshly proposed.

Patterns of understanding recovered by theologians from scripture or from past eras can become new keys of present-day explanation. But help toward coherent proposals and new organized systems must also come from contemporary nontheological thought. The personal culture of the theologian has to include as well a good knowledge of the philosophies and human sciences of his or her own day.[29]

The church's magisterium and theology are, thus, different in being differently positioned and differently endowed for serving believers. The basic difference, to be sure, does not exclude a degree of overlap. The pastoral magisterium gains much when its bearers bring to its work a deep theological culture, as now evident in the discourses, homilies, and pastoral writings of Pope Benedict XVI, who worked for two decades as an engaged and productive professor of theology. Theology, on its side, needs a vital relationship with the living church that professes its faith, worships God, and gives witness to God's generosity by dedicated service. But the characteristic contexts of the two contributions remain basically different, while the work of each complements that of the other.

4.3. THE THEOLOGIAN AND
MAGISTERIAL TEACHING

Theological research and reflection fuse together in concentration on what careful listening draws out of the Christian sources, or "places," that testify to God's word of revelation and work of saving grace. As developed in chapters 2 and 3 above, theology draws on scripture and the varied expressions of living and lived tradition in order to work out explanatory accounts of God's revelation and its implications for life. But these are for the Catholic theologian not the sole concern, for the church's magisterium has in the past offered, and continues to offer, guidance on interpreting God's gifts of saving truth and of his grace for living in a manner worthy of such gifts. Thus a final concern of this chapter is to describe the steps by which a theologian, by weighing and interpreting, deals with authoritative pronouncements by the teaching office on what God's revelation means both in itself and for us.[30]

In taking up this phase of doing theology, one can draw on helpful publications of the later twentieth century, such as "The Interpretation of Dogmas" (1990), a collaborative work of Catholic theologian-members of the International Theological Commission.[31] The document treats topics like contemporary theories of interpretation, the biblical and traditional foundations of church teaching on central tenets of the faith, and the criteria of adequate interpretation in the church.

Our previous chapters have gone over several areas treated in the commission's document. But a further topic remains, namely, the steps of theological work in the particular situation of response to a recent episcopal, conciliar, or papal teaching. Following a sketch offered by Juan Alfaro and attending to a key part of "The Interpretation of Dogmas," I distinguish two phases of the theological examination and interpretation of official church teaching.[32]

The combination and adaptation of these recent works gives the following sketch of two distinct theological investigations of church doctrine, with the first being a more technical analysis and the second a more constructive development of how a teaching contributes to the life of faith. Here is a particular case of the basic duality of theological work as listening and explaining, as present at the end of chapter 1 above.

Analysis of Church Teaching

A first cluster of concerns in a properly theological study of a church teaching, as in a document of a Council, a papal encyclical, or a declaration by the Congregation of the Doctrine of the Faith, centers on analysis. This aims to clarify the genesis of the intervention, its precise intent, and its binding authority.[33]

A first movement in working on a pronouncement of the magisterium is to clarify its place in the ongoing development of Catholic teaching. This involves examination of the need that called forth the declaration and of the situation that the teaching addresses, which is often a controversy. One has to seek out the sources on which the new proposal draws in formulating its teaching and to identify the underlying convictions and presuppositions motivating the authors in their choice of terms and of style in the text they issued.

A theological reading of a magisterial document has to be aware of previous church teaching on the same or related matters, so as to identify what is new in the most recent declaration. This kind of genetic study can gain a special depth of understanding if the theological researcher is able to study successive drafts of the text during its preparation, as is possible regarding teaching documents of the Councils of Trent, Vatican I, and Vatican II.[34]

Theological research into the genesis of a particular church teaching aims to identify and understand the historical conditions affecting an action of the magisterium. In such a study, the goal is to set in sharp relief the intention of the text, both in what it says and does not say. Such study may lead to identifying the combination of a traditional component reinforcing previous teaching along with an innovative aspect going beyond previous teaching in a creative manner.[35]

Theological research on church documents can be especially rewarding if one is able to identify new accents of magisterial teaching and give a plausible idea of their motivation and sources. In this line, helpful clarifications have emerged from the study of the movement of Catholic social teaching from Pope Leo XIII to Pope John Paul II.[36]

A second step in the analysis of a magisterial document is to clarify the exact doctrinal authority of the teaching, by study of how the magisterium sees itself acting and how the content of the teaching relates to the central components of God's word received in faith. Faith's response to God is an amazed and grateful acceptance of God's gift of himself and of the new life coming through Christ in the Holy Spirit. Faith is a "yes" to *what* God tells about himself and his work of salvation, a "yes" which leads to confessing faith in the public context of the life of the church. The creed, based on scripture and the rule of faith, delineates the basic coordinates of God's word received in the church, and later teachings have to be located with precision in their relation to what the creed professes to be the center of God's saving work and the believer's relation to God.

For such analysis of teaching by the church's teaching office, a key tool of theological work is the graded scale of doctrinal qualifications that express the weight of authority in church teachings.[37] To identify this doctrinal weight of a teaching is to draw a clear line between different spheres of obligation and freedom in our attempts to restate teaching for ourselves and for others in a way that enlightens personal situations.

Constructive Theological Thinking and Church Teaching

On church teaching, theology has to push ahead into the area of *meaning*, the meaning of teachings for individuals and different communities. In such theological work, the trained theologian often joins the concerned Catholic believer, who at times will set out on a theological quest of the meaning of faith and discipleship.

A helpful way to put order into this search for meaning is to follow the suggestion of Juan Alfaro by thinking in terms of past, present, and future, so as to give theological reflection three directions in which to work in deepening its grasp of a church teaching.

Theology has to have a *retrospective* moment, because every Christian doctrine springs from the events of God's revelation of himself in Israel and in his Son Jesus, who climaxes God's word and saving work for humankind. All doctrine tends ultimately to make present and contemporaneous for us the fundamental events of God's dealing with us as our Creator, Savior, and Sanctifier, as these basic interventions and works are attested in scripture and confessed in the church's creed. All moral teaching issued by the magisterium aims to give contemporary applications of the commandments given on Sinai, the instruction on practice imparted by Jesus, and the apostolic directives for life found in the New Testament Epistles.

Doctrine aims to guide faith toward hearing the original good news of Christ in a fresh and living way. Scripture, we recall, is not simply a record of past events over and done with, for it is the perennial sourcebook about the God who holds creation in being today, who draws us to his Son now risen to be life-giver, and who plants light and truth in our hearts by his Spirit. The theological quest moves along pathways that lead from present-day teaching back to the events witnessed to and the guidance given in scripture and then back again from them to their impact on Christian lives today.

Second, theological research seeks insight into the actual meaning now *in the present,* when the teaching authority has spoken to the rest of the church. Here the quest is for the light and life that a doctrine or moral norm can offer today to individuals and communities who take instruction from the teaching. God's word has not ceased to echo in human hearts and the Holy Spirit has not ceased teaching believers by letting the living voice of the Gospel resound now in the church and the world (DV 8). Church teaching aims to connect believers with God's project of salvation, which is still unfolding and continues to bless individuals. A work of salvation is present today with its call to conversion and its invitation to life in Christ as St. Paul repeatedly termed it. Theological service of the believing community has to recall this incessantly as it presents church teaching.

A powerfully concentrated emphasis on Jesus Christ pervades the major teachings of Vatican Council II, as in DV 1–4, LG 1–8, AG 1–5, and GS 10, 22, 32, 38–39, and 45. This should point the Catholic theologian to make every teaching throw light on the present-day relation that Christ indeed establishes with every believer. In Christ, "the entire revelation of the most high God is summed up" (DV 7), the revelation, that is, of God-with-us to save us from the darkness of sin and death and to raise us up to new life (DV 4).

The risen Christ is today still with his followers as the firstborn of the new humanity, as one who dwells in believing hearts (Matt 28:20; 2 Cor 13:5; Col 1:15, 18; Eph 3:15–16). The true shape of human life today is trinitarian, namely, that believers "should have access to the Father, through the Son, the Word made flesh, in the Holy Spirit, and thus become sharers in the divine nature" (DV 2).

Good theology, working from the church's teaching, connects doctrine with the death and resurrection of Christ to new life, a life he still lives for us and for our salvation. Teaching should, by good theological work on it, serve to introduce believers of today into a life-giving communion with God in three persons.

Third, theology takes a *prospective* view of church teaching by pointing to the future toward which believers are called. We are taught in the church, so as to be coherent and credible witnesses to God's full project of salvation for persons and for the world. When those who hear church teaching take it to heart and then speak and act more graciously and with greater dedication to benefit others, then the doctrinal tradition is showing its power to enhance and save individuals, families, and whole societies, as Pope John XXIII sketched in his hopeful commissioning of those who took part in Vatican Council II. Theology will search out how magisterial doctrine and moral teaching leads believers to be light for the world and salt of the earth.

Theological work oriented to the future will take the long view of an eschatological perspective, looking to the culmination of God's saving project, when the glory of Christ will be fully revealed and those following his way will be introduced into the final kingdom under God's sovereign rule, as God becomes in the end all in all (as in 1 Cor 15:20–28). Vatican II depicted the church as a people moving ahead in the present in search of a future permanent city (LG 9, echoing Heb 13:14). This perception is rife with implications for the church's teaching, most obviously in the way believers make it their own so as to freshly engender and intensify Christian trust in God's promises. Theology will move from what a church teaching presents now to look toward the time when doctrines will pass away because those who were believers will see God in face-to-face vision.

Doctrines, even though attested by God's prophets and apostles, indicated in inspired scripture, and taught by the Church, still do not provide a luminous vision of God's truth, for doctrines, to borrow words of Vatican II, are "like a mirror in which the church, during its pilgrim journey on earth, contemplates God, from whom she receives everything, until such time as she is brought to see him face to face as he really is" (DV 7, referring to 1 John 3:2). Theology remains on this essentially pilgrim journey.

The theological quest for meaning unfolds in the life of one who has heard about Jesus Christ, accepted the witness given to the same Christ, which is fundamentally the apostles' witness further taught by the Holy Spirit's anointing (1 John 2:20, 27). Present-day official teaching has its impact as guidance given to the Catholic community, but the theological quest looks further, going back to origins, probing present affirmations, and letting the future horizon of God's promises open up, from which comes light cast on the present by God's promised completion of our liberation and salvation.

Review Questions

1. Who were the "elders" or community "overseers" in the first era of Christianity, and what did St. Paul bring out as their chief responsibilities in Acts 20?

2. What do the New Testament texts on teachers contribute to an understanding of the church's magisterium?

3. What were some major contributions to Christian doctrine of the bishop-theologians of the fourth and fifth centuries?

4. How do Popes Innocent I and Leo I exemplify the early functioning of the teaching office of the bishop of Rome?

5. How do the magisterium (episcopal, conciliar, papal) and theologians relate to each other according to St. Thomas and Master Gratian?

6. How did Catholic theologians contribute to the Council of Trent during its sessions and then in the spread of its teaching?

7. How did Vatican Council II contribute to a new relationship between the magisterium and Catholic theology?

8. How do the magisterium (episcopal, conciliar, papal) and Catholic theologians converge in promoting the same goal?

9. What are the characteristic concerns of those who exercise the responsibilities of the church's magisterium?

10. What are the characteristic ways of analysis and constructive thought by which Catholic theologians respond to magisterial teaching?

Projects for Further Study

1. Study the First Epistle of John, guided by the annotations of the Jerusalem Bible or the New American Bible. Present, then, the different kinds of teaching that the author sees as given to the Christians to whom he writes.

2. Study the first four general Councils, that is, Nicea to Chalcedon, aiming to draw up an account of what each gave to the church's pastors and people. For this, use a short history of Councils, for example, by Norman Tanner (*The Councils of the Church*, 2001) or Hubert Jedin (*Ecumenical Councils of the Catholic Church*, 1960), or the entries about these Councils in the *New Catholic Encyclopedia* (1967, 2002) or *Oxford Dictionary of the Christian Church* (3rd ed., 1997).

3. Study Appendix 5 below to work out a list of the contributions to the teaching work of Vatican Council II made by the theologians who assisted the bishops who were the voting members of the Council.

4. In your college library, examine the theological dictionaries mentioned in note 26 of this chapter (page 259). Give examples of the influence of Vatican Council II on select entries in these works.

Chapter Five

Doing Theology amidst Life

A S A COUNTERPART to chapter 1 on historical models and ecclesial contexts of doing theology, this chapter draws out connections between doing theology and the broader realities of our human lives on earth and in history.

The life of a Christian has a corporate or community dimension, which is especially valued and accentuated in the Catholic tradition. To do theology in this tradition consequently involves a vital exchange within "the family of faith" in drawing on resources and experiences of communities of believers and then, through the results gained, in letting insights into theological meanings become an enrichment of others in a person's community of belief, worship, witness, and service of others. Section 5.2 below will develop this in greater detail.

The believer's life also develops within a thick matrix of personal situations, experiences, and decisions. Theology, thus, develops out of what is planted and grows in the soil of one's personal life and in the lives of other believers encountered along life's paths. Theology draws on personal experience, and it aims to contribute to enriching personal living, first in the person doing theology and then in the lives of those to whom the theologian tells what he or she has come to understand about God and about life under God's saving project that envelops all human lives. Section 5.3 below will sketch this dimension more at length.

But before relating theological listening and explaining to the horizon of life that surrounds our doing theology, a first section (5.1) will draw together the principal goals and activities of a theologian. This is the life that theology *is*.

5.1. THEOLOGY AS METHODICAL DISCIPLINE
AND AS WISDOM

The previous chapters have repeatedly described how doing theology involves probing the resources of faith to gain insight into the meaning of God's word of revelation and his work of renewing and saving his human creatures.

In the late second century, Irenaeus of Lyons insisted on taking the apostolic doctrinal tradition as foundational, while in the sixteenth century Melchior Cano showed that good theology, to grasp well God's word, has to draw upon many and varied testimonies. Vatican Council II proposed a genetic or developmental analysis and account of what the sources yield (OT 16), while taking account of a "hierarchical" ordering of the truths identified by the theological search.

More basically, a person engaged in the theological search studies the open book of scripture, both in detailed study of particular passages and in a global reading of the biblical message in tune with its reception by the Church Fathers and the living tradition (DV 12). But St. Thomas pointed out that particular truths received as articles of faith are not ends in themselves but instead vehicles to carry the believing human spirit toward encounter and communion with God himself.

A particular theological insight will also gain depth from finding it present in the liturgy and in the lives of holy people, since these too are "places" where God is speaking and working to bring salvation. Church teaching has to be studied in depth by concentrated study, which will be both attentive listening and more expansive construction of its meaning for life. Such activities make up a life dedicated to doing theology.

The following paragraphs develop further the initial sketch given in chapter 1, section 3 above, about the two phases of theological work, especially in its constructive or explanatory phase.

A Methodical Discipline of Perception

In all its activities, theology is the practice of critical and methodical search for meaning in God's revelation. Theology extends a person's "hearing in faith" (see Rom 10:17) in a more attentive listening to the witnesses and teachers, preeminently Jesus himself and his apostles, but also the others who speak to us out of the broad span of sources. In Catholic theology, a key moment has to be listening intelligently to the message and teaching that formulates what is held corporately as the faith of the church and the norms of living in Christ today.

Theology's initial moment is one of perception, as it lays hold of a reality that it did not create. This, however, is not done only passively, but in active questioning that follows steps of method proper to the sources consulted and heard. Still, the aim is always to identify and lay hold of a meaning expressed by another and then to express that meaning, meaningfully, for oneself and for others.

Theology searches and listens with the aim of attaining *well-grounded understanding* and then putting forth *solidly based discourse* about the meaning of God and of life in the light of his nearness in word and grace. Ultimately, the ground and basis of a valid theological proposal is the witness given by "the apostles and prophets" (Eph 2:20). Based on this witness, a theological explanation will have Jesus Christ as the cornerstone (ibid.), and the explainer will set in place stones quarried from the main "places," or *loci*, given us in the church and in human history.

Good theology, especially but not exclusively in the Catholic tradition, abhors the aridity of speculation about possible worlds that might have been or could still be. It turns quickly away from scenarios that could have, but in fact did not, develop at crucial points of the development of the church's teaching of faith, ways of worship, and following of Christ. The flight from idiosyncratic explanations has a long history beginning with the early Church Fathers and their rejection of gnostic lore about the soul's escape from this evil world, when they insisted on the apostolic message of creation and redemption by the Word incarnate in our flesh. In an often repeated movement, the mind of one engaged in doing theology moves toward the bedrock of the canonical scriptures and to the ecclesial places where the original witness has been set down to be perceived, understood, and further applied to living and acting in a manner worthy of the Gospel of Christ.

Explanation in the Theological Disciplines

From consulting the sources attentively in the quest of insights, theological work then turns to developing coherent explanations. In this second moment, the theologian dedicates his or her life to making, between the perceptions gained, intelligent connections by a broad-angle vision of the meaning attested in the sources.

God's word conveys in fact many different meanings, since its witnesses are many and varied and the work of salvation embraces the whole span of human life and action. But there is a coherence in God's word and work, for they come from one Savior God who guides his creation with consummate wisdom. The coherence, however, is often not immediately evident, and so theology keeps trying to bring it out by connecting the particulars. An overall design is needed, to show structures and cohesion. In such a design several or many particular truths meld into a single pattern of meaning, which shows something of the coherent wisdom embedded in what God says and does.

St. Thomas Aquinas produced an elegant design of the coherence of God's creative and saving work. He ordered the hundreds of short treatises, the "questions," of his *Summa of Theology* according to the scheme of a vast "coming out" (*exitus*) of creatures, especially human beings, from God the creator, and he gathered many doctrines under the further rubric of creatures' "return" (*reditus*), by loving attraction through the grace of Christ, to God as their final and fulfilling end. What God makes to issue forth into being and action, he then draws back to himself, especially his human, intellectually endowed, and free creatures, whom he unites in Christ and brings in love to the utterly fulfilling vision of his own goodness and glory.

In the twentieth century, the Swiss reformed theologian Karl Barth (1886–1968) gave an initial order to his huge *Church Dogmatics* by speaking of a threefold word of God to humans for them to lay hold of in faith. Christ is God's word in person, the scriptures God's word in written testimony, and the preached Gospel the spoken word of grace and salvation to otherwise lost human beings.

The German Jesuit Karl Rahner (1904–84) brought an ordered harmony into the hundreds of religious topics on which he wrote, doing this by repeatedly pondering them from a single perspective.

Rahner centered on the human person and reflected repeatedly on how our historical human nature is not a closed system but is in fact open to, and even expectant of, being called beyond its natural situation by God's gifts and graces, toward saving communion with God. God who reveals does not speak to us from a vast distance, but as the one who is an ultimate mystery present on the spiritual horizon of our lives. God's call, for Rahner, repeatedly finds human beings waiting for this loving invitation, which finds an echo in the way humans are made as "hearers of the word."[1]

St. Thomas, Karl Barth, and Karl Rahner, each in his own way, offer coherent and intelligently constructed explanations able to include many particular truths in systematic schemes that mirror the wisdom of God our Creator and Savior.

The Theological Areas and Basic Topics

The theological life of attentive, methodical listening and systematic explaining works itself out in different areas of research and communication of results on basic topics. Appendix 7 below gives a chart of the subject areas of Catholic theology, in which the central section of the four parts of systematic theology is most relevant to what follows here.

In *fundamental theology* one listens to testimonies and seeks to create ordered accounts of God's word of revelation and of the human condition in relation to God's call to faith in the Gospel. God's revelation comes close to a person by events and words, and fundamental theology tries especially to show the grounds for one to consider seriously and become ready to accept the message as a word of truth from God and about God. Such grounds or motives can arise from aspects of human existence itself, and they can be found in the way revelation makes its approach through history and credible witnesses. From the depths of our human yearning a place can open up where God's word fits in well. The word of God can give itself credibility by the luminous meaningfulness of what it presents about God and his saving work. Consideration of God's revealing word and of acceptance of this in faith then leads naturally to considering how individual witnesses and communities serve the further communication of God's word in this world.[2]

The listening and explaining of *dogmatic theology* attend to contents, that is, what the word of God says, as attested in scripture and the further sources of doctrine, about God and his gifts to and works for humankind. This is given to believers as fundamental tenets of faith. These include contents such as the following: (1) the life of the Triune God and God's creation of all that exists; (2) God's climactic entry into the human family in Christ and how Christ's life, death, and resurrection bring salvation to humankind; (3) the condition of human persons as created and graced by God, as fallen and impaired, as forgiven and justified through Christ, and as brought to virtuous living and holiness by God's Spirit; (4) the church as the people gathered into community by God's saving word and called to worship him and serve him prophetically in the world; (5) the sacramental events, celebrated liturgically, that both apply God's saving grace to his people and empower individuals for special service; and (6) the final destiny of God's creatures, especially human beings.

On each topic, to do theology is to hear how the sources speak of God and his works and then to make manifest the unity and coherence of God's overarching project for the world and humankind. The theologian, in each of these fields of hearing and explaining, will relate his or her accounts to the faith of the church by working in the stream of tradition and taking guidance from official church teaching. This is the vital context of Catholic teaching where theology has to push ahead the tasks of research and explanation.[3]

In *moral theology* the first concern is the complex of fundamental elements in the life of the Christian person called to live a life worthy of Christ and his Gospel. Central here is conversion to discipleship and to the graced freedom in which good moral choices put a Christian stamp on one's daily life. The moral conscience can draw on several resources, including biblical and church teaching along with the liturgy, prayer, and sacraments, which guide and motivate moral decisions that are both attuned to God's will and favor personal growth in virtuous character. The search for Christian moral wisdom then turns to the personal sphere of discipleship that embraces one's relation to God, the care of life, sexuality, and one's family. The public sphere of social realities, such as communications, the economy, and politics, offers numerous topics for conscience formation and guidance drawn from the Christian sources.[4]

A fourth area of theological life and work is *spiritual theology,* the study of spirituality, by a methodical examination of personal and communal life "in, with, and under" the healing and renewing Spirit of God. Here the biblical sources are ample as are many works of the Church Fathers, since both intertwined their accounts of God's gifts in themselves with insistence on the consequences of the same gifts for us and for each believer. Here the doing of theology becomes quite existential, by considering many personal applications of insights about the resources of life in the Spirit amid the passages of developing Christian discipleship.[5]

Wisdom for Living

Theology aims at well-grounded thinking, speaking based on evidence, and coherent explanations, but it does not stop there. This methodical activity looks further toward grasping and assembling a wisdom to guide everyday living. The coherent vision of a systematic theological explanation is more than a nicely assembled set of data. Values are involved, fundamental values that affect how people understand themselves personally and translate that self-understanding into moral and spiritual living. Successful theology orients human life, providing goals for striving and working, surrounded by a horizon for further thought and especially for prayer to God from the heart.

Good theology draws from the wellspring of trustworthy sources and expresses meaning coherently. Believers who enter the theological quest find values to be appropriated and to articulate in a vision of daily reality and focused choices and activity. Theology, when well developed, points the way toward knowing Jesus Christ and encountering him daily as the one "who became for us wisdom from God, and righteousness and sanctification and redemption" (1 Cor 1:30).

What was just said is one way to speak of the "wisdom for living" that arises out of the effort of doing theology. But there is another wisdom, one given as a gift from on high, which methodical listening and investigation cannot locate and even the most acute reflection cannot organize systematically. Some people have been given "wise hearts" by which they instinctively unfold their daily lives in profound coherence with values given by God. Israel's King Solomon prayed to God for wisdom as a gift that might accompany his royal projects (1 Kgs 3:5–14; Wis 9:1–12). St. Paul knelt in supplication to beg for his readers an interior gift to enlighten their understanding (Eph 3:14–19), a gift of a wholly different order than even the best explanations reached by doing theology.

Some people have knowledge of God's ways with themselves and of their own way to God, grasping this by an instinct given by the Holy Spirit, as St. Thomas explained.[6] The study and reflection of one doing theology also looks to affecting our understanding of how to live, but this requires more hard work than may be needed by those blessed with wise hearts. Theology ponders data and testimonies to clarify their meaning and then works out a coherent structure of what the quest has led one to discover. This is, admittedly, a secondary kind of wisdom, but it has the value of communicability and it *can* on its own level enrich human life, prayer, and action.

Theology can issue in wisdom, because it deals with resources given by the Creator for sane, humane, and holy living in the midst of his creation. Theology sets forth numerous points of doctrinal truth, across the panorama of its subject areas and topics, all of which relate to the life that "was the light of all people" from the beginning and became flesh in Jesus Christ, to bring us "grace and truth" (John 1:3, 14–17). Theology is a development of the teaching begun by Jesus and his apostles, worked out in the hope of taking hold of well-grounded pointers and principles of a good life.

Theology deals with our ultimate goal of consummate fulfillment and happiness in union with God, but also with the intermediate stages along the way, as a person encounters God's word and grace and moves through conversion and growth in commitment to God and dedication to serving the good of others. In all this, theology can and does articulate a wisdom to guide human living according to values that are given from above but that also resonate with our human make-up, so as to be guides toward a sane and sanctified style of life. Theology, ultimately, is for such a life.[7]

5.2. THEOLOGY IN THE COMMUNAL
LIFE OF FAITH

The variety of the Christian sources and the complexity of systematic reflection on their witness mean that few individuals will be complete theologians. One profound account, Bernard Lonergan's *Method in Theology*, presented no less than eight "functional specialties" that are required for carrying through to the end a complete theological project.

Four specialties are *disciplines of perception*: researching data, interpreting historical data, framing the relevant history, and showing how basic viewpoints had interacted in conflict with each other in a dialectical manner. Then follow four *specializations of understanding*: recognizing the horizon within which doctrines make sense, stating doctrines based on their evidence and reasons, putting doctrines into systematic connection with each other and with daily experience, and communicating the outcome of theological work in a way well adapted to different cultures.[8]

This suggests that today doing theology is at best a cooperative and collaborative undertaking. In fact, most theologians work within groups, in schools of theology or departments of theology. Here they have the collegial experience of association with their peers and of work on shared projects.

But another community, the church, is more significant than an academic group of associates in theological work. The church is the place of active communication of God's word and of its "hearing in faith" by individuals and local communities (see Rom 10:17). Vatican Council II's account of tradition retrieved the primacy of the active handing on of the message and form of life transmitted first by Jesus' apostles and even went so far as to speak of the church transmitting to every generation all that she herself *is* (DV 8). This affirmation makes it clear that the actions of the believing, worshiping, and witnessing church are contemporary "places" (*loci*) where one doing theology will gain insight into God's word and work and into human living shaped by God's Spirit.

This book's account of "doing theology" has from the beginning taken the ongoing life of the church as an essential context and point of reference. Biblical and traditional teaching, taken up in official church doctrine, is a testimony to be investigated, but this includes doctrine's connection with the church's liturgical worship, with her lived public witness, and with dedication to bettering human lives. Theology has to take account of, and be open to enrichment from, these dimensions of the church community.

Theology Enriched from the Ecclesial Community

Doing theology as a Catholic involves taking seriously what one's fellow believers actually hold and express as their faith convictions. Theological work is impoverished when it becomes one-sidedly critical of how believers manifest what they hold and seek to live by. The skills and broader religious culture of one long engaged in the practice of theology may well set a person apart from ordinary, less reflective believers, but the relation is skewed if theology is done with a supercilious disdain for the common run of church members. The instruction of Vatican II on the "sense of the faith" (*sensus fidei*) instilled by the Holy Spirit (LG 12) should inculcate in one doing theology not an aristocratic sense of superiority but a genuinely populist respect for people living the faith in their daily lives and devotions.

This "sense of the faith" is an instinctive feel for the truth of God and for his ways of working in human lives. Obviously this sense can atrophy and disappear in persons who do not regularly refresh themselves from the biblical, liturgical, and sacramental wellsprings of Christian life. These resources are given for renewing one's heart in faith and dedication to God's reign, with which a person develops a sensitive ability to perceive God's truth amid various testimonies and expressions.[9]

What believers generally hold as true is the objective "sense of the faithful" (*sensus fidelium*), which is important evidence for the validity of points of teaching. In 1950, before his dogmatic definition as a truth of faith that God assumed Mary, body and soul, into the life of heaven, Pope Pius XII questioned all the Catholic bishops of the world about the belief that they along with their people actually held regarding the extent to which the Mother of Jesus shared in the salvation brought by her Son.

The papal canvass had a positive outcome, allowing Pius XII to ascertain a widespread conviction, within the faith of the church, that Mary was truly assumed into heaven. Thus in the dogmatic decree of November 1, 1950, the pope said he was proceeding to the definition as a solemn act of the magisterium, because what he was defining was in fact held as true by the faith of the church, which is guided by the Spirit of truth. In this case, the conviction about God's crowning gift to Mary was found to be already planted deep in the souls of believers.[10]

There is therefore a disposition diffused throughout the church by which believers are able to recognize God's truth in particular expressions. One way in which this shows itself today is in the springing up of "movements" in the church, which in some cases take on stable and durable forms as new ways of dedication to Christ and to serving him, with the members mutually supporting each other. This occurred in past centuries under the lead of individuals who became founders of new religious communities, like Francis of Assisi, Dominic de Guzmán, Angela Merici, and Ignatius Loyola. In our own day, new movements of faith and dedication underlie the way of life and prayer of the Focolare Movement, the Community of Sant'Egidio, and the parish-based renewal communities spread across North America.

Theology worked out in an ecclesial context, attentive to what the Spirit in saying to the churches, will also have an *ecumenical* sensitivity. This follows from Vatican Council II's assertion that elements of truth and means of sanctification coming from Christ are indeed maintained and made operative unto salvation in the churches and ecclesial communities now outside the Catholic communion (LG 15, UR 3, 20–23). From this basis Vatican II committed the Catholic Church to engaged participation in the ecumenical movement, which had, before the Council, grown to considerable vitality between 1910 and 1960 without Catholic input and participation. After the Council, ecumenical activity has become a major factor in Catholic life, which Pope John Paul II confirmed and further accentuated in his encyclical *Ut unum sint* of 1995.

Theology done in a Catholic community setting can well learn from Protestant figures like Martin Luther and Karl Barth, as done on occasion in this book. The methodological orientation followed by Avery Dulles, namely, the ordered survey of recent and current "models" of theological understanding of a given topic, is enriched by its inclusion of Orthodox and Protestant thinkers in its panorama of approaches to theological understanding.[11] A first place for building on this wider basis, in tune with a Catholic esteem for values outside its own boundaries, is in biblical studies, where Catholic theology can gain much by consulting works of exegesis and biblical theology by scholars belonging to the Anglican Communion and formed in different Protestant traditions. Eastern Orthodox spirituality and patristic-based teaching are a fertile source of new insights from which all Christians can benefit.

A significant component of church life in the early twenty-first century is ecumenical collaboration, by which the churches are forging new bonds between themselves and promoting public witness and action in concert instead of being in competition with each other.

A part of ecumenical activity having particular relevance for those doing theology is the series of *bilateral dialogues* that have produced numerous insightful texts.[12] These statements of consensus and convergence frequently offer fresh insight into the biblical and traditional sources of theological understanding. They give more open and inclusive ways of expressing the doctrinal heritage of the Christian churches.[13] Fortunately, the churches have been generous in allowing the publication of statements formulated in these dialogues, which provide significant materials for use in the theological quest. And this provision of theological papers from joint groups continues to this day.[14]

Theology Contributing to the Church Community

When an individual believer sets out on a theological quest for meaning, probing the Christian sources and looking for the deeper significance of the faith, any good results of better understanding and increased wisdom are sure to become more than a private personal possession.

Being a Christian means to share with others, in a network of mutual influences, in communities in which one lives. A person's worship of God in liturgy with others can well take on more depth in the light of a better grasp of God's work of salvation, the work which the church's worship continues to make present and actual in celebration. Theology aims ultimately at greater wisdom for living, and this leads naturally to giving a witness that can well influence others.

The First Letter of Peter contains a section to which the New American Bible gives the title, "The Christian in a Hostile World" (2:11–4:11). In this situation, the recommended response to hostile opponents rests on believers having understood well their vocation and the hope they have in Christ. A degree of theological insight undergirds a considered answer and wisdom shown in patience.

> But even if you do suffer for doing what is right, you are blessed. Do not fear what they fear, and do not be intimidated, but in your hearts sanctify Christ as Lord. Always be ready to make your defense to anyone who demands from you an accounting for the hope that is in you; yet do it with gentleness and reverence. Keep your conscience clear, so that, when you are maligned, those who abuse you for your good conduct in Christ may be put to shame. For it is better to suffer for doing good, if suffering should be God's will, than to suffer for doing evil.
>
> (1 Pet 3:14–17)

Explaining to others opposed to the Christian way the reasons for our hope is, in fact, what theological research and reflection should give an individual the ability to do.

The contribution of a theological teacher to the church community builds on his or her personal appropriation of what goes into an "accounting for the hope" that is in us, our hope in Christ. The theologian aims to present insights and systematic accounts of God's work to the community of faith, the same community that nourishes and sustains the theological seeker in faith and life. Service as a theological teacher aims to help other believers by leading them to the foundational sources of the Christian message, scripture and tradition, with the light of official teaching, where they find testimony to God's saving work in the world and in their lives. Theology can help people clarify how God is active in their lives, as in the sacraments and in what the Holy Spirit is stirring in believing hearts.

St. Paul listed "teachers" (*didaskaloi*) after "apostles" and after "prophets," in the list of those who serve to build up the communal body of Christ in the world (1 Cor 12:28). The teachers were endowed with gifts and learning by which their instruction of believers and preaching gained greater depth and a better grounding in scripture. From this, the community's worship of God and witness in its milieu became more vibrant, by having a clearer basis in the sources and a clearer idea of how God intends the work of salvation to unfold.

A developed theological understanding of what Christians believe and how they worship can especially serve others by promoting awareness of the different realizations of the church, which is at the same time local, regional, and universal. Believers' lives unfold in all three contexts. The local community of the parish brings them into face-to-face sharing in worship and side-by-side witness and service in one limited locale. But a theological account of church life will alert people to the regional reality of the diocese, headed by the bishop as chief pastor who oversees teaching and pastoral service, whom Vatican II calls "the visible source and foundation of unity" in the particular church of the diocese (LG 23, also 26).

A good theology of the church, while bringing out the importance of what is immediate and local, will also expand believers' awareness beyond a narrow parochialism to take in the larger unity and the further realizations of the church both in the diocese and the universal body of the Catholic communion. The latter we confess to be a privileged form of the church of Christ, called "one, holy, catholic, and apostolic" in the creed. But Catholics make this confession, in actual fact, in the immediate setting of a worshiping community gathered in one place as a primary and concrete form of the church of Christ.

A theologian has to draw on particular traditions of a local church and be alert to what is held true and valued by the "sense of the faith" of its members. These are the immediate context of his or her work of probing the theological sources and developing explanations that connect the realities of revelation and faith. The primary Christian sources will be heard and read amid the realities of a surrounding religious culture, so that theological results can communicate the faith more deeply in a manner adapted to real people in a given place.

Vatican II's Decree on the Church's Missionary Activity speaks of a theological activity that is needed not just in the traditional mission lands, namely, the investigation of how the inherited ideals and wisdom of a given culture can be related to the fundamental tradition of Christianity, in order to contribute to developing in each major socio-cultural area an integral image and account of Christian existence and community life (AG 22).[15]

The theologian has to attend to numerous theological "places" (*loci*) where he or she finds testimonies to God's work for human salvation. In our global village, this means giving attention to ecclesial developments in other churches of the world, both others of the Catholic communion in other regions and those of other Christian communions. From this wider awareness and more expansive information, the theologian can enrich faith and life in his or her immediate locale. Theology is an area of beneficial exchange of gifts between the churches. By this, it serves as a means to foster the development of catholicity in particular churches where one contributes insights and explanations.

Personally, the author of these lines has at times had the delight of students finding well-grounded what he set forth theologically out of the Christian sources. Especially satisfying has been the knowledge that others have taken over my theological insights and explanations to further communicate them by preaching and teaching in communities of faith and worship.

But some major Catholic theologians of the past century had to wait years before their work was recognized as authentic contributions to the life and teaching of the Catholic Church. Figures of the stature of Henri de Lubac, Yves Congar, and John Courtney Murray were judged during the 1950s to be unreliable Catholic thinkers, and church superiors made them suspend some of their projects of theological publication.

But with Vatican Council II, these theologians were recognized as offering a valuable service to the teaching office of the Catholic Church. They lived to see their insights and explanations accepted, and they were called in as experts to help prepare documents eventually approved and promulgated by the Council as Catholic teaching. These theologians did more than probe the sources and draw up new accounts of God's word, human life in faith, and the relation of the church to the world. They suffered personally, but also patiently, which makes their contribution even more exemplary.[16]

5.3. THEOLOGY IN THE PERSONAL LIFE OF FAITH

In chapter 3, on the components of tradition, we urged the potential of lives lived in holiness for promoting a deeper understanding of God and his saving work. Here the horizon widens to bring out what underlies every discussion of the theological sources, namely, that they are ultimately presentations and interpretations of testimonies resting on personal experiences of the realities of sin and loss leading to rescue and renewed life and action. For they come from human beings who know of their own wanderings and, even more, of their being found by God and gathered to him in communion. This key characteristic of the theological sources comes to expression emblematically at the beginning of the apostolic letter 1 John, in words taken up in part into the prologue of Vatican II's Constitution on Divine Revelation:

> We declare to you what was from the beginning, what we have heard, what we have seen with our eyes, what we have looked upon and touched with our hands concerning the word of life — this life was revealed, and we have seen it and testify to it, and declare to you the eternal life that was with the Father and was made visible to us — we declare to you what we have seen and heard so that you also may have fellowship with us; and truly our fellowship is with the Father and with his son Jesus Christ.
> (1 John 1:1–3; see DV 1)

Doing theology is to work with what witnesses have experienced and understood as a result of their finding God's work, word, and grace active in their lives to give them fellowship, or communion, with God and Christ. The fundamental stratum of the theological sources is what believers have experienced and still do experience, as they live the drama of faith, repentance, joyful worship, and service of others. Such testimonies call up the same or similar realities in the theologian's own life, so that he or she may grasp as deeply meaningful what the witnesses relate and communicate.

The theologian's personal experience is not a theological source in the strict sense, because of its private nature, but it serves as an environment that can enrich theological insight into what one hears from the founding Christian witnesses. Experience adds depth to what comes from well-articulated explanations of God's saving work in human lives. Then, in a natural transition, theology opens on a service of helping others know the message of Christ more accurately and live lives of deeper coherence with that Gospel announcement and call.

Theology Enriched by Personal Experience

In the early twenty-first century, fortunately, the criteria of solid theological work by Catholics are no longer those that dominated ordinary Catholic theological work in the decades before Vatican Council II. The day has passed of insisting on theology as largely apologetic argument for positions of the church's magisterium, as Pope Pius XII's encyclical *Humani generis* laid this down in 1950.[17] Theology today takes seriously the nature of its sources, beginning with the many voices of scripture. The sources rest on recitals of God's saving work in history and are directed toward calling forth and solidifying a personal response to God's grace and call.

Theology remains a methodical activity, bound to being precise in its notions, as complete as possible in gathering testimonies, and coherent in its explanations. It has to examine everything that is relevant and submit to the rules of right thinking and coherent presentation. But theology unfolds beyond the intellectual sphere of well-grounded and well-connected explanations, since religious realities, its essential subject matter, enter human lives at decisive moments. Theology is about events and words that call for decision. It treats topics that include offers of a life in personal relations of love and in delight in inspiring and animating gifts beyond all our deserving.

One Catholic theologian working in fundamental theology, Gerald O'Collins, inserts in a key place a reflection on human experience, especially the strong experiences that lead to decisions that change the direction of a person's life. For some experiences bring to us a potential of living more coherently, beyond the all too common reality of living out disjointed fragments of life and work.[18]

Some narratives of the personal drama of faith and life under God's grace have entered the Christian tradition as brilliant illuminations of God's work in human lives, such as Augustine's *Confessions*, the *Pilgrim's Testament* of Ignatius Loyola, and the *Life... Written by Herself* (*Libro de la vida*) of Teresa of Avila. In these accounts, the experiences recounted can enrich greatly the theological quest of Christian wisdom. From them we can know the life of faith from the inside, by firsthand reports on guidance given by the Holy Spirit and on communion of life with God.

Some accounts of personal experience can thus carry us beyond the solely private sphere to show forth a personal identity that can positively contribute to how others, including myself, live. Some of our companions in the community of faith have lived with God in ways that enlarge the horizons of our aspirations beyond what we have to date sought as valuable. They make us and others aware of how fragile is our dedication to personal goals and to the good of others. They disclose at times a personal grandeur that others have made incarnate in their lives. Experiences described by perceptive and gifted believers can alert us and lead us to better contact with the mysterious presence working in us to affect our personal values and the direction of our prayer, work, and dealing with others.

A solid theology is not segregated from Christian spirituality, but draws on it as a valued source. Lived spirituality is not simply a matter of individual devotion isolated from, and without relevance for, understanding theological topics and issues. Fortunately, the proverbial "great divorce" of spiritual living from theological questions and answers, dominant during most of the second millennium in the West, is being overcome through a reconciliation and new interdependence. This should grow more intense, to the enrichment of those who set out on the theological quest.

For a person doing theology, the question is not whether his or her quest for meaning and wisdom can be enriched by taking account of personal experiences of others and of oneself. The issue is that of discovering the authentic traces of God in experience, which we have to admit is often a confused amalgam combining chaotic fragments with patterns of deeper coherence. Experience includes both sinful self-seeking and the healing integration of one's drives and wants. It combines our fears of evil and diminishment with flashes of assurance of God's light and blessing. This is the personal horizon within which the theologian probes the biblical and ecclesial sources of insight and wisdom. The sources, eminently the New Testament Gospels and apostolic letters, along with the Fathers, liturgy, and the saints, alert theologians to realities of their own lives which correspond to what the sources depict, and this promotes deeper insights into what they narrate, announce, and explain.

Theology Speaks to Personal Experience

A competent and concentrated reading of the theological sources and an elegant and coherent ordering of what one finds will lead to conclusions that naturally influence what believers experience as they journey onward in life in this world. Theology does not unfold its quest on a distant planet nor is it concerned with abstract thought, as in pure mathematics.

Ultimately, theological research and reflection are not privately personal and solely self-referential. They have to do with Jesus Christ, with the God and Father whom he praised and served, and with the word about him that has gone forth into our world to be planted in human hearts by the Spirit sent by the risen Christ. The experiences of this Spirit are both personal and social, for while the Spirit works in individuals, this work effects a gathering, a convocation, of many into communities. So, what individuals experience comes to be shared by many others. Theological discoveries have their own drive to be communicated to others and to influence their experiences of life in the world in which Christ is still present and his Spirit is forming communities of faith and witness.[19]

What an individual lays hold of during the theological quest, by drawing insight out of the sources and creatively organizing the elements discovered, leads to expression and communication, both by how one really lives and by one's spoken and written words to others. Since the result comes from a limited individual, it remains partial and incomplete. My own theological results need to be complemented by

those of others who have their own experiences, approaches to the
sources, and moments of seeing connections between different parts
of God's word and work.

The approach that emerges from this introduction to doing theology leads to claiming that the most basic location of what results
from a theological quest is not the university lecture or scholarly
essay. Good theology aims to find a dwelling place in minds and
hearts of persons who find its insights and explanations to be sources
of light in the lives they are living. Theology should intersect with
how we understand ourselves as we live in the social context of family, friends, and those with whom and for whom we are given work
to do. To be sure, Christian theology has to do with texts, from scripture, the Fathers, or church teaching, but it looks beyond "getting it
right" in accurate reports and correct explanations. Theology cries
out to be assimilated into the web of personal experiences and into
the way one prays, chooses, serves others, and looks to the future.

But a person setting out on the theological quest has to be ready to
wait patiently for clear results that affect life. We live in complex settings of myriad influences through our perceptions and daily practice.
But God's grace and mercy are also there, because his Son has come
into our human family and his Spirit has been poured out on the whole
of that family. Christ and the Spirit contribute to our personal surroundings, but with influences that are beyond rational calculation and
easy analysis. In communicating to others, the theological researcher
has to face incomprehension of insights and explanations proposed,
since a level of interest has to be there concerning ultimate features
of living. To accept and take hold of a theological account of life, a
person has to have a basic level of spiritual interest and experience.

But a solid theological result, the outcome of attentive hearing
by competent reading of the sources and of well-ordered reflection,
remains valid even when not appreciated as a source of personal light
in the lives of others. The theological "places" (*loci*) give authentic witness to God's project for humane and holy living. Jesus of
Nazareth lived an utterly coherent human life, while teaching profoundly about life in this world before God. He left a treasure for
all cultures that is relevant across the whole gamut of human situations, especially as he faced and went through the absolutely universal

experience of death. What Jesus was, what he taught, and how he lived to the end, leading to his risen life — this can make human life, any human life, meaningful and fundamentally livable, as Vatican II insistently affirmed in its Pastoral Constitution on the Church in the Modern World (*Gaudium et spes*).

The key passage is the conclusion of the constitution's chapter on human dignity (nos. 12–22), with its programmatic opening, "In reality, it is only in the mystery of the Word made flesh that the mystery of humanity truly becomes clear" (GS 22). The following chapters of the Pastoral Constitution, on human life in community and on human activity in the world, conclude in the same way with paragraphs on Christ, who undergirds human solidarity (GS 32) and is a normative source of human action fulfilled in the paschal mystery of his death and resurrection (GS 38)

In tandem with this claim about Christ, the New Testament offers ample witness to how the Spirit of God works in human lives, both in Gospel accounts of Jesus who was anointed by the Spirit and in Acts on the Spirit animating the apostles and gathering the first Christian communities of believers. In the apostolic letters, one hears a variety of accounts of new life in the Spirit, contrasted by Paul with the destructive "works of the flesh." Again, an absolutely universal sketch of good living appears, when Paul speaks of the healing and creative "fruits of the Spirit" (Gal 5:19–23). From the New Testament, we receive basic tests to apply to our lives, in the "discernment of spirits" which is a key part of a reflective and spiritually attentive life.[20]

With increased theological understanding, a person should become more perceptive of the light of God's truth that the Spirit has given to dwell in our minds and hearts to influence how we think and act.

Finally, a theological explanation, worked out systematically from the witness of the sources, can become a personal vision within which one can see and understand one's own life. Penetrating to the foundations of the beliefs we profess about God's work, and seeing their implications, opens the way to constructing a personal vision of faith. We profess the faith of the church on Sundays and major feast days, but we need a personal creed for weekday living.

Theological research can lead to insights into scripture and the other resources of the tradition that can fuse together into a coherent framework in which to recognize a personal vocation and to be alert to personal experiences of the truth and grace of God. A personal creed is then a horizon of understanding and a way to chart personal growth by what is offered when an individual hears and reads the scriptures and takes account of church teaching.

Theology is about influences that mean to shape a meaningful course of life into the future. It gives, for personal navigation, a "pole star" in the person of Christ. From the prophets and apostles, received in tradition, it clarifies numerous points on the horizon of life before God.

A Closing Word

This fifth chapter differs from the four chapters that preceded it, for it has been quite prescriptive of what ought to take place in the theological search. A longer descriptive account went ahead, on theology, scripture, tradition, and church teaching. But the transition was right and just, since what *is given* by myriad Christian witnesses is in fact the basis of *what ought to be* as operative conclusions emerge.

But insistence on what should be can become irksome. So it is time to close this discussion of how you ought to practice theology, before the rules and prescriptions become oppressive.

Instead let us turn afresh to practicing attentive and methodical listening to God's word. May insights into the reality of Christ and the work of the Spirit become personal possessions more widely held and treasured. May well-grounded thinking and speaking flourish; may the Gospel indeed become in our day and in our lives truly a vital word, a *viva vox evangelii* (DV 8).

Review Questions

1. A basic viewpoint of this book is given by St. Paul in Romans 10:17, "Faith comes from what is heard, and what is heard comes through the word of Christ." How does this give rise to the first phase of theological work?

2. What is the overall design by which St. Thomas shows the coherence of God's work and word? How did Karl Rahner bring unity into many of the theological topics that he investigated?

3. How do fundamental and dogmatic theology differ in their respective contents and goals?

4. What kind of wisdom does theology seek?

5. How can the ecclesial community contribute to doing theology?

6. What is the basis of an ecumenical sensitivity in Catholic theology?

7. How does 1 Peter 3:15 define a task for theology within the ecclesial community?

8. Although personal experience is not, strictly speaking, a theological source, how does it nevertheless enter into theological work?

9. Why must theology move beyond "getting it right" in correct interpretations of its texts and sources?

10. How does Vatican Council II's Pastoral Constitution on the Church in the Modern World, no. 22, contribute to a basic orientation in doing theology?

Projects for Further Study

1. Pondering the introduction to this chapter, describe the two horizons, communitarian and personal, that have been the setting of your personal journey of faith and life.

2. Drawing on the previous chapters of this book, work out an ordered account of the statement, "Theology's initial moment is one of perception" (page 119 above).

3. Study Appendix 7 below, along with the entries by Rahner and Mansini mentioned in note 3 on page 262, and from these explain the aims and content of the central area of theology, where it treats basic Christian doctrines.

4. Outline the main points you would treat in explaining to a class what is "the sense of the faith" and "the sense of the faithful."

5. Study one of the following works: St. Augustine, *Confessions*; St. Ignatius Loyola, *The Pilgrim's Testament*; or St. Teresa of Avila, *Her Life... Written by Herself*. From this, show different ways in which personal experience can enrich the quest for Christian wisdom.

Appendix 1

Opening Address of
the Second Vatican Council

Pope John XXIII
(October 11, 1962)

INTRODUCTION

On October 11, 1962, feast of the Maternity of Mary, at the opening session of Vatican Council II, Pope John XXIII delivered this address to the approximately twenty-five hundred Council members (bishops and superiors of clerical religious orders), Council experts, and approximately fifty-five delegated observers from other churches, all assembled in St. Peter's Basilica. In the following days the text was studied carefully by several Council members and experts, who found in it an unexpectedly pointed statement of what Vatican II should contribute to the church and the whole world. In the early weeks of the Council's deliberations, Council members began citing Pope John's address in their comments in St. Peter's as expressing the Council's purpose, namely, as assembled not to condemn errors, but to promote pastoral renewal and the cause of Christian unity. The address also served as a norm in some members' evaluation of draft texts prepared before the Council, for example, in positive assessments of the text on liturgical reform and in critical judgments on the text *The Sources of Revelation,* on scripture and tradition.

More than forty years after the close of the Council, Pope Benedict XVI referred to Pope John's opening address and drew from it his notion of a "hermeneutic of reform," as a principle to guide interpretation of the event and the documents of Vatican II (see Appendix 6 below). Pope Benedict presented Vatican II's approach to reform by citing no. 25 of the address that follows.

The following text gives Pope John's address in its entirety.[1]

GAUDET MATER ECCLESIA
(October 11, 1962)

[1] Mother Church rejoices [*Gaudet Mater Ecclesia*] that, by the singular gift of Divine Providence, the longed-for day has finally dawned when — under the auspices of the virgin Mother of God, whose maternal dignity is commemorated on this feast — the Second Vatican Ecumenical Council is being solemnly opened here beside St. Peter's tomb.

[The Ecumenical Councils of the Church]

[2] The Councils — both the twenty ecumenical ones and the numberless others, also important, of a provincial or regional character, which have been held down through the years — all prove clearly the vigor of the Catholic Church and are recorded as shining lights in her annals. In calling this vast assembly of bishops, the latest and humble successor to the Prince of the Apostles who is addressing you intended to assert once again the magisterium, which is unfailing and endures until the end of time, in order that this magisterium, taking into account the errors, the requirements, and the opportunities of our time, might be presented in an exceptional form to all people throughout the world.

[3] It is only natural that in opening this universal Council we should want to look to the past and to listen to the voices whose echo we hear in the memories and the merits of the more recent and ancient Pontiffs, our predecessors. These are solemn and venerable voices, throughout the East and the West, from the fourth century to the Middle Ages, and from there to modern times, which have handed down their witness to those Councils. They are voices which proclaim in perennial fervor the triumph of that divine and human institution, the Church of Christ, which from Jesus takes its name, its grace, and its meaning.

[4] Side by side with these motives for spiritual joy, however, there has also been for more than nineteen centuries a cloud of sorrows and of trials. Not without reason did the elderly Simeon announce to Mary the mother of Jesus that prophecy which has been and still is true: "Behold this child is set for the fall and the resurrection of many in Israel, and for a sign which shall be contradicted" (Luke 2:34). And Jesus himself, when he grew up, clearly outlined the manner in which the world would treat his person down through the succeeding centuries with the mysterious words: "He who hears you, hears me" (Luke 10:16), and with those others that the same evangelist relates: "He who is not with me is against me and he who does not gather with me scatters" (Luke 11:23).

[5] The great problem confronting the world after almost two thousand years remains unchanged. Christ is ever resplendent as the center of history and of life. Individuals are either with him and his Church, and then they enjoy light, goodness, order, and peace. Or else they are without him, or against him and deliberately opposed to his Church, and then they give rise to confusion, to bitterness in human relations, and to the constant danger of fratricidal wars.

[6] Ecumenical Councils, whenever they are assembled, are a solemn celebration of the union of Christ and his Church, and hence lead to the universal radiation of truth, to the proper guidance of individuals in domestic and social life, to the strengthening of spiritual energies for a perennial uplift toward real and everlasting goodness.

[7] The testimony of this extraordinary magisterium of the Church in the succeeding epochs of these twenty centuries of Christian history stands before us collected in numerous and imposing volumes, which are the sacred patrimony of our ecclesiastical archives, here in Rome and in the more noted libraries of the entire world.

[The Origin and Reason for the Second Vatican Council]

[8] Regarding the initiative for the great event which gathers us here, it will suffice to repeat as historical documentation our personal account of the first sudden springing up in our heart and on our lips of the simple words, "Ecumenical Council." We uttered those words in the presence of the Sacred College of Cardinals on that memorable January 25, 1959, the feast of the Conversion of St. Paul,

in the basilica dedicated to him. It was completely unexpected, like a flash of heavenly light, shedding sweetness in eyes and hearts. And at the same time it gave rise to a great fervor throughout the world in expectation of the holding of the Council.

[9] Three years of laborious preparation have elapsed, during which a wide and profound examination was made regarding modern conditions of faith and religious practice, and of Christian and especially Catholic vitality. These years have seemed to us a first sign, an initial gift of celestial grace.

[10] Illumined by the light of this Council, the Church — we confidently trust — will become greater in spiritual riches and by gaining strength and new energies from it, she will look to the future without fear. In fact, by bringing herself up to date where required, and by the wise organization of mutual co-operation, the Church will make individuals, families, and peoples really turn their minds to heavenly things.

[11] And thus the holding of the Council becomes a motive for wholehearted thanksgiving to the Giver of every good gift, in order to celebrate with joyous canticles the glory of Christ our Lord, the glorious and immortal king of ages and of peoples.

[The Opportuneness of Holding the Council]

[12] There is, moreover, venerable brothers, another subject which it is useful to propose for your consideration. Namely, in order to render our joy more complete, we wish to narrate before this great assembly our assessment of the happy circumstances under which the Ecumenical Council commences.

[13] In the daily exercise of our pastoral office, we sometimes have to listen, much to our regret, to voices of persons who, though burning with zeal, are not endowed with too much sense of discretion or measure. In these modern times they can see nothing but prevarication and ruin. They say that our era, in comparison with past eras, is getting worse, and they behave as though they had learned nothing from history, which is, nonetheless, the teacher of life. They behave as though at the time of former Councils everything was a full triumph for the Christian idea and life and for proper religious liberty.

[14] We feel we must disagree with those prophets of gloom, who are always forecasting disaster, as though the end of the world were at hand.

[15] In the present order of things, Divine Providence is leading us to a new order of human relations which, by human efforts and even beyond what people expect, are directed toward the fulfillment of God's superior and inscrutable designs. And everything, even human differences, leads to the greater good of the Church.

[16] It is easy to discern this reality if we consider attentively the world of today, which is so busy with politics and controversies in the economic order that it does not find time to attend to the care of spiritual reality, with which the Church's magisterium is concerned. Such a way of acting is certainly not right, and must justly be disapproved.

[17] It cannot be denied, however, that these new conditions of modern life have at least the advantage of having eliminated those innumerable obstacles by which, at one time, the sons of this world impeded the free action of the Church. In fact, it suffices to leaf even cursorily through the pages of ecclesiastical history to note clearly how the Ecumenical Councils themselves, while constituting a series of true glories for the Catholic Church, were often held to the accompaniment of most serious difficulties and sufferings because of the undue interference of civil authorities. The princes of this world, indeed, sometimes in all sincerity, intended thus to protect the Church. But more frequently this occurred not without spiritual damage and danger, since their interest therein was guided by the views of a selfish and perilous policy.

[18] In this regard, we confess to you that we feel most poignant sorrow over the fact that very many bishops, so dear to us, are noticeable here today by their absence, because they are imprisoned for their faithfulness to Christ or impeded by other restraints. The thought of them impels us to raise most fervent prayer to God. Nevertheless, we see today, not without great hopes and to our immense consolation, that the Church, finally freed from so many obstacles of a profane nature such as trammeled her in the past, can from this Vatican Basilica, as if from a second apostolic cenacle, and through your intermediary, raise her voice resonant with majesty and greatness.

[Principal Duty of the Council:
The Defense and Advancement of Truth]

[19] The greatest concern of this Ecumenical Council is this: that the sacred deposit of Christian doctrine should be guarded and taught more efficaciously. That doctrine embraces the whole human person, composed of body and soul. And, since we are pilgrims on this earth, it commands us to tend always toward heaven. This demonstrates how our mortal life is to be ordered in such a way as to fulfill our duties as citizens of earth and of heaven, and thus to attain the aim of life as established by God. That is, all people, whether taken singly or as united in society, today have the duty of tending ceaselessly during their lifetime toward the attainment of heavenly things and to use, for this purpose only, earthly goods, the employment of which must not prejudice their eternal happiness.

[20] The Lord has said, "Seek first the kingdom of God and his justice" (Matt 6:33). The word "first" expresses the direction in which our thoughts and energies must move. We must not, however, neglect the other words of this exhortation of our Lord, namely, "And all these things shall be given you besides." In reality, there always have been in the Church, and there are still today, those who, while seeking the practice of evangelical perfection with all their might, do not fail to make themselves useful to society. Indeed, it is from their constant example of life and their charitable undertakings that all that is highest and noblest in human society takes its strength and growth.

[21] In order, however, that this doctrine may influence the numerous fields of human activity, with reference to individuals, to families, and to social life, it is necessary first of all that the Church should never depart from the sacred patrimony of truth received from the Fathers. But at the same time she must ever look to the present, to the new conditions and new forms of life introduced into the modern world, which have opened new avenues to the Catholic apostolate.

[22] For this reason, the Church has not watched inertly the marvelous progress of the discoveries of human genius, and has not been backward in evaluating them rightly. But, while following these developments, she does not neglect to admonish everyone so that, over and above the realm of the senses — things we perceive — they may raise

their eyes to God, the source of all wisdom and all beauty. And may they, to whom it was said, "Subdue the earth and have dominion" (Gen 1:28), never forget the most serious command: "The Lord thy God shall thou worship, and Him only shall thou serve" (Matt 4:10; Luke 4:8), so that it may not happen that the fleeting fascination of visible things should impede true progress.

[The Way toward Doctrinal Progress]

[23] This having been established, it becomes clear how much is expected from the Council in regard to doctrine. The twenty-first Ecumenical Council, which will draw upon the effective and important wealth of juridical, liturgical, apostolic, and administrative experiences, wishes to transmit the doctrine, pure and integral, without any attenuation or distortion, which throughout twenty centuries, notwithstanding difficulties and contrasts, has become the common patrimony of all. It is a patrimony not well received by all, but always a rich treasure available to persons of good will.

[24] Our duty is not only to guard this precious treasure, as if we were concerned only with antiquity, but to dedicate ourselves with an earnest will and without fear to that work which our era demands of us, pursuing thus the path which the Church has followed for twenty centuries. The salient point of this Council is not, therefore, a discussion of one article or another of the fundamental doctrine of the Church which has repeatedly been taught by the Church Fathers and by ancient and modern theologians, and which is presumed to be well known and familiar to all.

[25] For this a Council was not necessary. But from the renewed, serene, and tranquil adherence to all the teaching of the Church in its entirety and preciseness, as it still shines forth in the Acts of the Council of Trent and First Vatican Council, the Christian, Catholic, and apostolic spirit of the whole world expects a leap forward toward a doctrinal penetration and a formation of consciences in faithful and perfect conformity to the authentic doctrine, which, however, should be studied and expounded through the methods of research and through the literary forms of modern thought. The deposit of faith is one thing, namely, the truths contained in our venerable teaching,

but the manner in which they are formulated is another, always keeping the same meaning and same understanding. And it is the latter that must be taken into great consideration, with patience if necessary, assessing everything according to the forms and proportions of a magisterium which is predominantly pastoral in character.

[How to Repress Errors]

[26] At the outset of the Second Vatican Council, it is evident, as always, that the truth of the Lord will remain forever. We see, in fact, as one age succeeds another, that human opinions follow one another and exclude each other. Often errors vanish as quickly as they arise, like fog before the sun. The Church has always opposed these errors. Frequently she has condemned them with the greatest severity. Nowadays however, the Spouse of Christ prefers to make use of the medicine of mercy rather than that of severity. She considers that she meets the needs of the present day by demonstrating the validity of her teaching rather than by condemnations.

[27] Not, certainly, because there are no fallacious teachings, opinions, and dangerous concepts to be guarded against and dissipated. But these are so obviously in contrast with the sound norm of right living, and have produced such lethal fruits, that by now it seems that people are spontaneously inclined to condemn them, particularly those ways of life which despise God and his law or place excessive confidence in technical progress and a well-being based exclusively on the comforts of life. People are ever more deeply convinced of the paramount dignity of the human person and of his perfection as well as of the duties which that implies. Even more important, experience has taught people that violence inflicted on others, the might of arms, and political domination, are of no help at all in finding a happy solution to the grave problems which afflict them.

[28] That being so, the Catholic Church, in raising the torch of religious truth by means of this Ecumenical Council, desires to show herself to be the loving mother of all, benign, patient, full of mercy and goodness toward the brethren who are separated from her. To the human family, oppressed by so many difficulties, the Church says, as Peter said to the poor man who begged alms from him, "I have

neither gold nor silver, but what I have I give you; in the name of Jesus Christ of Nazareth, rise and walk" (Acts 3:6).

[29] In other words, the Church does not offer to people of today riches that pass away, nor does she promise them merely earthly happiness. But she distributes to them the goods of divine grace which, raising them to the dignity of children of God, are the most efficacious safeguards and aids toward a more humane life. She opens the fountain of her life-giving doctrine which allows men and women, enlightened by the light of Christ, to understand well what they really are, what their lofty dignity and their purpose are, and, finally, through her children, she spreads everywhere the fullness of Christian charity, than which nothing is more effective in eradicating the seeds of discord, nothing more efficacious in promoting concord, just peace, and the brotherly unity of all.

[The Unity of the Christian and Human Family Must Be Promoted]

[30] The Church's solicitude to promote and defend truth derives from the fact that, according to the plan of God, who wills all people to be saved and to come to the knowledge of the truth (1 Tim 2:4), without the assistance of the whole of revealed doctrine men and women cannot reach a complete and firm unity of minds, with which are associated true peace and eternal salvation.

[31] Unfortunately, the entire Christian family has not yet fully attained this visible unity in truth. The Catholic Church, therefore, considers it her duty to work actively so that there may be fulfilled the great mystery of that unity which Jesus Christ invoked with fervent prayer from his heavenly Father on the eve of his sacrifice. She rejoices in peace, knowing well that she is intimately associated with that prayer, and then exults greatly at seeing that invocation extend its efficacy with salutary fruit, even among those who are outside her fold.

[32] Indeed, if one considers well this same unity which Christ implored for his Church, it seems to shine, as it were, with a triple ray of beneficent heavenly light: namely, the unity of Catholics among themselves, which must always be kept exemplary and most firm; the unity of prayers and ardent desires with which those Christians

separated from this Apostolic See aspire to be united with us; and the unity in esteem and respect for the Catholic Church which animates those who follow non-Christian religions.

[33] In this regard, it is a source of considerable sorrow to see that the greater part of the human race — although everyone who is born was redeemed by the blood of Christ — does not yet participate in those sources of divine grace which exist in the Catholic Church. Hence the Church, whose light illumines all, whose strength of supernatural unity redounds to the advantage of all humanity, is rightly described in these beautiful words of St. Cyprian:

> The Church, surrounded by divine light, spreads her rays over the entire earth. This light, however, is one and unique and shines everywhere without causing any separation in the unity of the body. She extends her branches over the whole world. By her fruitfulness she sends ever farther afield her rivulets. Nevertheless, the head is always one, the origin one for she is the one mother, abundantly fruitful. We are born of her, are nourished by her milk, we live of her spirit. (*The Unity of the Catholic Church*, no. 5)

[Conclusion]

[34] Venerable brothers, such is the aim of the Second Vatican Ecumenical Council, which, while bringing together the Church's best energies and striving to have people welcome more favorably the good tidings of salvation, prepares, as it were, and consolidates the path toward that unity of the human family that is required as a necessary foundation, in order that the earthly city may be brought to the resemblance of that heavenly city where truth reigns, charity is the law, and whose extent is eternity (cf. St. Augustine, Epistle 138, 3).

[35] Now, "our voice is directed to you" (2 Cor 6:11), venerable brothers in the episcopate. Behold, we are gathered together in this Vatican Basilica, upon which hinges the history of the Church where heaven and earth are closely joined, here near the tomb of Peter and near so many of the tombs of our holy predecessors, whose ashes in this solemn hour seem to thrill in mystic exultation.

[36] The Council now beginning rises in the Church like daybreak, a forerunner of most splendid light. It is now only dawn. And already at this first announcement of the rising day, how much sweetness fills our heart. Everything here breathes sanctity and arouses great joy. Let us contemplate the stars, which with their brightness augment the majesty of this temple. These stars, according to the testimony of the apostle John (Rev 1:20), are you, and with you we see shining around the tomb of the Prince of the Apostles, the golden candelabra. That is, the Church that is confided to you (ibid.).

[37] We see here with you important personalities, present in an attitude of great respect and cordial expectation, having come together in Rome from the five continents to represent the nations of the world. We might say that heaven and earth are united in the holding of the Council — the saints of heaven to protect our work, the faithful of the earth continuing in prayer to the Lord, and you, seconding the inspiration of the Holy Spirit in order that the work of all may correspond to the modern expectations and needs of the various peoples of the world.

[38] This requires of you serenity of mind, brotherly concord, moderation in proposals, dignity in discussion, and wisdom of deliberation. God grant that your labors and your work, toward which the eyes of all peoples and the hopes of the entire world are turned, may abundantly fulfill the aspirations of all.

[39] Almighty God! In thee we place all our confidence, not trusting in our own strength. Look down benignly upon these pastors of thy Church. May the light of thy heavenly grace aid us in taking decisions and in making laws. Graciously hear the prayers which we pour forth to thee in unanimity of faith, of voice, and of mind.

[40] O Mary, Help of Christians, Help of Bishops, of whose love we have recently had particular proof in thy temple of Loreto, where we venerated the mystery of the incarnation: dispose all things for a happy and propitious outcome and, with thy spouse, St. Joseph, the holy apostles Peter and Paul, St. John the Baptist and St. John the Evangelist, intercede for us to God.

[41] To Jesus Christ, our most amiable Redeemer, immortal King of peoples and of times, be love, power, and glory forever and ever.

Appendix 2

Opening of the Second Period of Vatican Council II

Pope Paul VI
(September 29, 1963)

INTRODUCTION

After Vatican II's first period closed on December 8, 1962, the Council's commissions undertook intense work of revising the prepared draft texts to conform to the goals and priorities that Pope John XXIII had expressed and were embraced by a majority of the Council members during the 1962 working period. Pope John followed and encouraged this work of revision, but his health declined, and he died on June 3, 1963. His successor, Giovanni Battista Montini, cardinal-archbishop of Milan, was elected on June 21 and took the name Paul VI. The second period of Vatican Council II opened September 29, about which this Appendix reprints with permission two reports from the *Tablet* (*www.thetablet.co.uk*), volume 217, pages 1056–59, from the issue of October 5, 1963. The second report digests Paul VI's opening address, with some passages in English translation, into which J. Wicks has inserted section headings.[1]

1. STREAMLINING IN ST. PETER'S
The Effects of the First Session

The second session has opened, and from the first day we know how much had been in fact achieved by the first. A year ago the bishops met in St. Peter's full of expectation, awaiting a great and novel experience which they had never expected, but quite uncertain what its character would be. If 1870 [The First Vatican Council] gave any guidance, the conservative genius of the Church would quickly assert itself, and the opponents of change, being in possession of most of the machinery and with a long tradition of commands unquestionably obeyed, would keep the reins firmly in their hands. A year later the expectation is all the other way: the forces making for reform have shown their formidable strength, and a fresh and forward-looking pope wears the mantle of Pope John and has made it clear that the Council is to go on in the spirit in which the late pope summoned it.

There is no question that many, particularly among the bishops from North America, who a year ago had a general readiness to follow whatever lead they were given from the Holy See, with a certain personal bias in favor of keeping things as they are, have returned to Rome feeling very differently and anxious to range themselves where they think the New World should always be, in the van of progress. The real question is how far the conservative elements have also changed, being realistic men and recognizing that they are in the presence of a pope and a Council resolved to grapple with all the matters set out in the schemata [draft texts], beginning with the nature of the church, and that they will not be deterred from amending the language of the schemata where it is old-fashioned and formalized. It is already clear that it will be much easier to follow the second session. . . .

The streamlining is everywhere in evidence. The seventy documents of last year have been reduced to seventeen schemata that will be the texts of this session. The one on the church is of two volumes of some fifty pages each and is understood to have a good deal to say about bishops in groups — the authority, that is, of national hierarchies. There is the intention to emphasize that the bishops are an order who ought to develop much more capacity for joint action, to correct the natural tendency for them to agree to leave each other alone, each to be a monarch in his own diocese, in a way that has prevented the development of a common mind. In general, there is recognition that the language is much fresher. One of last year's documents on the deposit of faith, an old style demolition of bygone Modernists like Tyrrell, has been quietly buried.

The four cardinals who have been appointed by the pope as stage managers of the sessions are really more important than the cardinals [presidents] who preside morning by morning....[2]

...Although the physical presence of the very great man who started it all [Pope John XXIII] has been taken from us, his noble spirit securely lingers. It was the last hour of this long ceremony [on September 29], during which Paul VI spoke in a voice sometimes hoarse with deep feeling, that put the seal on this conviction. Everywhere in this city the speech was received with a quiet but warm and grateful admiration.... In the hands of a pope who so clearly understands the inner spirit of his unique predecessor... the future of the Council seems assured.

The contrast between these two figures, between these two voices, between these two manners, lends savor to the firm sense of continuity. The new pope left us with the conviction of a vast work ahead but not of cloud-capped impossibilities. The church lives in Christ, Christ in the church; it is here that we must concentrate our gaze and see clearly the ground of our hope, the spur of effort, the source of continuing energy, the spirit of the charity which makes all approaches, all reconciliations conceivable, though truths, pleasant or unpleasant, be firmly stated. It was in the breadth, the magnanimity that informed all, that one felt the abiding spirit of John. The personal contribution was a judgment very individual — detached and keen — yet warm and embracing.

2. THE ROAD BEFORE THE COUNCIL
Pope Paul's Opening Speech
(Report, with Excerpts Cited)

A four-point summary of the objectives of the Council, a discussion of some of the questions raised by the schema *De ecclesia* [draft text *The Church*] with which the Council was to begin its deliberations, an indication of the church's respect for non-Christian religions — these were among the features of the speech delivered by Pope Paul on Sunday for the opening of the second session.

The Council and Pope John XXIII

Welcoming the Fathers of the Council, the pope dwelt on the fitting-ness of the word *ecclesia* — "a coming together or a meeting" — to describe the church met in Council. Around the man "who is the last in time and merit, but identified with the first apostle in authority and mission, the successor of Peter," were gathered the Fathers [Council members], who too were "apostles, descended from the apostolic col-lege and its authentic successors." Pope Paul compared the assembly to a "new cenacle" [upper room of Jesus' Last Supper and of the coming of the Holy Spirit on Pentecost] where "all tongues will be united in one voice and one voice alone will bring the message to all the world." Referring to himself as "the least among you, the servant of the servants of God, even though he bears the keys of the supreme office consigned to Peter by Christ the Lord," the pope went on: "The Lord is our witness when, at the first moment of the second session of the great synod, we declare to you that in our mind there is no intention of human predominance, no jealously of exclusive power, but only the desire and the will to carry out the divine man-date which makes us, from among you, my brethren, the supreme shepherd. . . . "

He had intended to send them all his first encyclical letter, but this present address would have to serve as a prelude both to the Council and to his pontificate. Paying tribute to his predecessor, he said that John XXIII's speech opening the first session had "seemed like a prophetic voice for our century." "That speech still echoes in our minds, pointing out to the Council the path it has to take, thereby freeing us from all doubt and weariness which we may encounter along the difficult road we have undertaken."

Pope John deserved gratitude and praise for having resolved to convoke this Council "in order to open to the Church new horizons and to tap the fresh spiritual water of the doctrine and grace of Christ our Lord and let it flow over the earth." By gathering up the broken thread of the First Vatican Council he had "banished the fear wrongly deduced from that Council, as if the supreme powers conferred by Christ on the Roman Pontiff to govern and vivify the Church were sufficient without the assistance of the Ecumenical Councils."[3]

Pope Paul also emphasized the pastoral aim that Pope John had given to the Council: "You [John XXIII] have awakened in the conscience of the magisterium of the Church the conviction that Christian doctrine is not merely truth to be investigated by reason illumined by faith, but teaching that can generate life and action, and that the authority of the Church is not limited to condemning contrary errors but extends to the communication of positive and vital doctrine, the source of its fruitfulness."

Confessing Jesus Christ, Beginning and End of Everything

Calling on the Fathers to go forward, Pope Paul emphasized that Christ was the starting point, Christ was the road they must follow, and Christ was their final goal. He wanted the Council to be fully aware of this relationship between ourselves and Jesus, a relationship at once multiple and unique, fixed and stimulating, mysterious and crystal-clear, binding and beautifying, a relationship between the church they constituted and Christ from whom they came, by whom they lived, and towards whom they tended.

"Let no other light be shed on this Council but Christ the light of the world; let no other truth be of interest to our minds but the words of our Lord, our only master; let no other aspiration guide us but the desire to be absolutely faithful to him." The Council should have as its starting point the vision of Christ as *Pantocrator* (Creator of All Things) "which acknowledges him as the Incarnate Word, the Son of God and the Son of Man, the redeemer of the world, the hope of humanity and its supreme master, the Good Shepherd, the Bread of Life, the High Priest and Victim, the one Mediator between God and man, the Savior of the World, the eternal King of the ages; and which declares that we are his chosen ones, his disciples, his apostles, his witnesses, his ministers, his representatives, and his living members together with the whole company of the faithful, united in an immense and unique mystical body, his Church, which he is forming by means of faith and the sacraments, as generations of mankind succeed one another; a Church which is spiritual and visible, fraternal and hierarchical, temporal today and eternal tomorrow."

Topic 1 of the Council's Work:
The Nature of the Church

Such a concept of Christ and his Mystical Body helps one better to understand the objectives of the Council, which he summarized thus: "The knowledge or, if you will, the self-awareness of the Church; its reform; the bringing together of all Christians in unity; the dialogue of the Church with the contemporary world." Quoting the biblical images used to describe the church, Pope Paul said that the church had come to see itself as a historic, visible, and hierarchically organized society, animated by a mysterious principle of life. Pius XII's encyclical *Mystici corporis* (the Mystical Body) had partly answered the Church's longing to express its nature in full doctrinal form. The First Vatican Council discussed the subject, and many external influences had caused it to be studied both inside and outside the Church.

Pope Paul went on,

> It should not come as a surprise that, after twenty centuries in which both the Catholic Church and other Christian bodies distinguished by the name of Church have seen such great geographical and historical development, there should still be a need to enunciate a more precise definition of the true, profound, and complete nature of the Church which Christ founded and the apostles began to build. The Church is a mystery; she is a reality imbued with the divine presence and, for that reason, she is ever susceptible of new and deeper investigation. Human thought moves forward. Man advances from empirically observed fact to scientific truth, from one truth he derives another by logical deduction, and, confronted by the complexity and permanence of reality, he bends his mind now to one of its aspects, now to another. It is thus that thought evolves. The course of its evolution can be traced in history.
>
> The time has now come, we believe, when the truth regarding the Church of Christ should be examined, coordinated, and expressed. The expression should not, perhaps, take the form of a solemn dogmatic definition, but of a declaration, making known by means of the Church's magisterium, in a more explicit

and authoritative form, what the Church considers herself to be. This self-awareness of the Church is clarified by faithful adherence to the words and thought of Christ, by respectful attention to the teaching of ecclesiastical tradition, and by docility to the interior illumination of the Holy Spirit, who seems to be requiring of the Church today that she should do all she can to make known what she really is. . . .

For this reason, the principal concern of this session of the Council will be to examine the intimate nature of the Church and to express in human language, as far as that is possible, a definition which will best reveal the Church's real, fundamental constitution and manifest her manifold mission of salvation. This theological doctrine has the possibility of magnificent developments, which merit the attentive consideration of our separated brethren also and which, as we ardently hope, may make the path towards common agreement easier.

First among the various questions that this consideration will raise, venerable brethren, is one which affects all of you as bishops of the Church of God. We have no hesitation in saying that we look forward with expectation and confidence to this discussion which, taking for granted the dogmatic declarations of the First Vatican Council regarding the Roman Pontiff, will go on to develop the doctrine regarding the episcopate, its function, and its relationship to Peter. For us personally it will provide doctrinal and practical standards by which our apostolic office, endowed as it is by Christ with the fullness and sufficiency of power, may receive more help and support, in ways to be determined, from more effective collaboration with our beloved and venerable brothers in the episcopate.

Next it will be necessary to elucidate the teaching regarding the different components of the visible and mystical Body, the pilgrim, militant Church on earth, that is, priests, religious, the faithful, and also the separated brethren who are also called to adhere to it more fully and completely.

Topic 2: Renewal of the Church's Life

Another chief subject of the Council's deliberations is the renewal of
the church, something which must follow from our awareness of the
relationship whereby Christ is united to his church. If the bride of
Christ were to discover some shadow, defect, or stain upon her wed-
ding garment, her primary duty would be to reform, correct, and set
herself to rights in conformity with her divine model. Jesus' saying, "I
consecrate myself, that they also may be consecrated in truth" (John
17:19), is the essential attitude, desired by Christ, that the Council must adopt. It is only after this internal sanctification has been
accomplished that the church can show herself to the whole world
and say, "Who sees me, sees Christ."

In this sense the Council is to be a new springtime, a reawaken-
ing of the mighty spiritual and moral energies which at present lie
dormant. The Council is evidence of a determination to bring about
a rejuvenation both of the interior forces of the church and of the
regulations by which her canonical structure and liturgical forms are
governed. The Council, that is, is striving to enhance in the church
that beauty of perfection and holiness which imitation of Christ and
mystical union with Him in the Holy Spirit can alone confer.

> Yes, the Council aims at renewal. Note well, however, that
> in saying and desiring this we do not imply that the Catho-
> lic Church of today can be accused of substantial infidelity to
> the mind of her divine Founder. Rather it is the deeper realiza-
> tion of her substantial faithfulness that fills her with gratitude
> and humility and inspires her with the courage to correct those
> imperfections that are proper to human weakness. The reform
> at which the Council aims is not, therefore, a turning upside
> down of the Church's present way of life or a breaking with
> what is essential and worthy of veneration in her tradition, but
> it is rather an honoring of tradition by stripping it of what is
> unworthy or defective so that it may be rendered firm and fruit-
> ful. Did not Jesus say to his disciples, "I am the true vine, and
> my Father is the vine-dresser. Every branch of mine that bears
> no fruit, he takes away, and every branch that does bear fruit,
> he prunes, that it may bear more fruit" (John 15:1–2)?

This verse summarizes the process of perfection desired by the Church. The living Church should be conformed to the living Christ, with faith and charity as the principle of her life. No pains must be spared to make faith strong and joyful and to make Christian instruction and teaching methods more effective. The first requirement is certainly a more diligent study and a more intensive proclamation of the word of God, and on this foundation an education in charity will be built up.

Topic 3: Promoting Ecumenism

After a passing reference to the probability that a third session would be necessary, Pope Paul turned to the question of Christian unity. Addressing the observers, after mentioning the consolation and hope aroused by their presence as well as the deep sadness he felt at their prolonged separation, he continued:

> If we are in any way to blame for that separation, we humbly beg God's forgiveness and ask pardon too of our brethren who feel themselves to be injured by us. For our part, we willingly forgive the injuries which the Catholic Church has suffered, and forget the grief endured during the long series of dissensions and separations. . . . [4]
>
> We are aware that serious and complicated questions remain to be studied, treated, and resolved. We would wish that this could be done immediately on account of the love of Christ that "urges us on" (2 Cor 5:14). But we also realize that these problems require many conditions before satisfactory solutions can be reached, conditions which are as yet premature. Hence we are not afraid to wait patiently the blessed hour of perfect reconciliation.

Pope Paul then addressed both the observers in St. Peter's, as representatives of their various communions, as well as "those other venerable Christian communities separated from us which did not accept the invitation to attend the Council," on the Catholic attitude toward reunion: "Our manner of speaking towards them is friendly, completely sincere, and loyal. We lay no snares: we are not motivated by temporal interests.... We do not wish to make of our faith an occasion for polemics. Secondly we look with reverence upon the true religious patrimony which we share in common and upon what has been preserved — and in part even well developed — among our separated brethren," and Pope Paul expressed the hope that they would want to study more closely Catholic doctrine and its logical derivation from the deposit of revelation. Finally, "aware of the enormous difficulties still in the way of the desired union, we humbly put our trust in God": "What is impossible with men is possible with God" (Luke 18:27).

Topic 4: The Church in Dialogue with the World

In conclusion, Pope Paul discussed the "dialogue with the modern world." The Council would build a bridge toward the contemporary world. By her interior renewal she was distinguishing and separating herself from the secular society in which she existed, while at the same time being the life-giving leaven in the world. The Council's desire to conduct a dialogue with the world — witness the message to mankind given at the beginning of the first session — meant that the present Council was characterized by love, by the universal love of Christ. Nevertheless they must be realists and not close their eyes to the evils of the world. The absence of certain bishops indicated that religious liberty was being oppressed in the countries concerned, while there was also the "emptiness, sadness, and despair" to be found in some societies.

The church looks towards certain categories of people with particular solicitude: the poor, the needy, the afflicted, the hungry, the suffering, and the sorrowing. She looks towards men of culture and learning, scientists, artists; towards the workers, to the mission which may be recognized as theirs, if it is good, if it is Christian, of creating a new world of free individuals and brothers and sisters; to the leaders of nations, reminding them of their opportunity to give their peoples many good things necessary for their life.[5]

> And then the Catholic Church looks further still, beyond the confines of the Christian horizon — for how can she put limits to her love if she would make her own the love of God the Father

who rains down his grace on all people alike and who so loved the world as to give his only-begotten Son? She looks, then, beyond her own sphere and sees those other religions which preserve the sense and notion of the one supreme, transcendent God, creator and sustainer, and which worship Him with acts of sincere piety and base their moral and social life on their beliefs and religious practices. It is true that the Catholic Church sees in such religions omissions, insufficiencies, and errors which cause her sadness, yet she cannot exclude them from her thoughts and would have them know that she esteems what they contain of truth and goodness and humanity.[6] For the Catholic Church is in the forefront of those who, as a necessary duty of true civilization, strive to preserve religion and worship of God in modern society. She is the most vigorous upholder of God's rights over mankind.

Other vast fields of humanity fall under her gaze: the new generations of youth desirous of living and expressing themselves: the new peoples now coming to self-awareness, independence, and civil organization; the innumerable men and women who feel isolated in a troubled society that has no message for their spirit. To all without exception she proclaims the good news of salvation and hope, to all she offers the light of truth and life and salvation, for God "desires all men to be saved, and to come to the knowledge of the truth" (1 Tim 2:4).

Appendix 3

Address at the Last Meeting of Vatican Council II

Pope Paul VI
(December 7, 1965)

INTRODUCTION

At a final public session, on December 7, 1965, the Council took concluding votes on four documents: Religious Liberty (DH), Missionary Activity of the Church (AG), Priests: Their Ministry and Life (PO), and the Pastoral Constitution on the Church in the Modern World (GS). Paul VI's promulgation of these documents followed.

Also the Catholic Church formally "consigned to oblivion" the excommunication of AD 1054 of the Orthodox Church of Constantinople, which was at the same moment reciprocated by the ecumenical patriarch of Constantinople.

Then followed the pope's address, mentioning most of the Council documents, but speaking at length on the style, outlook, and central themes of *Gaudium et spes,* the Pastoral Constitution on the Church in the Modern World.[1]

• • •

Today we are concluding the Second Vatican Council. We bring it to a close at the fullness of its efficiency: the presence of so many of you here clearly demonstrates it; the well-ordered pattern of this assembly bears testimony to it; the normal conclusion of the work done by the Council confirms it; the harmony of sentiments and decisions proclaims it. And if quite a few questions raised during the course of the Council itself still await appropriate answers, this shows that its labors are now coming to a close not out of weariness, but in

163

a state of vitality which this universal synod has awakened. In the postconciliar period this vitality will apply, God willing, its generous and well-regulated energies to the study of such questions.

This Council bequeaths to history an image of the Catholic Church symbolized by this hall, filled, as it is, with shepherds of souls professing the same faith, breathing the same charity, associated in the same communion of prayer, discipline and activity and — what is marvelous — all desiring one thing: namely, to offer themselves like Christ, our Master and Lord, for the life of the Church and for the salvation of the world. This Council hands over to posterity not only the image of the Church but also the patrimony of her doctrine and of her commandments, the "deposit" received from Christ and meditated upon through centuries, lived and expressed now and clarified in so many of its parts, settled and arranged in its integrity. The deposit, that is, which lives on by the divine power of truth and of grace which constitutes it, and is, therefore, able to vivify anyone who receives it and nourishes with it his own human existence.

What then was the Council? What has it accomplished? The answer to these questions would be the logical theme of our present meditation. But it would require too much of our attention and time. This final and stupendous hour would not perhaps give us enough tranquility of mind to make such a synthesis. We should like to devote this precious moment to one single thought which bends down our spirits in humility and at the same time raises them up to the summit of our aspirations. And that thought is this: what is the religious value of this Council? We refer to it as religious because of its direct relationship with the living God, that relationship which is the raison d'être of the Church, of all that she believes, hopes and loves; of all that she is and does.

Could we speak of having given glory to God, of having sought knowledge and love of him, of having made progress in our effort of contemplating him, in our eagerness for honoring him and in the art of proclaiming him to men and women who look up to us as to pastors and masters of the life of God? In all sincerity we think the answer is yes. Also because from this basic purpose there developed the guiding principle which was to give direction to the Council. Still fresh in our memory are the words uttered in this basilica by our venerated predecessor, John XXIII, whom we may in truth call the originator of this great synod. In his opening address to the Council he had this to say: "The greatest concern of the Ecumenical Council is this: that the sacred deposit of Christian doctrine be guarded and taught more effectively.... The Lord has said: 'Seek first the kingdom of God and His justice.' The word 'first' expresses the direction in which our thoughts and energies must move" (Opening Discourse, October 11, 1962).

His great purpose has now been achieved. To appreciate it properly it is necessary to remember the time in which it was realized: a time which everyone admits is oriented toward the conquest of the kingdom of earth rather than that of heaven; a time in which forgetfulness of God has become habitual, and seems, quite wrongly, to be prompted by the progress of science; a time in which the fundamental act of the human person, more conscious now of himself and of his liberty, tends to pronounce in favor of his own absolute autonomy, in emancipation from every transcendent law; a time in which secularism seems the legitimate consequence of modern thought and the highest wisdom in the temporal ordering of society; a time, moreover, in which the human soul has plumbed the depths of irrationality and desolation; a time, finally, which is characterized by upheavals and a hitherto unknown decline even in the great world religions.

It was at such a time as this that our Council was held to the honor of God, in the name of Christ and under the impulse of the Spirit: who "searches all things," "making us understand God's gifts to us" (Cf. 1 Cor 2:10–12), and who is now quickening the Church, giving her a vision at once profound and all-embracing of the life of the world. The theocentric and theological concept of the human person and the universe, almost in defiance of the charge of anachronism and irrelevance, has been given a new prominence by the Council, through claims which the world will at first judge to be foolish, but which, we hope, it will later come to recognize as being truly human, wise and salutary: namely, God is — and more, he is real, he lives, a personal, provident God, infinitely good; and not only good in himself, but also immeasurably good to us. He will be recognized as our Creator, our truth, our happiness; so much so that the effort to look on him, and to center our heart in him, which we call contemplation, is the highest, the most perfect act of the spirit, the act which even today can and must be at the apex of all human activity.

People will realize that the Council devoted its attention not so much to divine truths, but rather, and principally, to the Church — her nature and composition, her ecumenical vocation, her apostolic and missionary activity. This secular religious society, which is the Church, has endeavored to carry out an act of reflection about herself, to know herself better, to define herself better and, in consequence, to set aright what she feels and what she commands. So much is true. But this introspection has not been an end in itself and has not been simply an exercise of human understanding or of a merely worldly culture. The Church has gathered herself together in deep spiritual awareness, not to produce a learned analysis of religious psychology, or an account of her own experiences, not even to devote herself to reaffirming her rights and explaining her laws. Rather, it was to find in herself, active and alive, the Holy Spirit, the word of Christ; and to probe more deeply still the mystery, the plan and the presence of God above and within herself; to revitalize in herself that faith which is the secret of her confidence and of her wisdom, and that love which impels her to sing without ceasing the praises of God. *"Cantare amantis est"* (To sing is the expression of a lover), says St. Augustine (Sermon 336; *Patrologia Latina,* 38, 1472).

The Council documents — especially the ones on divine revelation, the liturgy, the Church, priests, religious, and the laity — leave wide open to view this primary and focal religious intention, and show how clear and fresh and rich is the spiritual stream which contact with the living God causes to well up in the heart of the Church, and flow out from it over the dry wastes of our world.

But we cannot pass over one important consideration in our analysis of the religious meaning of the Council: it has been deeply committed to the study of the modern world. Never before perhaps so much as on this occasion has the Church felt the need to know, to draw near to, to understand, to penetrate, serve and evangelize the society in which she lives; and to come to grips with it, almost to run after it, in its rapid and continuous change.

This attitude, a response to the distances and divisions we have witnessed over recent centuries, in the last century and in our own especially, between the Church and secular society — this attitude has been strongly and unceasingly at work in the Council; so much so that some have been inclined to suspect that an easygoing and excessive responsiveness to the outside world, to passing events, cultural fashions, temporary needs, an alien way of thinking, may have swayed persons and acts of the ecumenical synod, at the expense of the fidelity which is due to tradition, and this to the detriment of the religious orientation of the Council itself. We do not believe that this shortcoming should be imputed to it, to its real and deep intentions, to its authentic manifestations.

We prefer to point out how charity has been the principal religious feature of this Council. Now, no one can reprove as want of religion or infidelity to the Gospel such a basic orientation, when we recall that it is Christ himself who taught us that love for our brothers is the distinctive mark of his disciples (cf. John 13:35); when we listen to the words of the apostle: "Religion that is pure and undefiled before God and the Father is this: to visit orphans and widows in their affliction, and keep oneself unstained by the world" (James 1:27) and again: "One who does not love his brother whom he has seen, cannot love God whom he has not seen" (1 John 4:20).

Yes, the church of the Council has been concerned, not just with herself and with her relationship of union with God, but with man — man as he really is today: living man, man all wrapped up in himself, man who makes himself not only the center of his every interest but dares to claim that he is the principle and explanation of all reality. Every perceptible element in man, every one of the countless guises in which he appears, has, in a sense, been displayed in full view of the Council Fathers, who, in their turn, are mere men, and yet all of them are pastors and brothers whose position accordingly fills them with solicitude and love.

Among these guises we may cite man as the tragic actor of his own dramas; man as the superman of yesterday and today, ever frail, unreal, selfish, and savage; man unhappy with himself as he laughs and cries; man the versatile actor ready to perform any part; man the narrow devotee of nothing but scientific reality; man as he is, a creature who thinks and loves and toils and is always waiting for something, the "growing son" (Gen 49:22); man sacred because of the innocence of his childhood, because of the mystery of his poverty, because of the dedication of his suffering; man as an individual and man in society; man who lives in the glories of the past and dreams of those of the future; man the sinner and man the saint, and so on.

Secular humanism, revealing itself in its horrible anticlerical reality has, in a certain sense, defied the Council. The religion of the God who became human has met the religion (for such it is) of humans who make themselves God. And what happened? Was there a clash, a battle, a condemnation? There could have been, but there was none. The parable of the Samaritan has been the model of the spirituality of the Council. A feeling of boundless sympathy has permeated the whole of it. The attention of our Council has been absorbed by the discovery of human needs (and these needs grow in proportion to the greatness which the sons and daughters of the earth claim for themselves). But we call upon those who term themselves modern humanists, and who have renounced the transcendent value of the highest realities, to give the Council credit at least for one quality and to recognize our own new type of humanism: we, too, in fact, we more than any others, honor humankind.

And what aspect of humanity has this august senate studied? What goal under divine inspiration did it set for itself? It also dwelt upon humanity's ever twofold facet, namely, man's wretchedness and his greatness, his profound weakness — which is undeniable and cannot be cured by himself — and the good that survives in him which is ever marked by a hidden beauty and an invincible serenity.

But one must realize that this Council, which exposed itself to human judgment, insisted very much more upon this pleasant side of man, rather than on his unpleasant one. Its attitude was very much and deliberately optimistic. A wave of affection and admiration flowed from the Council over the modern world of humanity. Errors were condemned, indeed, because charity demanded this no less than did truth, but for the persons themselves there was only warm respect and love. Instead of depressing diagnoses, encouraging remedies; instead of direful prognostications, messages of trust issued from the Council to the present-day world. The modern world's values were not only respected but honored, its efforts approved, its aspirations purified and blessed.

You see, for example, how the countless different languages of peoples existing today were admitted for the liturgical expression of our communication with God and God's communication with us: to human persons as such was recognized their fundamental claim to enjoy full possession of their rights and transcendental destiny. Their supreme aspirations to life, to personal dignity, to just liberty, to culture, to the renewal of the social order, to justice and peace were purified and promoted; and to all men and women was addressed the pastoral and missionary invitation to the light of the Gospel.

We can now speak only too briefly on the very many and vast questions, relative to human welfare, with which the Council dealt. It did not attempt to resolve all the urgent problems of modern life; some of these have been reserved for a further study which the Church intends to make of them, many of them were presented in very restricted and general terms, and for that reason are open to further investigation and various applications.

But one thing must be noted here, namely, that the teaching authority of the Church, even though not wishing to issue extraordinary dogmatic pronouncements, has made thoroughly known its authoritative teaching on a number of questions that today weigh upon people's conscience and activity, descending, so to speak, into a dialogue with them, but ever preserving its own authority and force. It has spoken with the accommodating friendly voice of pastoral charity; its desire has been to be heard and understood by everyone; it has not merely concentrated on intellectual understanding but has also sought to express itself in simple, up-to-date, conversational style, derived from actual experience and a cordial approach which make it more vital, attractive and persuasive; it has spoken to modern men and women as they are.

Another point we must stress is this: all this rich teaching is channeled in one direction, the service of humankind, of every condition, in every weakness and need. The Church has, so to say, declared herself the servant of humanity, at the very time when her teaching role and her pastoral government have, by reason of the Council's solemnity, assumed greater splendor and vigor. The idea of service has been central.

It might be said that all this and everything else we might say about the human values of the Council have diverted the attention of the Church in Council to the trend of modern culture, centered on humanity. We would say not diverted, but rather directed. Any careful observer of the Council's prevailing interest for human and temporal values cannot deny that it is from its pastoral character that the Council has virtually made its program, and must recognize that the same interest is never divorced from the most genuine religious interest, whether by reason of charity, its sole inspiration (where charity is, God is!), or the Council's constant, explicit attempts to link human and temporal values with those that are specifically spiritual, religious and everlasting; its concern is with man and with earth, but it rises to the kingdom of God.

The modern mind, accustomed to assess everything in terms of usefulness, will readily admit that the Council's value is great if only because everything has been referred to human usefulness. Hence no one should ever say that a religion like the Catholic religion is without use, seeing that when it has its greatest self-awareness and effectiveness, as it has in Council, it declares itself entirely on the side of human beings and in their service.

In this way the Catholic religion and human life reaffirm their alliance with one another, the fact that they converge on one single human reality: the Catholic religion is for humankind. In a certain sense it is the life of humankind. It is so by the extremely precise and sublime interpretation that our religion gives of humanity (surely man by himself is a mystery to himself) and gives this interpretation in virtue of its knowledge of God; for a knowledge of God is a prerequisite for a knowledge of man as he really is, in all his fullness. For proof of this let it suffice for now to recall the ardent expression of St. Catherine of Siena, "In your nature, eternal God, I shall know my own." The Catholic religion is human life because it determines life's nature and destiny; it gives life its real meaning, it establishes the supreme law of life and infuses it with that mysterious activity which we may say divinizes it.

Consequently, if we remember, venerable brothers and all of you, our children, gathered here, how in everyone we can and must recognize the countenance of Christ (cf. Matt 25:40), the Son of Man, especially when tears and sorrows make it plain to see, and if we can and must recognize in Christ's countenance the countenance of our heavenly Father — "He who sees me," Our Lord said, "sees also the Father" (John 14:9) — our humanism becomes Christianity, our Christianity becomes centered on God; in such sort that we may say, to put it differently, a knowledge of man is a prerequisite for a knowledge of God.

Would not this Council, then, which has concentrated principally on man, be destined to propose again to the world of today the ladder leading to freedom and consolation? Would it not be, in short, a simple, new and solemn teaching to love other humans in order to love God? To love man, we say, not as a means but as the first step toward the final and transcendent goal which is the basis and cause of every love.

And so this Council can be summed up in its ultimate religious meaning, which is none other than a pressing and friendly invitation to humankind of today to rediscover in fraternal love the God "whom to turn away from, is to fall; whom to turn to, is to rise again; whom to remain in, is to be secure...; whom to return to, is to be born again; in whom to dwell is to live" (St. Augustine, *Soliloquies*, I, 1, 3; *Patrologia Latina* 32, 870).

This is our hope at the conclusion of this Second Vatican Ecumenical Council and at the beginning of the human and religious renewal which the Council proposed to study and promote; this is our hope for you, brothers and Fathers of the Council; this is our hope for the whole of humankind which here we have learned to love more and to serve better.

To this end we again invoke the intercession of St. John the Baptist and of St. Joseph, who are the patrons of the Ecumenical Council; of the holy apostles Peter and Paul, the foundations and pillars of the Holy Church; and with them of St. Ambrose, the bishop whose feast we celebrate today, as it were uniting in him the Church of the East and of the West. We also earnestly implore the protection of the most Blessed Mary, the Mother of Christ and therefore called by us also Mother of the Church. With one voice and with one heart we give thanks and glory to the living and true God, to the one and sovereign God, to the Father, to the Son and to the Holy Spirit. Amen.

Appendix 4

Catholic Doctrine
on Revelation and Faith
The Conciliar Texts

INTRODUCTION TO VATICAN COUNCIL I (1869–70)

The early Ecumenical Councils of the fourth and fifth centuries AD had major roles in the development of Christian doctrine. They clarified central contents of what Christians received from God's word, namely, what came first to Israel through Moses and the prophets, to be transmitted in the Old Testament, and then came to the world through the teaching and work of Jesus as is transmitted by his apostles and their associates in the New Testament.

The early conciliar clarifications became central affirmations in the creed professed to this day in Christian worship of the East and West: confessing God, as Father, Son, and Holy Spirit, and Jesus Christ as truly the Son of God but also as truly human, born of the Virgin Mary, to carry out a mission of redemption for the good of the whole human family.[1]

Valued works of theology by Christian writers, for example, by St. Augustine (d. AD 430), set forth basic principles about the Christian faith and life, the sacraments, and the role of God's interior grace in lives of faith and love. These doctrines were widely received in the churches of Western Christianity and were put into systematic form by leading theologians of the Middle Ages, for example, Peter Lombard (d. 1160), St. Bonaventure (d. 1274), and St. Thomas Aquinas (d. 1274). But disputes broke out over these points when Martin Luther issued in 1517 his program of church reform. To this challenge, the Council of Trent gave several well-developed doctrinal answers during its three working sessions, 1545–47, 1551, 1562–63, adding a series of reform decrees that had the effect of profoundly shaping Catholic life until well into the twentieth century.

The intellectual movement of the European enlightenment, especially in the eighteenth and early nineteenth centuries, raised new challenges to faith in God's revelation and to church teaching, on the basis of philosophical claims for the powers of human reason to understand the world and to chart properly humane ways of personal, social, and political life. Pope Pius IX convened Vatican Council I, which met from December 1869 until July 1870, when it had to suspend work because of the war that had broken out between France and Prussia. Vatican I gave a Catholic response to enlightenment challenges in teaching that combines respect for human reason with clear indications of how human beings have to go beyond reason to accept God's revelation in faith. From several draft texts proposed for deliberation at Vatican I, only two were discussed, revised, voted on, and promulgated as Catholic doctrine. The first document responds to the enlightenment on faith and reason, treating in four chapters (1) the nature of God, (2) divine revelation and its communication in scripture and tradition, (3) the need of faith and how humans are helped toward coming to believe, and (4) the mutual and coordinate relations between faith and human reason. This is a dogmatic constitution, that is, a document of solemn teaching, and is called *Dei Filius* ("The Son of God"), from the opening words of its Preface.

In its second constitution, Vatican Council I gave to the church a teaching from only one chapter of what had been drawn up in a longer preliminary draft on the nature of the church. Singled out for clarification were two issues, responding to views of the church long circulating in France (as "Gallicanism"), which had presented church authority as a dispersed reality, which the Vatican I majority saw as obscuring the fundamental role of the bishop of Rome, the successor of Peter. Thus, the second document promulgated at Vatican I, called *Pastor aeternus* ("The eternal Shepherd"), speaks of the pope's primacy in authority as he governs the church and of his special prerogative of being able, under certain well-defined conditions, to teach central truths of God's revelation in a way protected from error ("infallibility").

For the purposes of this introduction to doing theology, the first of Vatican I's constitutions, *Dei Filius,* serves to show the starting point of modern Catholic teaching on God's revelation and the response of faith. Vatican Council I responded to the challenge of its age by formulating the nature of revelation as supernatural instruction which God gives to human beings, who must submit to this teaching in order to know the truth about their supernatural vocation and about God's plan and work for their salvation.[2]

VATICAN COUNCIL I
Dogmatic Constitution on the Catholic Faith
(April 24, 1870)

Preface[3]

The Son of God [*Dei Filius*], redeemer of the human race, our lord Jesus Christ, promised, when about to return to his heavenly Father, that he would be with his church militant upon earth all days even to the end of the world (see Matt 28:20). Hence never at any time has he ceased to stand by his beloved bride, assisting her when she teaches, blessing her in her labors, and bringing her help when she is in danger. Now this redemptive providence appears very clearly in unnumbered benefits, but most especially is it manifested in the advantages which have been secured for the Christian world by Ecumenical Councils, among which the Council of Trent requires special mention.

> [On the Council of Trent (1545–63), the Preface enumerates benefits given to Catholics by the Tridentine clarifications of doctrine and decrees on reforms of Catholic life, regarding both the clergy and the laity. But the Preface laments that outside the church Trent was rejected by Protestants, who allowed religious topics to be decided by individuals exercising their own "private judgment" about the meaning of the Bible. As modern times progressed, many intellectuals came to deny the authority of the Bible under the influence of naturalist philosophies of the enlightenment, which called in question God's coming to us in Christ, our Lord and Savior, and went on to treat the Bible as merely human writing infected with myths. Viewing its own

century, the Preface relates that atheist views have been circulating which deny the norms of right human action and threaten the good order of society.

Amid the spread of false doctrines and opinions, even some teachers of Catholic doctrine have become confused about basic truths, and so Vatican Council I intends to clarify fundamental Catholic doctrines on the basis of God's word, as this is found in scripture, in the tradition received in the church, and in previous accounts of doctrine by the church's teaching authority.]

Chapter 1 – God the Creator of All Things

[1. The Nature of God]

The holy, catholic, apostolic, and Roman church believes and acknowledges that there is one true and living God, creator and lord of heaven and earth, almighty, eternal, immeasurable, incomprehensible, infinite in will, understanding and every perfection. Since he is one, singular, completely simple and unchangeable spiritual substance, he must be declared to be, in reality and in essence, distinct from the world, supremely happy in himself and from himself, and inexpressibly loftier than anything besides himself which either exists or can be imagined.

[2. Creation by God]

This one true God, by his goodness and almighty power, not with the intention of increasing his happiness, nor indeed of obtaining happiness, but in order to manifest his perfection by the good things which he bestows on what he creates, by an absolutely free plan, "together from the beginning of time brought into being from nothing the twofold created order, that is the spiritual and the bodily, the angelic and the earthly, and thereafter the human which is, in a way, common to both since it is composed of spirit and body."[4]

[3. God's Providence over Creation]

Everything that God has brought into being he protects and governs by his providence, "which reaches from one end of the earth to the other and orders all things well" (Wis 8:1). "All things are open and laid bare to his eyes" (Heb 4:13), even those which will be brought about by the free activity of creatures.

Chapter 2 – Revelation

[4. Natural Knowledge of God and Supernatural Revelation]

The same holy mother church holds and teaches that God, the source and end of all things, can be known with certainty from the consideration of created things, by the natural power of human reason, for "ever since the creation of the world, his invisible nature has been clearly perceived in the things that have been made" (Rom 1:20). It was, however, pleasing to his wisdom and goodness to reveal himself and the eternal laws of his will to the human race by another, and that a supernatural, way. This is how the apostle puts it: "In many and various ways God spoke of old to our fathers by the prophets; but in these last days he has spoken to us by a Son" (Heb 1:1–2).

[5. The Human Need of Divine Revelation]

It is indeed thanks to this divine revelation, that those matters concerning God which are not of themselves beyond the scope of human reason, can, even in the present state of the human race, be known by everyone without difficulty, with firm certitude and with no intermingling of error. It is not because of this that one must hold revelation to be absolutely necessary; but the reason is that God has directed human beings to a supernatural end, that is, to share in the good things of God that utterly surpass the understanding of the human mind; indeed, "Eye has not seen, nor ear heard, nor the human heart conceived, what God prepared for those who love him" (1 Cor 2:9).

> [Paragraphs 6 and 7 then treat the communication to us of God's revelation, namely, by the scriptures and "unwritten traditions" coming from the apostles of Jesus. Here Vatican I restates a text of the Council of Trent. But it adds to this its own teaching on the divine inspiration of scripture, before repeating Trent on how scripture should be interpreted.]

Chapter 3 – Faith

[8. Definition of Faith]

Since human beings are totally dependent on God as their creator and lord, and created reason is completely subject to uncreated truth, we are obliged to yield to God the revealer full submission of intellect and will by faith. This faith, which is the "beginning of human salvation,"[5] the Catholic Church professes to be a supernatural virtue, by means of which, with the grace of God inspiring and assisting us, we believe to be true what he has revealed, not because we perceive its intrinsic truth by the natural light of reason, but because of the authority of God himself, who makes the revelation and can neither deceive nor be deceived. Faith, declares the apostle, is "the assurance of things hoped for, the conviction of things not seen" (Heb 11:1).

[9. Internal and External Helps toward Assenting in Faith]

Nevertheless, in order that the submission of our faith should be in accordance with reason, it was God's will that there should be linked to the internal assistance of the Holy Spirit outward indications of his revelation, that is to say divine acts, and first and foremost miracles and prophecies, which clearly demonstrating as they do the omnipotence and infinite knowledge of God, are the most certain signs of revelation and are suited to the understanding of all. Hence Moses and the prophets, and especially Christ our Lord himself, worked many absolutely clear miracles and delivered prophecies; while of the apostles we read: "And they went forth and preached everywhere, while the Lord worked with them and confirmed the message by the signs that attended it" (Mark 16:20). Again it is written: "We have the prophetic word made more sure; you will do well to pay attention to this as to a lamp shining in a dark place" (2 Pet 1:19).

[10. Faith as God's Gift]

Now, although the assent of faith is by no means a blind movement of the mind, yet no one can "accept the Gospel preaching" in the way that is necessary for reaching salvation "without the inspiration and illumination of the Holy Spirit, who gives to all facility in accepting and believing the truth."[6] And so faith in itself, even though it may not work through charity, is a gift of God, and its operation is a work belonging to the order of salvation, in that a person yields true obedience to God himself when he accepts and collaborates with his grace which he could have rejected.

[11. The Object of the Assent of Faith]

Wherefore, by divine and catholic faith all those things are to be believed which are contained in the word of God as found in scripture and tradition, and which are proposed by the church as matters to be believed as divinely revealed, whether by her solemn judgment or in her ordinary and universal magisterium.

[12. Faith Necessary for Salvation]

Since, then, "without faith it is impossible to please God" (Heb 11:6) and reach the fellowship of his sons and daughters, it follows that no one can ever achieve justification without it, neither can anyone attain eternal life unless he or she perseveres in it to the end (see Matt 10:22, 24:13). So that we could fulfill our duty of embracing the true faith and of persevering unwaveringly in it, God, through his only begotten Son, founded the church, and he endowed his institution with clear notes to the end that she might be recognized by all as the guardian and teacher of the revealed word.

[13. The Church as a Motive of Credibility]

To the Catholic Church alone belong all those things, so many and so marvelous, which have been divinely ordained to make for the manifest credibility of the Christian faith. What is more, the church herself by reason of her astonishing propagation, her outstanding holiness and her inexhaustible fertility in every kind of goodness, by her catholic unity and her unconquerable stability, is a kind of great and perpetual motive of credibility and an incontrovertible evidence of her own divine mission. So it comes about that, like a standard lifted up for the nations (see Isa 11:12), she both invites to herself those who have not yet believed, and likewise assures her sons and daughters that the faith they profess rests on the firmest of foundations.

[14. Interior Grace and Perseverance in Faith]

To this witness is added the effective help of power from on high. For, the kind Lord stirs up those who go astray and helps them by his grace so that they may come to the knowledge of the truth (see 1 Tim 2:4); and also confirms by his grace those whom "he has called out of darkness into his admirable light" (1 Pet 2:9), so that they may persevere in this light, not abandoning them unless he is first abandoned. Consequently, the situation of those, who by the heavenly gift of faith have embraced catholic truth, is by no means the same as that of those who, led by human opinions, follow a false religion; for those who have accepted the faith under the guidance of the church can never have any just cause for changing this faith or for calling it into question. This being so, "giving thanks to God the Father who has made us worthy to share with the saints in light" (Col 1:12), let us not neglect so great a salvation (cf. Heb 2:3), but "looking unto Jesus the author and finisher of our faith" (Heb 12:2), "let us hold the unshakeable confession of our hope" (Heb 10:23).

[Chapter 4 completes the constitution by giving a further account of how natural reason and supernatural faith in God's revelation are different but still relate to one another. The believer can investigate the revealed mysteries of salvation by applying his reason once it is enlightened by faith.[7] Reason and faith both come from God and, while they differ in their objects and ways of operating, no true opposition can arise between them. Rightly understood, they support and help each other. In the Church, the teaching authority, while exercising vigilance regarding ideas contrary to faith, favors the sciences, as long as they are practiced in their proper areas. However, the main concern of church teaching is to protect God's revelation from false understandings, to declare the meaning of revealed truths, and to promote sound development in their understanding.]

INTRODUCTION TO VATICAN II
ON REVELATION, FAITH, AND SCRIPTURE

In 1962, during its first working period, Vatican Council II took up a draft text on scripture and tradition as the two sources of our knowledge of God's revelation. The text was sharply criticized for not promoting the goals that Pope John had set for the Council, and the pope had it sent back to a newly formed drafting commission for revision. Responding to requests from the Council members, the commission added an initial chapter on the nature of divine revelation itself. Vatican II draws extensively on scripture to present God's revelation in Christ as the loving self-manifestation of God-with-us to free us from sin and spiritual death. God's revealed word is an invitation, given through Christ and in the Holy Spirit, to personal communion. Vatican II advances beyond Vatican I's teaching on revelation and faith by adopting biblical language in order to show God's revealing work as attractive and powerful to save otherwise lost human beings. Furthermore, looking to promote a vital faith in God's revelation, the Council concluded its constitution on revelation, in chapter 6, with pastoral directives aiming to give scripture a central place in Catholic faith, teaching, and life. The following texts are chapters 1 and 6 of Vatican II's *Dei Verbum*.[8]

VATICAN COUNCIL II
Dogmatic Constitution on Divine Revelation
(November 18, 1965)

Prologue

[The Council's Intention]

1. Hearing the word of God reverently and proclaiming it confidently, this holy synod makes its own the words of St. John: "We proclaim to you the eternal life which was with the Father and was made manifest to us — that which we have seen and heard we proclaim also to you, so that you may have fellowship with us; and our fellowship is with the Father and with his Son Jesus Christ" (1 John 1:2–3). Following then in the steps of the Councils of Trent and Vatican I, this synod wishes to set forth the authentic teaching on divine

revelation and its transmission. For it wants the whole world to hear the summons to salvation, so that through hearing it may believe, through belief it may hope, and through hoping it may come to love.[9]

Chapter 1 – Divine Revelation Itself

[The Nature and Central Content of God's Revelation]

2. It pleased God, in his goodness and wisdom, to reveal himself and to make known the mystery of his will (see Eph 1:9), which was that people can draw near to the Father, through Christ, the Word made flesh, in the Holy Spirit, and thus become sharers in the divine nature (see Eph 2:18; 2 Pet 1:4). By this revelation, then, the invisible God (see Col 1:15; 1 Tim 1:17), from the fullness of his love, addresses men and women as his friends (see Exod 33:11; John 15:14–15), and lives among them (see Bar 3:38), in order to invite and receive them into his own company. The pattern of this revelation unfolds through deeds and words which are intrinsically connected: the works performed by God in the history of salvation show forth and confirm the doctrine and realities signified by the words; the words, for their part, proclaim the works and bring to light the mystery they contain. The most intimate truth thus revealed about God and human salvation shines forth for us in Christ, who is himself both the mediator and the sum total of revelation.[10]

[The Preparation for Revelation in Christ]

3. God, who creates and conserves all things by his Word (see John 1:3), provides constant evidence of himself in created realities (see Rom 1:19–20). Furthermore, wishing to open up the way to heavenly salvation, he manifested himself to our first parents from the very beginning. After the fall, he buoyed them up with the hope of salvation, by promising redemption (see Gen 3:15); and he has never ceased to take care of the human race, in order to give eternal life to all those who seek salvation by persevering in doing good (see Rom 2:6–7). In his own time, God called Abraham and made him into a great nation (see Gen 12:2). After the era of the patriarchs, he taught this nation, through Moses and the prophets, to recognize him as the only living and true God, as a provident Father and just

judge. He taught them, too, to look for the promised Savior. And so, throughout the ages, he prepared the way for the Gospel.

[God's Supreme and Definitive Revelation in Christ]

4. After God had spoken many times and in various ways through the prophets, "in these last days he has spoken to us by a Son" (Heb 1:1–2). For he sent his Son, the eternal Word who enlightens all humankind, to live among them and to tell them about the inner life of God (see John 1:1–18). Hence, Jesus Christ, the Word made flesh, was sent as "a man to men and women,"[11] "speaks the words of God" (John 3:34), and accomplishes the saving work which his Father gave him to do (see John 5:36; 17:4). As a result, he himself — to see whom is to see the Father (see John 14:9) — completed and perfected revelation and confirmed it with divine guarantees. Everything to do with his presence and his manifestation of himself was involved in achieving this: his words and works, signs and miracles, but above all his death and glorious resurrection from the dead, and finally his sending of the Spirit of truth. He revealed that God is with us, to deliver us from the darkness of sin and death, and to raise us up to life eternal.

The Christian dispensation, therefore, since it is the new and definitive covenant, will never pass away; and no new public revelation is to be expected before the glorious manifestation of our Lord, Jesus Christ (see 1 Tim 6:14 and Titus 2:13).

[The Response of Faith to God's Revelation]

5. "The obedience of faith" (see Rom 16:26; compare Rom 1:5; 2 Cor 10:5–6) must be our response to God who reveals. By faith one freely commits oneself entirely to God, making "the full submission of intellect and will to God who reveals,"[12] and willingly assenting to the revelation given by God. For this faith to be accorded we need the grace of God, anticipating it and assisting it, as well as the interior helps of the Holy Spirit, who moves the heart and converts it to God, and opens the eyes of the mind and "makes it easy for all to accept and believe in the truth."[13] The same Holy Spirit constantly perfects faith by his gifts, so that revelation may be more and more deeply understood.

[The Revealed Truths]

6. By divine revelation God wishes to manifest and communicate both himself and the eternal decrees of his will concerning the salvation of humankind. He wished, in other words, "to share with us divine benefits which entirely surpass the powers of the human mind to understand."[14]

The holy synod professes that "God, the first principle and last end of all things, can be known with certainty from the created world, by the natural light of human reason" (see Rom 1:20). It teaches that it is to his revelation that we must attribute the fact "that those things, which in themselves are not beyond the grasp of human reason, can, in the present condition of the human race, be known by all with ease, with firm certainty, and without the contamination of error."[15]

[Chapter 2 of the constitution is on the initial apostolic and the ongoing ecclesial communication of revelation by means of living tradition and scripture, with no. 10 describing the role of the church's teaching authority in authentically interpreting the word of God.[16] But "this magisterium is not superior to the word of God, but is rather its servant." Chapter 3 states Catholic doctrine on sacred scripture, that is, on its inspiration by the Holy Spirit, its content of truth meant for our salvation, and how to rightly interpret the sacred books.[17] Chapter 4 affirms the role of the Old Testament in witnessing to God's revelation in Israel and in preparing for Christ, for "the books of the Old Testament, all of them given a place in the preaching of the Gospel, attain and display their full meaning in the New Testament and, in their turn, they shed light on it and explain it" (no. 16). Chapter 5 speaks of the New Testament, with a notable account in no. 19 of how the words and deeds of Jesus were passed on orally before the evangelists wrote them down in the Gospels for the benefit of the churches of the apostolic age. The constitution then outlines a pastoral program in chapter 6, given here, by which Catholics should come to take the scriptures as their rule of faith, their guide in living, and source of their spirituality.]

Chapter VI – Sacred Scripture in the Life of the Church

[Why the Church Venerates Scripture]

21. The Church has always venerated the divine scriptures as it has venerated the Body of the Lord, in that it never ceases, above all in the sacred liturgy, to partake of the bread of life and to offer it to the faithful from the one table of the word of God and the Body of Christ. It has always regarded, and continues to regard the scriptures, taken together with sacred tradition, as the supreme rule of its faith. For, since they are inspired by God and committed to writing once and for all time, they present God's own word in an inalterable form, and they make the voice of the Holy Spirit sound again and again in the words of the prophets and apostles. It follows that all the preaching of the Church, as indeed the entire Christian religion, should be nourished and ruled by sacred scripture. In the sacred books the Father who is in heaven comes lovingly to meet his children, and talks with them. And such is the force and power of the word of God that it is the Church's support and strength, imparting robustness to the faith of its daughters and sons and providing food for their souls. It is a pure and unfailing fount of spiritual life. It is eminently true of holy scripture that: "The word of God is living and active" (Heb 4:12), and "is able to build you up and to give you the inheritance among all those who are sanctified" (Acts 20:32; see 1 Thess 2:13).

[Attention to Preparing Good Translations]

22. Access to sacred scripture ought to be widely available to the Christian faithful. For this reason the Church, from the very beginning, made its own the ancient Greek translation of the Old Testament called the Septuagint; it honors also the other Eastern translations, and the Latin translations, especially that known as the Vulgate. But since the word of God must be readily accessible at all times, the Church, with motherly concern, sees to it that suitable and correct translations are made into various languages, especially from the original texts of the sacred books. If, when the opportunity presents itself and the authorities of the Church agree, these translations are made jointly with churches separated from us, they can then be used by all Christians.

[Making Scripture Study Fruitful for Believers]

23. Taught by the Holy Spirit, the spouse of the incarnate Word, which is the Church, strives to reach an increasingly more profound understanding of the sacred scriptures, in order to nourish its children with God's words. For this reason also it duly encourages the study of the Fathers, both Eastern and Western, and of the sacred liturgies. Catholic exegetes and other workers in the field of sacred theology should work diligently together and under the watchful eye of the sacred magisterium. Using appropriate techniques they should together set about examining and explaining the sacred texts in such a way that as many as possible of those who are ministers of God's word may be able to dispense fruitfully the nourishment of the scriptures to the people of God. This nourishment enlightens the mind, strengthens the will, and fires the hearts of men and women with the love of God.[18] The holy synod encourages those members of the Church who are engaged in biblical studies constantly to renew their efforts, in order to carry on, with complete dedication and in accordance with the mind of the Church,[19] the work they have so happily begun.

[The Role of Scripture in Theology]

24. Sacred theology relies on the written word of God, taken together with sacred tradition, as its permanent foundation. By this word it is powerfully strengthened and constantly rejuvenated, as it searches out, under the light of faith, all truth stored up in the mystery of Christ. The sacred scriptures contain the word of God, and, because they are inspired, they truly are the word of God; therefore the study of the sacred page should be the very soul of sacred theology.[20] The ministry of word, too — pastoral preaching, catechetics and all forms of Christian instruction, among which the liturgical homily should hold pride of place — gains healthy nourishment and holy vitality from the word of scripture.

[Exhortation to Read Scripture Regularly]

25. Therefore, all clerics, particularly priests of Christ and others who, as deacons or catechists, are officially engaged in the ministry of the word, should immerse themselves in the scriptures by constant spiritual reading and diligent study. For it must not happen

that any of them become "empty preachers of the word of God to others, not being hearers of the word in their own hearts,"[21] when they ought to be sharing the boundless riches of the divine word with the faithful committed to their care, especially in the sacred liturgy. Likewise, the holy synod forcefully and specifically exhorts all the Christian faithful, especially those who live the religious life, to learn "the surpassing knowledge of Jesus Christ" (Phil 3:8) by frequent reading of the divine scriptures. "Ignorance of the scriptures is ignorance of Christ."[22] Therefore, let them go gladly to the sacred text itself, whether in the sacred liturgy, which is full of the divine words, or in devout reading, or in such suitable exercises and various other helps which, with the approval and guidance of the pastors of the Church, are happily spreading everywhere in our day. Let them remember, however, that prayer should accompany the reading of sacred scripture, so that it becomes a dialogue between God and the human reader. For, "we speak to him when we pray; we listen to him when we read the divine oracles."[23] It is the duty of bishops, "with whom the apostolic doctrine resides"[24] suitably to instruct the faithful entrusted to them in the correct use of the divine books, especially the New Testament and in particular the Gospels. This is done by translations of the sacred texts which are equipped with necessary and really adequate explanations. Thus, the children of the Church can familiarize themselves safely and profitably with the sacred scriptures and become steeped in their spirit.

Moreover, editions of sacred scripture, provided with suitable notes, should be prepared for the use even of non-Christians, and adapted to their circumstances. These should be prudently circulated, either by pastors of souls, or by Christians of any walk of life.

[Conclusion]

26. So may it come that, by the reading and study of the sacred books "the word of God may speed on and triumph" (2 Thess 3:1) and the treasure of revelation entrusted to the Church may more and more fill people's hearts. Just as from constant attendance at the eucharistic mystery the life of the Church draws increase, so a new impulse of spiritual life may be expected from increased veneration of the word of God, which "stands forever" (Isa 40:8; see 1 Pet 1:23–25).

Appendix 5

Theologians at Vatican Council II
Jared Wicks, SJ

INTRODUCTION

The following account rests on research on Vatican II, both by the author and by doctoral candidates who studied the Council for their dissertations at the Gregorian University in Rome. The text first took shape as a lecture in Brescia, Italy, in February 2004.[1] It is given here, with recent additions on contributions by Professor Joseph Ratzinger, then at Bonn but now Pope Benedict XVI. The aim is to complement presentations of the Council that give extensive attention to factors other than the theologians whose expertise also contributed to the Council. The details related in what follows serve to document an intense and fruitful collaboration between the church's teaching office, especially the bishops who were members of the Council, and theologians who served as experts (*periti*) at Vatican II.

♦ ♦ ♦

Popular accounts of the Second Vatican Council at times emphasize the critical, and even combative, activity of the theologian-experts, especially during the first period (October–December 1962). Individual Council theologians such as Karl Rahner, Yves Congar, and Eduard Schillebeeckx appear as significant protagonists in the conciliar drama. In fact, the papers of these theologians document their considerable involvement, just before the Council opened and then during its first weeks, when they circulated among the Council Fathers and other experts their critiques of the initial draft texts and some alternative texts on the sources of revelation, the deposit of faith, and the nature of the church.

187

But more than three years before Vatican II began on October 11, 1962, the conciliar activity of theologians had begun with lectures and writings aiming to sketch the context of the coming Council, to identify its priorities, and to propose topics that it should treat. Numerous theologians worked for the preparatory commissions in the period from mid-1960 into the summer of 1962.

During the four autumn periods of Council sessions (1962–65), and for some during the three intersessions, Vatican II demanded of numerous theologians a variety of services, including consultations offered to the Council members and composition of their Latin interventions in the Aula and of the comments they handed in on draft texts under discussion. *Periti*) were invited to give lectures to groups of bishops on the Council topics. As the Council moved ahead, more and more *periti* were called into service of the conciliar commissions, including several mixed commissions and numerous subcommissions. The commissions asked their theologian-associates to examine in detail the oral and written interventions of the Fathers on the draft texts and to draw up proposed revisions reflecting the interventions.

But in all this, the ultimate outcome of the theologians' work was decided by others, that is, by the Council members who were the members of the commissions and who voted in the Aula. The ideas, preferences, and texts drawn up by the theologians were consultative proposals of experts, about which the Council members in different moments decided whether, and in what form, these theological contributions might appear in the schemata placed before the Council and then in the documents approved by the Council.

My aim here is to indicate the principal moments in which *periti* contributed to the huge ecclesial event that was the Second Vatican Council. To stay within reasonable limits, I will say practically nothing about the decisive influence exercised on the Council by Popes John XXIII and Paul VI, nor will I tell much about major players in Vatican II such as Cardinals Augustin Bea, Leo Josef Suenens, and Julius Döpfner. Other accounts of the Council treat them amply. Here the emphasis is on the "ways and means" by which theologians influenced the Council, with examples of the topics they presented, both in preparation for and during Vatican II. I hope to verify the actual degree, beyond mythic narratives, of the influence of the *periti* on the work of the Council and on its results.[2]

Announcement, First Responses, and the Ante-preparatory Phase, 1959–60

As is well known, Pope John XXIII announced on January 25, 1959, his intention of convoking an Ecumenical Council of the Catholic Church. He spoke to a gathering of cardinals, at the Basilica of St. Paul's Outside the Walls, after prayers concluding the Week of Prayer for Christian Unity. Around the world, people were still getting used to the new pope, Angelo Giuseppe Roncalli, who had been papal nuncio in Bulgaria, Turkey, and France, but most recently was patriarch of Venice, when he was elected to succeed Pius XII (pope, 1939–59) on October 28, 1958, just eighty-eight days before he announced the coming Council. But some theologians went into action quickly, and many followed in the next three and a half years with contributions to help prepare the Council.

In France, Yves Congar, OP, was in print by mid-February 1959, with a survey on Councils in the life of the church, to which he added his hopes that the coming Council would refrain from any new definition of privileges given to the Blessed Virgin Mary, that it would create a better balance in church governance between the wide scope of papal action and the restricted roles of bishops, that it would manifest a genuine solicitude for the good of human life in this world, and that it would give a positive impulse to better relations with non-Catholic Christians, for whom at the moment there was no designated office for contact and dialogue in the Vatican.[3]

In autumn 1959, Congar was at an ecumenical congress at the Benedictine Abbey of Chevetogne, Belgium, where the topic was general Councils, and Congar stressed the importance of the first four such Councils, because of the overriding significance for both Eastern Orthodox and Catholics of their dogmatic teachings. For the new Council for which the Catholic Church was preparing, Congar named two doctrinal topics calling for further clarification because of their ecumenical import: the "collegiality" of all the bishops in governing the whole church, and a clarification of the relations between holy scripture and the tradition coming from the apostles and preserved in the church.[4]

Another theologian who went quickly to work after Pope John's announcement was Hubert Jedin, historian of the Council of Trent, then professor of modern church history in the faculty of Catholic theology of Bonn, Germany. Jedin wrote a concise history of the church's general Councils in a book translated into seven languages beyond its original German. Jedin also recommended to his Italian scholar-friends that they prepare a handy one-volume edition of all the decrees of the general Councils from Nicea (325) to Vatican I (1869–70).[5]

Hans Küng spent his summer vacation of 1959 composing his widely read book on the just-announced Council's potential for initiating reform in the Catholic Church in ways which would pave the way to the reunion of the presently divided Christian churches.[6] By a happy accident, Küng had been invited to Basel in January 1959 by the Reformed theologian Karl Barth and lectured there on ongoing reform of the church (*ecclesia semper reformanda*), just a week before Pope John announced the coming Council. His book on reform and reunion was also influenced by a meeting around July 1, 1959, with two Dutch priests, Jan Willebrands and Frans Thijssen, the coordinators of the Catholic Committee on Ecumenical Questions, which had been quietly promoting ecumenism among European Catholic theologians during the 1950s. Küng stressed in his book that the very holding of a Council signaled a change of climate in the Catholic Church, in which there was now good reason to hope for concrete changes, in a new receptivity to the justified proposals of the Protestant Reformation, which would then lead toward recomposing the fractured unity of Western Christianity.

A young professor of fundamental theology in the theology faculty of the University of Bonn, Germany, Joseph Ratzinger, anticipated a major theme of Vatican II in an early lecture on the Council as expressing the collegial nature of the church's pastoral leadership, on the model of the twelve apostles. Many had forgotten this after Vatican I had time in 1870 to treat only the Successor of Peter and his infallibility in certain moments of his teaching. Still, the Council is not a parliament of the peoples' representatives, since the bishops gathered in Council are the body bearing a primary responsibility in this later age for giving witness to the word of Christ from which believers live.[7]

In the Vatican, Pope John had a "pre-preparatory" commission formed in May 1959, as announced publicly on Pentecost Sunday. It included the "number two" of each of the ten offices or congregations of the church's central government, with the cardinal secretary of state, Domenico Tardini, directing the group and reporting on its work to Pope John. An unknown monsignor from the Vatican marriage tribunal, the Rota, Pericle Felici, became secretary of this pre-preparatory group, in the first of his tasks as indefatigable coordinator of the daily work of the Second Vatican Council.

Cardinal Tardini got the Council machinery moving with a letter of June 18, 1959, to 2,594 bishops and major superiors of clerical religious orders, who by canon law would be called to be participating members of the Council. The letter expressed Pope John's desire to hear from the future Council members their views, advice, and suggestions regarding the questions and topics that the Council should take up.

The survey begun in 1959 had a 77 percent level of response from those contacted (2,150 answers). The responses differed greatly, from short indications of one or two points of church doctrine, law, and administration to lengthy proposals with arguments to back them up. The letter of June asked for a response in September, but in fact the answers from the bishops of the world kept arriving well into spring 1960, which gave the pre-preparatory commission the needed time to organize the vast material, eventually made up of about nine thousand different proposals, with many items coming from several or more respondents, under a chosen set of headings. In the letter of request, Cardinal Tardini said explicitly that in preparing the answer, the bishop or religious superior could conduct a consultation with persons who were experts in the various ecclesiastical fields.

In the Proposals of 1959–60: Scattered Signs of Theologians' Input

The suggestions of the bishops and religious superiors for the Council agenda were published in the Vatican II *Acta et Documenta* (series 1, vol. 2, in 8 parts). These were originally for use in the second phase of preparation, in composing draft texts of decrees to put before the Council members. But recently these texts of 1959–60 have begun attracting the attention of those interested in Catholic history, because they present a portrait of the church's leadership at the moment of its transition from the pontificate of Pope Pius XII to that of John XXIII and Vatican II. Recent studies of the proposals, often treating those from one nation, indicate that the future Fathers of the Council were not widely interested in gathering ideas from a consultation of experts in theology. This, at least, is implied in reviews of the proposals that came from France, England, Spain, Canada, and Italy.

But there were exceptions. In the Netherlands, four bishops proposed that the Council sanction a positive Catholic engagement in the ecumenical movement. The bishops used for this a memorandum drawn up by Fathers Willebrands and Thijssen, of the Catholic Committee on Ecumenical Questions.[8]

In Strasbourg, France, Archbishop Jean Julien Weber inserted into his proposal several suggestions of Y. Congar, who was then living in Strasbourg. The Council should center its teaching on the Gospel, proclaiming before the world the lordship of Jesus Christ, and stressing the great truths of God as Trinity and his redemptive work that are held in common with Christians of other confessions. In this recentering, the church would present itself as the "gathered congregation of those joined to Christ by faith and baptism," with such an ample vision allowing Catholics to acknowledge the saving action of the Holy Spirit, not just in their own life and sacraments, but in other Christian bodies as well. Here is thinking that puts into practice, even before Vatican II urged it, the principle of "the hierarchy of truths" (UR 11), intending thereby to offer a corrective to overemphasis in Catholic piety on special devotions, especially to the Virgin Mary.[9]

In his study of the responses from the United States, Joseph Komonchak discovered some documentation of the American bishops' consultations of theologians.[10] Cardinal Richard Cushing of Boston formed a committee of ten, including four theologians of St. John's Seminary, to draw up possible proposals for the Council. The cardinal selected twenty items, including a request for a new systematic account of the church as the mystical body of Christ, which should lead to social conclusions, for example, toward overcoming exaggerated nationalism in one part of the body.

Cardinal Francis Spellman of New York asked his seminary professors for a list of possible suggestions. Among the topics submitted, the cardinal declined to pass on to Rome proposals to restore the diaconate as a permanent ministry in the church and to let the vernacular take the place of Latin in the celebration of the Catholic liturgy. One of the professors proposed that the Council bring clarity in an area then under discussion, namely, whether ideally a government is obliged to favor the true faith, while only tolerating heretical and schismatic sects. Cardinal Spellman, who later brought Father John Courtney Murray, SJ, to Vatican II as his advisor, crossed out with a big X the topic of the state favoring one religious confession.

At Catholic University of America, the moral theologian Father Francis Connell, CSsR, drafted twenty points of doctrine for the Council, from which Archbishop O'Boyle of Washington selected nine for inclusion in his proposal, including a request that the Council solemnly condemn racism and all discrimination against persons of other races. But these cases of theologians' influence are, in fact, very few among the 138 responses that came from U.S. bishops.

Among the suggestions of the future Council members, two can be mentioned because of the roles that those responsible would have at Vatican II.

At Milan, the deadline of September 1959, fixed by Cardinal Tardini, was not observed, since it left little time for ideas to grow to maturity. The theological faculty of Milan held regular meetings on proposals for Vatican II from October 1959 into April 1960, with regular reports being presented to the archbishop, Cardinal Giovanni Battista Montini (the future Pope Paul VI). This interaction resulted in two documents sent to the Vatican in early May 1960, showing an elegant complementarity between the faculty's doctrinal proposals and the cardinal's comprehensive pastoral suggestions. Cardinal Montini said it was time to adopt a new policy regarding men who left the priesthood to marry, offering them reconciliation and a dispensation from celibacy. To ensure real progress toward the ecumenical hopes that John XXIII had been mentioning in talks on the Council, Cardinal Montini urged the holding of preconciliar "hearings" with representatives of the Eastern Orthodox and Protestant churches, so that at the coming Council Catholic bishops would have accurate ideas of the faith and life of other Christians and not think of them and their communities in ways derived from outdated textbooks.[11]

In Münster, Germany, Bishop Michael Keller incorporated into his proposal a series of topics worked out by professors of the Catholic theology faculty of the University of Münster. In teaching on what the church is, the Council should draw more widely on scripture than is ordinarily done, so that the topic of the Body of Christ, from St. Paul, would be accompanied by insistence on the Holy Spirit who unites and gives life to the community and on the notion of "the people of God" who are on pilgrimage toward the fullness of God's kingdom and reign.

Bishop Keller took over a paragraph composed by Professor Hermann Volk, who was then dean of the Münster faculty:

> The Council should declare solemnly that sacred scripture is the principal source of Catholic truth, while tradition, although not creative of divine revelation, is for us a source from which God's revealed truths become manifested. The Council should show that the popular idea is not right that the Catholic Church lives from the sacraments, while Protestants live from the word they hear read and preached. Taking its cue from the Letter to Hebrews, "The word of God is living and active, sharper than any two-edged sword" (Heb 4:12), the Council should acknowledge the saving efficacy of the word, as it is read during the liturgy, applied in the homily, and explained in catechesis, always according to the meaning that the church holds to be true.

Together with this topic, well known from writings of Professor Volk, Bishop Keller took over another idea of the faculty, namely, that Catholic seriousness about the value of scripture should lead to a revision of the liturgical lectionary, so that people would not hear the same Sunday readings every year, but should be exposed to many more biblical passages by selections arranged in a three-year cycle of readings.[12]

After contributing these preparatory proposals for Vatican II, H. Volk was named bishop of Mainz in the spring of 1962 and so became a member of the Second Vatican Council, where he contributed to the work of the Secretariat for Promoting Christian Unity and the Council's doctrinal commission. In October 1965, when the commission was working on the final revisions of its constitution on Divine Revelation, Volk voiced his dissatisfaction over the way the beginning of text then stood, that is, by naming the Council as the subject or speaker of the teaching (*Sacrosancta Synodus...*). For Volk the opening words should indicate briefly the topic and should not call attention to the Council. In a short consultation between Volk and the Louvain theologian Gerard Philips, a new opening phrase was formulated that the commission members immediately voted to accept: "Hearing the word of God reverently and proclaiming it confidently, this holy synod..." (*Dei verbum religiose audiens et fidenter proclamans...*). In this way, one theologian affected Vatican II both early in its preparation and later near the end of its work.[13]

The Studies Submitted by the Theological Faculties

The second part of the pre-preparatory survey was the collection of proposals by professors teaching in Catholic theology faculties. In July 1959, Cardinal Tardini wrote to sixty-two such bodies around the world, to ask for "brief studies, clear and precise, looking to practical conclusions that the Council might decide to adopt." The deadline was set for April 1960 and fifty-three faculty groups submitted responses, now published in the *Acta et Documenta* (series 1, vol. 4, in 3 parts). The majority of these studies were collegial products, coming out of discussions of proposals by individuals and amendments accepted by vote in faculty meetings, as was done in Milan and Münster.

A notable exception was the packet of sixteen individually signed studies by professors of theology at the Pontifical Lateran University in Rome, where Pope John had studied as a young priest of the diocese of Bergamo. One of these studies, by a Spanish Capuchin professor of Old Testament, Father Teófilo García, urged the Council to give a good example, one that would encourage all Catholic theologians to follow suit, by adopting biblical themes and biblical theology in its documents of teaching and renewal of pastoral practice.[14] But Father Garcia died in spring of 1960 and so had no chance for a personal influence on the work of the Council.

The case of the rector of the Lateran University, Msgr. Antonio Piolanti, was different, for in 1960 he became a member of the Preparatory Theological Commission, and from 1962 to 1965 he was an officially named expert of Vatican II. In his personal study submitted in early 1960, Piolanti decried tendencies that he found in present-day Catholic theology toward an autonomy that was subversive of the faith. The Council should intervene, to reaffirm the clear principles laid down by the popes, beginning with Gregory XVI and Pius IX in the nineteenth century and continuing in the twentieth century in teachings by Pius X and most recently by Pius XII in the encyclical *Humani generis* (August 1950). The tendencies needing correction were especially of French origin, in the work of theologians whom Piolanti named, like Henri Bouillard, SJ, and Marie-Dominic Chenu, OP, who relativized the meaning of doctrinal terms by holding that they are tied to thinking of past ages. Another tendency was the work of Jesuits based at Lyon, like Henri de Lubac, Jean Daniélou, and Hans Urs von Balthasar, who promoted a return to the theology of the early Church Fathers as an alternative to the disciplined thought of scholastic theology. This group, in Piolanti's reading, advanced the idea that theological statements derive their validity, not from objective grounds of fact and reason, but from their correspondence with the religious experience that gives rise to positions and that theological discourse intends to explain.

Msgr. Piolanti called for the Council to censure these tendencies, by affirming the immutability of the truths of faith, which sound theology receives from the authoritative teaching office of the Successor of Peter. This gives theology its positive basis, and, as Pius XII said in *Humani generis,* theology's task is then to show how the truths now being taught were already present in some real way in the Bible and the works of the Church Fathers. Then, in a second methodological step, theology should investigate the deposit of doctrine to discover by rational reflection further truths that are there by implication.[15]

Msgr. Piolanti was a typical member of one stream of theology then in vogue in Rome, and he had the satisfaction of seeing his recommendation of a censure of the "new theology" of French origin taken over in the Council proposal of the Vatican Congregation for Seminaries and Studies, for which Piolanti was a consultant. The Congregation, after erasing the names of the theologians mentioned, submitted the main parts of Piolanti's study as one of its own proposals for the Vatican II conciliar agenda.[16]

Msgr. Piolanti's colleague at the Lateran, Father Francesco Spadafora, handed in a demonstration of why the Council should affirm the absolute "inerrancy" of scripture, which was being called in question in recent works of Catholic scholars writing in French, who take the Bible as relating a sacred history of God's actions to save human beings, without concerns for precision on the historical details. Some of these authors, not named by Spadafora, go so far as to claim that we actually know little of what Jesus did or said, since the Gospels, these writers claim, relate only what the early Christian communities believed about him and passed on as they adopted certain "literary forms."[17]

We turn now to some of the other proposals made by theological faculties in early 1960, selecting three of interest because of their subsequent influence during the Council, for example, through the service of their members as experts associated with the Council's commissions or by the work of Council members formed by contacts with these schools of theology.

The Catholic theology faculty of Montreal, Canada, was the formative milieu of Montreal's archbishop, Cardinal Paul-Emile Léger, who during the Council became an influential exponent of reform ideas coming from Pope John XXIII. In the pre-preparatory phase, the theologians of Montreal proposed that the Council initiate preparation of a new universal Catholic catechism, which would revise the four-hundred-year-old *Catechism of the Council of Trent,* to include instruction on doctrines which had become official church teaching since Trent, to treat scripture passages on the basis of solid recent biblical exegesis, and above all to draw amply on the "kerygmatic theology" then being promoted in Austria and Germany.

The Montreal theologians also called for the Council to issue a doctrinal text, *On the Sources of Revelation,* in order to set forth the Catholic understanding of how God's Word comes to us. Here, the nature of "tradition" needs clarification, since it is a term with various meanings. According to the meaning one uses, there follow different ways of explaining the interrelation of tradition with scripture. On the biblical source of revelation, the Council should aim to reconcile two different attitudes, namely, the church's religious veneration of the inspired books of the Bible and the technical study of the words, style, and historical background of the biblical books that is proper to exegesis. Regarding scholarly study of the Bible, since new methods were becoming widely used, the professors of Montreal suggested that the Council should move Catholic teaching beyond the directives given in the two encyclicals on biblical studies, Leo XIII's *Providentissimus Deus* (1893) and Pius XII's *Divino afflante Spiritu* (1943).[18]

In Rome, the Pontifical Biblical Institute, with its staff of Jesuit professors, became influential during the Council by circulating memoranda in evaluation of the use of scripture in draft texts coming up for discussion. Among the Institute's alumni were Cardinals Bernard Alfrink of Utrecht, the Netherlands, and Albert Gregory Meyer of Chicago. The rector of the Institute, Father Ernst Vogt, a Swiss Jesuit, had taught in Brazil, and the large episcopal conference of Brazil regularly took over memoranda of the Institute as bases of their interventions commenting on draft texts. Also, a major player in the Council, Cardinal Augustin Bea, SJ, president of the Secretariat for Promoting Christian Unity, had been professor for years at the Institute and was its rector before Father Vogt.

In the preparatory phase of Vatican II, the Biblical Institute offered a five-point proposal for the Council agenda regarding sacred scripture.

1. The Council should explain how both scripture and the tradition initiated by the apostles come from a single source, namely, the Gospel of Christ, and in the further life of the church scripture and tradition are never separated but stand in close mutual interrelation.

2. From the letters of St. Paul, the Council should underscore how faith, as trusting adherence to the good news of Christ, is central in our acceptance of salvation, for such teaching is of considerable ecumenical importance.

3. To show the basis of the church's esteem of scripture, the Council should teach about the saving efficacy of the proclaimed word of God, which scripture records. (Here the Biblical Institute echoed, without knowing it, the proposal from Münster.)

4. In teaching on the Gospels as historical documents about Jesus, the Council should remind Catholics that after Easter, before the Gospels were composed, the Holy Spirit was guiding the apostles and their associates to a progressively deeper understanding of the person and work of Jesus, an understanding that the Gospels express in various ways.

5. The Institute, where the scriptures of Israel were studied intensively, called for the Council to mince no words in condemning all forms of antisemitism.[19]

Finally, among the theology faculties, we must hear from Louvain, in view of the huge influence on Vatican II exercised by Cardinal Leo Josef Suenens, with other Belgian bishops such as André-Marie Charue of Namur and Emile De Smedt of Brugge, as well as by the Louvain theologians associated with the conciliar commissions, like Gérard Philips, Lucien Cerfaux, Charles Moeller, and the canonist Willy Onclin. In early 1960, the Louvain proposal for Vatican II followed the outline of the attributes of the church, which the Council should set forth in a way that would show the true face of the church to the world. As "one and catholic," the church should actively promote ecumenical relations with other Christians. As "holy" the church should look optimistically upon the world, not seeing it as the source of myriad errors, but as God's good creation, which Christ has redeemed.

Louvain gave the note of "apostolic" special treatment, first urging a renewed Catholic fidelity to scripture, which combines the sacred books of Israel — which served Jesus and his apostles as their own Bible — with the New Testament books coming directly or indirectly from the apostles. Second, since the bishops are today successors of the apostles, the Council should work out a doctrine of the episcopate, to complete Vatican I, which treated only the pope. It would be important to treat bishops not only as chief pastors of individual dioceses, but also as together forming the universal episcopal college, which would be in action in the Council itself. Finally, to make clear that it is "apostolic," the church should receive from the Council a concentrated teaching on Jesus Christ himself, and this should go beyond treating Jesus as the supreme mediator and communicator of revelation about God and human life, to treat his very person and work as the revelation itself of God. Therefore, in Christ the church finds the deep roots of every dogma and doctrine that it teaches. He is the founder of the church, in a past action, its present-day guide, and in the final consummation God plans to unite all things under his headship (Eph 1:10).[20]

In the studies sent in from theology faculties in 1960, the attentive reader is sure to note some differences of opinion, even oppositions, which during Vatican II's working periods (1962–65), both in the Aula and in the Council's commissions, burst forth in disputes between their respective exponents.

Vatican II's Preparatory Phase (1960–62)

On Pentecost Sunday, June 5, 1960, Pope John XXIII declared the end of the pre-preparatory phase and instituted the groups that would have responsibility for drawing up draft texts for Vatican Council II. He formed ten preparatory commissions, roughly corresponding to the ten congregations of the Roman Curia, making the cardinal prefect of the congregation the president of the respective commission.[21] In an action of far-reaching impact, John XXIII also instituted the Secretariat for Promoting Christian Unity, which was also to function in ways still undefined in preparing the Council. Its first president was Cardinal Augustin Bea, SJ.[22]

Beginning in September 1959 and working into March 1960, the pre-preparatory commission had analyzed the proposals sent in by the future members of the Council and organized them under the headings of current systematic theology, moral teaching, and the Code of Canon Law. Many of the proposals were easy to group together, but others lost their biblical and spiritual content by adaptation into these established categories. Mimeographed summaries of the proposals from the different geographical areas were prepared and sent to the Vatican congregations, in anticipation of the work of actual preparation of draft texts. A two-volume *Analyticus Conspectus,* detailing the approximately nine thousand particular proposals, was printed in early 1961 for use by the preparatory commissions.[23]

On the basis of further summaries, Pope John XXIII formulated topics that each of the preparatory commissions should treat in preparing draft texts based on the proposals and on their own further perceptions of needed Council actions.

One of the last actions of the pre-preparatory group, working under Cardinal Tardini in the spring of 1960, was to draw up lists of possible members and consultants whom the heads of the preparatory commissions could invite to take part in their work. Tardini foresaw the problem posed by the close relation between the Roman Curia's congregations and the conciliar preparatory commissions, and so he urged the commission presidents to gather bishops and experts from the whole Catholic world, not just men already associated with the Curia's congregations. But this did not prevent some of the commissions from being dominated by members and consultants who also served the Curia's offices. In fact, in June 1962 one perceptive observer of the preparation called the near identity of the preparatory commissions with the curial congregations the "original sin" of the preparation. Then in the preparation there followed several "actual sins," such as the claim and practice of autonomy by the commissions, especially that for theology, which refused to collaborate with other commissions and the Secretariat for Promoting Christian Unity on topics of common responsibility, such as the liturgy, theological education, and the Catholic understanding of the sacraments and life of the Eastern Orthodox and Protestant Churches.[24]

But along with the particular preparatory commissions, John XXIII also created a large central preparatory commission, with over one hundred members, including numerous presidents of episcopal conferences of the world. This group was to receive the draft texts of the individual preparatory commissions and to evaluate them with a view to recommending either their further revision or passing them on to the pope for distribution to all the future members for deliberation in the Council itself.[25]

Theologians Working for the Particular Preparatory Commissions (1960–62)

Regarding the preparatory commissions that prepared the draft texts for Vatican II, it is important not to be carried along toward easy generalizations based on partial perceptions of their work. To be sure, there were groups, like the Commission on Clergy and the Christian People and the Commission on the Sacraments, that were controlled by individuals closed to new directions and that proposed simply that Vatican II confirm the doctrine and law then in force. And, among the ten bodies, the theological commission was a special case, which I will treat below.

The Preparatory Commission on the Liturgy had an excellent group of theological consultants oriented to the renewal of Catholic worship, such as Josef Andreas Jungmann, Theodor Klausner, Frederick McManus, Bernard Botte, Godfrey Dieckman, Cipriano Vagaggini, Johannes Hofinger, and Johannes Wagner. They gave Vatican II in 1962 its model draft text based on fifty years of liturgical research that flowed together with a fresh perception of the Christian community as the priestly people called through Christ to worship the Father in the Holy Spirit. The Commission for the Lay Apostolate included Bishops Emilio Guano (Livorno, Italy), Franz Hengsbach (Essen, Germany), and Gabriel Garrone (Toulouse, France), with the social thinkers Pietro Pavan and Agostino Ferrari Toniolo, and had consultors like Ferdinand Klostermann, Johannes Hirschmann, SJ, and Roberto Tucci, SJ, all of whom in time made solid contributions to the Pastoral Constitution on the Church in the Modern World, *Gaudium et spes.*

Clearly the Secretariat for Promoting Christian Unity was a special case, as a new invention in 1960. It was prepared by the Catholic Committee led by Fathers Willebrands and Thijssen, and it had the extraordinary leadership of Cardinal Bea, who was supported by Bishops Lorenz Jaeger (Paderborn), François Charriére (Lausanne-Geneva), and Emile De Smedt (Brugge), with competent theologians like Hermann Volk, Johannes Feiner, Eduard Stakemeier, Christoph

Dumont, OP, Jerôme Hamer, OP, Maurice Bevenot, SJ, and George Tavard, AA. This group prepared excellent texts for Vatican II, like its draft of a pastoral decree *The Word of God*, and then it added new co-workers during the Council for the taxing labors of seeing three significant documents through successive revisions to completion: the Decree on Ecumenism (UR), the Declaration on the Church and Non-Christian Religions (NA), and the Decree on Religious Liberty (DH). But during the preparatory phase of 1960–62, the secretariat had to struggle to establish itself as a body with competence to contribute draft texts.

Some theologians found themselves unable to contribute much to the preparatory commissions with which they were associated. The historian of the Council of Trent, Hubert Jedin, was in a minority on the Commission on Seminaries, with his ideas for reform of seminary studies.[26] Karl Rahner was not a consultor of the Theological Commission, but of that on sacraments, for which he was asked only to prepare a document on the restoration of the permanent diaconate, to which married men could be ordained. This was a topic requested with some frequency by bishops in the proposals of 1959–60, and Rahner prepared a written text in collaboration with Bishop Franjo Seper of Zagreb, Croatia, which in time became the basis of no. 29 of the Dogmatic Constitution on the Church (LG).[27]

Now we take up the Preparatory Theological Commission, which usually dominates perceptions of the preparatory work of 1960–62. Cardinal Alfredo Ottaviani presided over its work, along with his main collaborator from the Holy Office, Archbishop Pietro Parente. Father Sebastian Tromp, SJ, longtime professor of fundamental theology at the Gregorian University, was chosen by Cardinal Ottaviani as the commission's secretary. Tromp played a central role in coordinating contact with the commission members, parceling out assignments, preparing meetings, and overseeing the movement of draft texts through the stages of composition.[28] There were twenty-seven members, of whom eleven were bishops and sixteen were veteran theologians like Antonio Piolanti, Salvador Garofalo, Lucien Cerfaux, Joseph Fenton, Franz Hürth, SJ, Luigi Chappi, OP, and Karel Balic, OFM. The twenty-nine consultants did include major figures of twentieth-century theology, like Yves Congar, OP, Henri de Lubac, SJ, Bernard Häring, CSsR, and Joseph Lécuyer, CSSp.

The Theological Commission prepared six draft texts, which in time were distributed to the members of Second Vatican Council:

1. The Sources of Revelation (drafting coordinated by S. Garofalo)

2. Guarding the Purity of the Deposit of Faith (L. Ciappi)

3. The Christian Moral Order (F. Hürth)

4. Chastity, Matrimony, the Family, and Virginity (E. Lio, OFM)

5. The Church (R. Gagnebet, OP)

6. The Blessed Virgin Mary (K. Balic)

However, not one of these six drafts made its way successfully through the phases of the Council's procedure of open discussion, written comments by the members, revision, a second discussion, further revision, and voting with the possibility of offering final amendments, followed by promulgation as a constitution or decree of the Council. All six documents of the Theological Commission were either replaced by new drafts made during the Council or were dismantled for partial inclusion in other draft texts. In a real sense, the Preparatory Theological Commission was a failure, and for understanding the theological problematic of Vatican II, much light comes from identifying the reasons for this failure. Fortunately, Y. Congar was an acute observer who saw problems in the commission, and he jotted them down in his diary, well before they came to the notice of the Council and the wider world.

1. The mentality that dominated the Preparatory Theological Commission of 1960–62 was, according to Congar, deeply formed by the style of work of the Holy Office, the Curia's office of doctrinal vigilance, where the priorities differed greatly from what John XXIII was proposing, in his own way, as goals of the Council. A clear sign of Holy Office influence was the draft text *Guarding the Purity of the Deposit of Faith*, which went out to all the Council members in 1962, along with six other draft texts, some weeks before Vatican II opened. The text on the deposit of faith had ten chapters, each of which set out to correct an erroneous belief, as on human knowledge of truth,

creation and evolution, God's objective word of revelation spoken to human beings, the right distinction between the supernatural and natural orders, original sin, and other points. This seemed to many to be a new "syllabus of errors" like the list of modern ideas that Pope Pius IX declared alien to Catholic truth in 1864. People reading the discourses of John XXIII during 1961 gradually came to sense a serious disconnect between his hopes for Vatican II and this document of the Preparatory Theological Commission.

2. The Theological Commission divided its consultants into small subcommissions for drafting texts, in which the coordinators asked individuals to prepare short sections. Much of this work went on between the plenary meetings of the commission, when only those residing in Rome had easy contact with each other and with Father Tromp. This impeded the proposals made earlier by the Biblical Institute and the Louvain faculty from influencing the overall direction of work. Congar noted that he was asked only for comments on short sections of the drafts that were developing. In 1962, when criticisms of the theological drafts began circulating and Congar joined his voice to them, he had to defend himself against an accusation by Cardinal Ottaviani of disloyalty to the commission. Congar told the cardinal that the method of preparatory work never gave him an occasion for speaking to the overall orientation of the documents or even to points on which he had done research and published, like the role of Mary, the nature of tradition, and the fundamental nature of the church itself.

3. Congar was formed in the tradition of the Dominicans of northern France, in the school of Saulchoir, which prized "returning to the sources" where the Christian mystery was expressed more simply, more concretely, and more vigorously than in recent scholastic theological manuals. This orientation alerted Congar early on in the preparation of Vatican II to a method that dominated the Theological Commission, namely, that of composing draft texts that brought together the positive teaching and censure of errors expressed in the encyclicals and discourses of the popes of the previous seventy years, from Leo XIII through Pius XII.[29] Congar's diary entry registers his profound disturbance at seeing the source of teaching not being the word of God addressed to the church, but instead in the word of the

church itself, in the limited form of recent papal documents. Compared with the classics of Christian theology from the early Fathers through the medieval masters like St. Thomas and St. Bonaventure, the Preparatory Theological Commission was in fact introducing an innovation quite discontinuous with the great tradition of Catholic thought nourished from the authentic sources.[30]

4. Finally, there was the refusal of the Preparatory Theological Commission of 1960–62 to form mixed commissions with other preparatory bodies like the Liturgy Commission or the Secretariat for Promoting Christian Unity. Concerns over the church's life of worship or ecumenical issues were not allowed to disturb work in the sealed-off doctrinal area. Congar saw the absence of ecumenical sensibilities in the Theological Commission posing a threat to Pope John's frequently expressed hopes that Vatican II would pave the way to future reunion with the now separated churches. In July 1961, he wrote to the pope about this narrowness of the Preparatory Theological Commission, and some months later he heard from Cardinal Bea that Pope John was disappointed over the absence of cooperation in preparing the Council between the bodies headed by Cardinals Ottaviani and Bea.

But there was also the large Central Preparatory Commission to which the Preparatory Theological Commission began submitting its draft texts in November 1961.

Theologians Consulted by Members of the Central Preparatory Commission

Some members of the Central Commission, which met for several days in sessions from June 1961 to June 1962, were pleased with the two initial draft texts of the Theological Commission, namely, *The Sources of Revelation* and *Guarding the Purity of the Deposit of Faith,* but other members were not satisfied. In fact at the meetings of this commission a critical opposition gradually formed, especially against the texts of the Theological Commission and against the mentality of their drafters. Cardinal Bea exercised an increasing influence over many members, since he arrived at some meetings with detailed criticisms that he had worked out with the theologians of the secretariat before sessions of the central commission. On the draft text *The*

Sources of Revelation, Bea said it should be withdrawn, because in treating the topics of biblical inspiration and interpretation it issued censures of positions held by a few Catholic exegetes, but by so small a number that Vatican II should not even take notice. But most of all, when the draft text spoke of interpretation of the Bible, it gave only admonitions and no signs of appreciation and encouragement for the work of the great majority of Catholic exegetes and biblical theologians.[31]

Other critical opponents of the drafts of the Preparatory Theological Commission spoke out during meetings of the Central Commission, such as Cardinals Julius Döpfner (Munich), Joseph Frings (Cologne), Bernard Alfrink (Utrecht), Franz König (Vienna), along with Bishop Dennis Hurley, OMI (Durban, South Africa) and Patriarch Paul Cheikho of the Chaldean Church. On November 10, 1961, the Central Preparatory Commission took a vote on *The Sources,* revealing that sixty-one of the seventy-seven members present associated themselves with the sharp criticisms voiced by Cardinal Bea. This was eleven months before Vatican II opened, and it signaled division among leading members of the coming Council over the work of the Preparatory Theological Commission. The wider world was informed of this a year later, when many of the criticisms of *The Sources* were voiced in open sessions during Vatican II's first working period.

Cardinal König prepared his interventions at meetings of the Central Preparatory Commission by obtaining evaluative comments from Karl Rahner on the draft texts.[32] Using comments coming from Rahner, König lamented that *The Sources* begins by treating *our* knowledge of God's word, from scripture and tradition, and not by an account of God's word *in itself,* which should be the true source of Vatican II's renewal of doctrine and church life. Further, the draft goes to such lengths to defend the role of tradition as a source that it leaves scripture in a shadow, while in fact the church places scripture first, which it venerates as a sacred and inspired text. Also, the draft should show appreciation for the efforts of Catholics in the hard work of biblical exegesis instead of laying down admonitions about their work. König concluded that the Theological Commission should have an exchange with the Pontifical Biblical Commission to get input by experts in the biblical field, and then the draft could be presented a second time to the Central Preparatory Commission.

In January 1962, König used arguments coming from Rahner in criticizing the draft on the deposit of faith, because it offered apologetic arguments against ideas considered wrong, when what our contemporaries really need is a positive synthetic presentation of revealed truths, with attention to the difficulties that sincere people have with some of the intricacies of Catholic doctrine.

During the time of the Central Commission's work, Cardinal Frings of Cologne was consulting with Joseph Ratzinger, then a professor in Bonn. This was especially necessary because Cardinal Frings was almost totally blind, which was compensated for by his total recall of what he heard. From these consultations, the cardinal of Cologne prepared numerous incisive interventions both before and during Vatican II. Ratzinger composed for Frings an analysis of the world in which Vatican II would meet, which the cardinal gave as a lecture in Genoa on November 20, 1961, and which came out in a booklet that Pope John XXIII read. In February 1962 the pope told the cardinal that he was delighted with his, that is, Ratzinger's, analysis, which set goals for the Council that coincided with the pope's own hopes.[33]

In another consultation with a Bonn professor, Frings heard from Hubert Jedin a reminder of the great importance, once the Council began, of the new commissions that would oversee revisions of texts in the light of the Council members' interventions. This led to Frings's dramatic intervention on the first working day of Vatican II, October 13, 1962, to call for a postponement of the elections of the new commission members, so the members could get to know who were the most competent on the different Council topics among the bishops from other nations.[34]

Theologians at Work During the Council (1962–65)

When the Council opened, two hundred experts were named as official advisors to the Council. Many other theologians came to Rome as personal consultants of individual bishops or of episcopal conferences. For many of these men what began in October 1962 was a singular experience of intense theological work, both in exchanges with colleagues from around the world and in response to requests by the pastoral leaders of the church for help based on their theological competence. The diaries of two Jesuit experts, Otto Semmelroth and Pieter Smulders, contain expressions of amazement over the number of other theologians they were meeting each day to exchange news and receive stimulating ideas about the topics the Council would be discussing. It was also deeply satisfying to be actively involved in an undertaking of such magnitude and long-range importance as an Ecumenical Council of the Catholic Church.

Otto Semmelroth taught dogmatic theology at the Jesuit faculty of Sankt Georgen in Frankfurt, Germany, and was called to Rome for the Council to assist Bishop Hermann Volk of Mainz. During his years of teaching in Münster, Volk had given lectures and held seminars in German, and so he regularly asked Semmelroth, who used Latin at Sankt Georgen, to prepare Latin analyses of the draft texts and to put into good Latin the interventions Volk wanted to make. Semmelroth's Vatican II experience was intensified by his living at the German College, a residence for seminarians and student-priests, where Cardinal Döpfner and Karl Rahner also lived during the Council.[35]

Pieter Smulders taught dogmatic theology and patristics at the Jesuit faculty of Maastrict in the Netherlands, from which he was called to Vatican II by a former student, the Jesuit archbishop Adrianus Djajasepoetra of Jakarta, Indonesia, who made Smulders part of a four-man "brain trust" for the thirty bishops of Indonesia. Smulders lived at a Franciscan sisters' *pensione* on Via Cassia, along with some Indonesian bishops and a group of bishops and their experts from Brazil.[36]

First I will sketch something of the myriad services given by theologians to the Council members and to the episcopal conferences. A following section will relate the specialized work demanded of the theologians who were taken on as co-workers of the different Council commissions.

Theologians Serving Council Bishops and Episcopal Conferences

Before the Council's formal opening on October 11, 1962, a powerful stimulus to theological work during August was the mailing out to the members a booklet containing seven draft texts, of which four came from the Preparatory Theological Commission. Many bishops quickly called on theologians to study and evaluate these texts proposed for discussion at the first working period of Vatican II.

Karl Rahner continued his consultative help of Cardinal König after the arrival of the first draft texts, and Cardinal Döpfner asked for copies of Rahner's remarks.[37] In a similar way Yves Congar gave his critical comments on the drafts to Archbishop J. J. Weber of Strasbourg.[38] Jean Daniélou evaluated the drafts for the coadjutor archbishop of Paris, Pierre Veuillot, who had Daniélou's critical remarks translated into Latin and sent on to the Council secretariat before Vatican II opened.[39] In the same way, Cardinal Frings sent to the Council secretariat, a month before Vatican II opened, an incisive evaluation of the first drafts written by Joseph Ratzinger, who found only two (on liturgy and ecumenism) of the initial seven texts manifesting agreement with Pope John's goals and composed in a manner likely to deepen the life and worship of the church.[40]

In Freiburg, Germany, Bishop Hermann Schäuffele got from Professor Friedrich Stegmüller thirty-three pages of analysis and criticism of the drafts, along with an alternative draft text on what was lacking in the preparation, namely, a text on God as sovereign Creator and Lord, a topic that needed treatment to counteract a spirituality too absorbed in personal psychology and horizontal relations in the church.[41] In The Netherlands, P. Smulders studied the seven draft texts at the request of the papal nucio, Archbishop Giuseppe Beltrami, for whom he wrote sixty-seven pages of evaluations. Smulders praised the draft on the liturgy, but expressed serious reservations about the content and tone of the four drafts from the Preparatory Theological Commission.[42]

As the opening of the Council drew near, some theologians enlarged the scope of their critical work on the first draft texts. In The Netherlands in late August, Bishop Willem Bekkers (Den Bosch) had asked for comments on the draft texts from Eduard Schillebeeckx, OP, of the University of Nijmegen's theology faculty. In mid-September Bishop Bekkers brought together seventeen missionary bishops of Dutch origin to whom Schillebeeckx made an oral presentation of his criticisms. This prompted the secretary of the

Dutch Episcopal Conference, Father Jan Brouwers, to initiate action looking to distribute theological information to the whole group of twenty-five hundred Council members. Schillebeeckx wrote up a fifty-page text in Dutch, incorporating some of what Smulders had sent to Nuncio Beltrami. Brouwers got friends to make translations from Dutch into Latin and English, and these two texts were typed onto mimeograph stencils. In Rome, at the residential college for Dutch student-priests, Brouwers ran off some twenty-seven hundred copies of the texts in Latin and English, which circulated widely in October 1962 among the episcopal conferences and theologian-experts.[43]

Among other points, Schillebeeckx said that the draft *The Sources* lacked a necessary first chapter on God's revelation itself in the history of salvation. The Preparatory Theological Commission also shows no sign of having followed the pre-preparatory proposals of the future Council members, which the Preparatory Commission on Liturgy did do, to the enrichment of the draft text on liturgy. Where *The Sources* deals with the word of God, it takes this as God's speaking (*locutio*) which evolves into true propositions concerning God and human life, while seriously neglecting the revelation of God in events and the "real tradition," beyond the oral, through the practice of believing Christians in their communities. At a fundamental level, the texts on the sources and the deposit of faith have an inadequate notion of God's revelation, which comes to supreme expression in the incarnation of the Son of God, for Christ *is* the revelation of God well before he opens his mouth to teach. To be sure, oral communication is necessary, but it is narrative and explanation of the living Truth present in Jesus. The texts of the Preparatory Theological Commission suffer greatly when set beside the text on liturgy, which for Schillebeeckx is "an admirable piece of work."[44]

To keep this essay within reasonable limits, I will simply mention three other texts by theologians that were circulated as alternative drafts during the first weeks of Vatican II. Joseph Ratzinger and Karl Rahner composed an exposition of the revelation in Christ of God and of humans, in a text that was mimeographed and read widely in November 1962.[45] Y. Congar's "conciliar creed" gave vital reaffirmations of the central Christian truths.[46] Congar also contributed a beautiful short text on tradition and scripture, as an alternative to *The Sources,* for a group of French bishops, who gladly accepted Congar's emphasis on the living tradition of the believing community, by which the church becomes the corporate subject that passes on its own faith and life to successive generations.[47]

Along with these writings created under the stimulus of the Council's beginning, theologians gave numerous lectures around Rome to groups of bishops during the first working period. On October 10, the day before the Council's formal opening, Joseph Ratzinger spoke to the German-speaking bishops on the serious problems in the draft text *The Sources of Revelation.* Difficulties begin with the title itself, which shows more interest in the places where we come to know God's word than in God's own action, which comes before any human effort to pass on the witness in scripture and tradition.[48] Y. Congar's diary records that he lectured during the first weeks of the Council on scripture and tradition before the French bishops, the Melkites, the French-speaking bishops of Africa, and the Episcopal Conference of Argentina.

The Indonesian bishops lived during Vatican II in houses scattered around Rome, but they came together one afternoon each week to discuss Council topics, especially in the light of presentations by experts, like Hermann Schmidt, SJ (Gregorian University), on the liturgy, Ignace de la Potterie, SJ (Biblical Institute), on Gospel interpretation, and Frans Thijssen (Secretariat for Promoting Christian Unity) on ecumenism. The American Passionist Barnabas M. Ahern gave the U.S. bishops lectures on the methods and results of contemporary scripture studies, which raised their awareness of the narrowness of *The Sources* in its passages on Bible interpretation.

Personal contacts between theologians from different countries stimulated the circulation of theological ideas and new proposals during the first working period of Vatican II. Many Council members, individually and in their episcopal conferences, added to the intensity by the welcome they gave to experts who offered them theological updating. The texts under discussion were also stimulating, but in many cases this called for the formulation of concise alternatives well grounded in the early sources. It was no time for the theologians to offer brilliant personal insights, but instead texts with potential to find wide acceptance among the Council members because of what they could contribute to renewing Catholic doctrine, catechesis, and preaching.

During the first period of autumn 1962, P. Smulders was not yet an official expert of the Council and so he could not go to St. Peter's to hear the oral interventions at the morning sessions. But this left him free to move around Rome to gather information for the Indonesian bishops on positions emerging in other episcopates. On October 30, Smulders went to see Cardinal Bea, who was glad to pass on advice through Smulders to the bishops. Bea urged them to discuss thoroughly among themselves the upcoming draft texts until they reached a consensus, and then to choose one member to speak in the Aula in the name of the thirty. Bea advised against proposing any of the alternative texts then in circulation, since there was no realistic chance for them to be officially proposed. The bishops' "brain trust" should study carefully Pope John XXIII's opening discourse of October 11, since citations of this by Indonesian bishops would have a wide impact.

Some of the Council members were good Latinists and could easily prepare concise interventions, like Cardinal Ruffini of Palermo, the man who made the most oral interventions of any Council member. But others needed help, given by their theologians, in drafting correct and forceful Latin addresses, limited to ten minutes. On the first day of debate on *The Sources of Revelation*, November 14, 1962, Archbishop Gabriel Manek, SVD, of Endeh, spoke in the name of all the Indonesian bishops, giving both general and specific reasons for rejecting the draft text. The intervention had been written by P. Smulders and lightly revised at the November 9 meeting of the Indonesian bishops.[49] The Italian Franciscan Umberto Betti recorded in his diary four different times that the archbishop of Florence, Ermenegildo Florit, had delivered in the Aula "the comments that I drafted," which was also the case for Archbishop Florit's important introductory presentation before the Council, on September 30, 1964, of the emended text on revelation, which had replaced *The Sources of Revelation*.[50]

As the Council proceeded, the draft texts were revised in the light of the oral and written interventions of the members. In time, the revisions came up for vote, when a Council member voting in favor of the text could ask for a further amendment (a *modus*) which he thought would improve the text without changing its substance. Numerous theologians drafted these proposed amendments, often at the request of members but also on their own in the hope that a Council member would adopt then and append them to his favorable vote. In the last votes on the constitution *The Church* in 1964, Y. Congar circulated among numerous French bishops a text that would add to the document a full Catholic recognition of the episcopate in the Eastern Orthodox Churches, both in terms of their orders and their jurisdiction over their dioceses.[51]

Theologians as Consultants and Redactors of Texts for the Conciliar Commissions

With the opening of the Council, the ten preparatory commissions ceased to exist, and new conciliar commissions of twenty-five members were chosen from among the Council Fathers, with sixteen being elected and nine, including the president, appointed by the pope. The work of these conciliar commissions began slowly, but for some theologians this changed toward the end of the first period of 1962. A crucial event was the rejection by the Council, in early December 1962 without need of even taking a vote, of the draft text from the Preparatory Theological Commission, *The Church*. Within a few weeks, at the request of different episcopates, no less that five new draft texts were worked out by groups of theologians, along with four further texts on important particular points of ecclesiology.[52]

After the first period, at the end of January 1963, Yves Congar went to Mainz, where Bishop Hermann Volk called together the German theologians who were working on a new draft on the nature of the church. Karl Rahner was a principal contributor, but Congar found the text more academic than conciliar, hardly such as to build consensus in the Council.[53] But the French bishops had not asked Congar to work on a text, and besides he was not at that time taken into the service of a conciliar commission. But this changed on March 1, 1963, when Congar was urgently called to Rome to become an expert of the Doctrinal Commission, which was holding the first of its many working sessions during the times between the autumn gatherings of the whole Council.

When Congar arrived, the commission had just decided to take as the basis of a new working text on the church the draft composed, at the request of Cardinal Suenens, by the Louvain systematic theologian Gérard Philips. Congar became one of the seven theologians, along with seven commission members, formed into a subcommission to amend the Philips draft by incorporating useful ideas and texts from other proposed drafts that had come in from France, Germany, Rome, and Chile. Congar's diary is a record of intense work with other *periti,* such as Karl Rahner, SJ (Innsbruck), Rosario Gagnebet, OP (Rome, Angelicum), Gustave Thils (Louvain), Charles Moeller (Louvain), Pierre Lafortune (Montreal), and G. Philips (Louvain). The Belgians came to the meetings well prepared, and within three days the first two chapters of the new draft could be presented to the full commission.

Congar, now a commission *peritus,* was able to attend the meetings of the Doctrinal Commission of the Council, which at times he described in his diary. In a hall in the papal palace, the twenty-five members were seated at a quadrilateral of tables in the center, with Cardinal Ottaviani at the head, and the commission's secretary, Father Sebastian Tromp, at his side. The theologians sat on simple chairs around the wall, mainly as observers, but with the right to speak if invited by a member.

At one point during the review of the new draft on the church, Congar was asked to contribute, and he suggested that the paragraph on the church's magisterium (eventually LG 25) insert a phrase taken from the papal definitions of the Immaculate Conception (Pius IX, 1854) and Assumption of the Blessed Virgin Mary (Pius XII, 1950), namely, that church teaching arises from a *conspiratio,* or consensus, existing between the church's pastors and the body of the faithful. But Cardinal Ruffini objected that such a *conspiratio* is not an essential and universal factor in the development of magisterial teaching. Congar answered that the notion had biblical backing, on the need of two or three witnesses (Deut 19:15), but the president, Cardinal Ottaviani, questioned whether such a biblical rule had juridical force in the church. Sitting next to Congar was Msgr. Salvatore Garofalo, scripture teacher and rector of the Urban University in Rome, who supported Cardinal Ottaviani with the assurance that the text in question, in its setting in the Old Testament, comes from a wholly other context.[54]

At the end of the meeting, during which the full commission reviewed quite positively the work of the ecclesiology subcommission of seven members and seven experts, Father Tromp told the members to hand in to his office their proposed amendments in writing, which would be examined by the subcommission and its theologians, before a new version would be presented to the full commission for its approval with a view to distributing the new draft text *The Church* to all the Council members.

During Vatican II's second working period in autumn 1963, Pieter Smulders was named a Council expert at the request of the Indonesian episcopate, in the hope that by his attending the morning sessions in St. Peter's he could better assist the bishops. But soon he was called to work for the Doctrinal Commission, which found itself inundated with hundreds of comments by the Council members on the new draft on the church, after the Aula discussion through most of October 1963. Smulders was assigned to a subcommission working on the paragraphs treating priests and deacons, which in time became nos. 28–29 of *Lumen gentium*. The members were Bishops Maurice Roy (Quebec), Franjo Franic (Split, Croatia), and Vicente Scherer (Porto Alegre, Brazil). The other theological experts were the two Jesuits Alois Grillmeier and Otto Semmelroth, who handled proposals for revision of the paragraphs on priests, while Smulders worked with the Brazilian Franciscan Boaventura Kloppenburg on a new text on deacons.

Smulders first studied the cards on which the commission's secretarial staff had recorded each of the 120 oral and written interventions that had touched on deacons, that is, their roles as church ministers, the reintroduction of them as a permanent order of the Latin Church, and whether married men could become permanent deacons. Smulders worked in his room at the *pensione* on the Via Cassia, classifying the positions taken, finding 45 interventions favoring restoration of the permanent diaconate, but because a good number of these were made in the name of groups of bishops, he counted 714 Council members in this category. Twenty-five had spoken against this innovation, with a further sixty-seven signing on to their negative votes. In fact, a vote taken October 30, 1963, showed 1,588 favoring restoration of the diaconate, but a sizeable minority of 525 against it, mainly, it seemed, because the permanent deacons would be men given sacramental ordination but not obliged to celibacy.

On November 15–16, Smulders typed a ten-page single-space analysis of the arguments, indicating the names of the proponents or opponents after each consideration. Out of these, Smulders formulated five questions for decision by the three episcopal members of the subcommission before he and Kloppenburg could draft a revised text incorporating many views of Council members. On November 19, the three bishops reached a partial agreement, that is, that the Council should not decree the restoration, but only the *possibility* of such a change, but they had different ideas on the roles of episcopal conferences and the Holy See in any future process of making the diaconate a permanent feature of the Catholic Church. After this, Smulders rewrote his analysis to show the backing present for the views of the three subcommission members, and he composed a first proposal of a revised paragraph for the draft text.

In the meetings, Bishop Franic, a dogged opponent of having permanent deacons, criticized Smulders for inserting into his analysis some of his own ideas not documented by what the Council members had proposed. So when Smulders reworked his text, he was extra careful to give the name of a bishop or conference as responsible for every point introduced into the text. On November 21, the three episcopal members of the subcommission approved Smulders's analysis and new text, and on November 30 the full doctrinal commission followed suit, but they also introduced some modifications of Smulders's wording, when two-thirds of the members approved changes introduced during the meeting. So Smulders once more typed out the text of the paragraph on deacons that first went into the second complete draft text *The Church,* and then during 1964 remained with few modifications as what now stands in LG 29.

December 1, 1963, was a Sunday, and Smulders brought his text, with the note cards, to the Belgian College to return them to Gérard Philips, who was overseeing the revision. Later he went to the Gregorian to visit Father Tromp, his fellow Dutch Jesuit. He found Tromp tired and depressed, but quite ready to talk, mainly with laments over the preponderant influence of the Louvainians on the Doctrinal Commission. Tromp had lost influence, even with Cardinal Ottaviani, who now followed the suggestions of G. Philips and Archbishop Parente. The next day, December 2, the new configuration of the commission was confirmed by the election of Bishop A.-M. Charue (Namur, Belgium) as second vice-president of the Doctrinal Commission and of G. Philips of Louvain as adjunct secretary along with S. Tromp.

At the end of the December 2 commission meeting, Smulders was told to come to Rome in February–March, 1964, to work for the commission. This led to him being named to assist a new subcommission on divine revelation, for which during March–April 1964 he did for the future chapter 1 of *Dei Verbum,* on revelation itself, a work of analysis and composition like his work on the diaconate for the eventual *Lumen gentium.* In the fourth period of 1965, Smulders had a similar task of studying interventions and composing a new text based on them for what became part 1, chapter 3, on human activity in the universe, in the Pastoral Constitution *Gaudium et spes.*

In early 1964 Congar noted in his diary that the Council was overloading its experts, who already had their regular work as teachers and writers. But, nonetheless, Congar accepted further requests to assist conciliar commissions. In February 1964, he helped the Secretariat for Promoting Christian Unity revise the text on ecumenism, in the light of interventions by Council members commenting on a first draft during the second period.

In March–April 1964 Congar was with the subcommission on revelation, to which he made important contributions, in collaboration with Karl Rahner and Umberto Betti, to the account of tradition in chapter 2 of the future *Dei Verbum.* Congar was in a good position for this, since among the Council members' interventions there was a three-paragraph text which he had himself written in 1962. The text had been submitted to the commission over the signatures of a group of bishops of western France as a good way to fill out the undeveloped idea of tradition in the draft under discussion. It also helped that the subcommission on revelation had as members some bishops with backgrounds in theology like A.-M. Charue (Namur), Georges Pelletier (Trois Rivières, Canada), and

Joseph Heuschen (Liege, Belgium), along with Abbot Christopher Butler, OSB (Downside, England).

In September 1964 Congar joined the subcommission responsible for the chapter on human dignity in the future *Gaudium et spes*. Earlier, he had made critical comments on the draft text on the life and ministry of priests, and so he was drawn into revising this text as well, about which he later complained that the bishop-members of the commission on priests were a do-nothing lot, while all the work of the future decree *Presbyterium ordinis* was done by three *periti*, Joseph Lécuyer, Willy Onclin, and himself. Another weak draft text was the one treating the missions, whose first draft reflected more the approach of the Vatican Congregation for the Propagation of the Faith than a good ecclesiology. Congar threw himself into this work, becoming appreciative of his fellow *peritus* Joseph Ratzinger. Their work led to the Vatican II decree on missionary activity *Ad gentes* being a mature ecclesiological text, little affected by the turmoil, especially over episcopal collegiality, that had accompanied the genesis of the Dogmatic Constitution *The Church*.

Congar knew well what Smulders learned while working on the diaconate, namely, to subordinate his own ideas to what Council members were proposing. Every amendment had to rest on a member's intervention, and not be contradicted by that of another Council member. Compositional work by the *periti* had to produce texts backed by proposals of Council members which would in the next discussion win wide adherence among the Council members, and on doctrine this meant a near unanimity.

In October 1964 Congar saw the revised draft text on religious liberty, and right away he recognized in it numerous personal ideas of the principal expert-redactors, Pietro Pavan and John Courtney Murray, SJ. For Congar these were improvements, but their backing was weak in the previous interventions on the topic made by Council members. The revision was good, but the members should have an opportunity to react to its new passages, at least in writing. So Congar agreed with the decision of Paul VI in November 1964 to postpone voting to the fourth period, an action that infuriated the bishops from the United States.[55] In the intersession of early 1965, new comments came in, and Congar worked on a further revision, which turned out so well that the opponents of this initially controversial document were reduced to less than 5 percent of the Council members.

Final Considerations

Recalling the limitation imposed at the beginning of this essay, namely, to omit interventions at Vatican II by the popes, John XXIII and Paul VI, and by Council members of major influence, I offer here some wide-angle views of the contributions of the theologians to the Council.[56] According to the perspective taken, the perceptions differ notably.

If we look at the Council from the early preparations in 1959 and ponder its step-by-step development, a first contrast emerges between dominant mentalities among the theologians involved. On the one hand, some Council theologians were deeply formed by the anti-modernist orientation of the early twentieth-century Catholic Church and so they set out to plan a Council in continuity with Pius XII's cautionary encyclical *Humani generis* of 1950 (A. Piolanti; the drafters of *Guarding the Purity of the Deposit of Faith*). But other voices, in contrast, called for renewal based on more ancient sources, to make Catholic teaching more biblical, more coherent with fundamental liturgical structures, and better able to ground an ecumenical engagement (Congar; proposals from the Biblical Institute; topics submitted from theologians in Münster and Louvain).

During the three-year preparation of the Council (1959–62), the proponents of renewal were dispersed, even isolated. Only the assembling of the theologians in Rome in October 1962 allowed their lines of thought to unite in an intense and fruitful exchange, leading to the alternative drafts of 1962 that helped focus opposition to the draft texts of the Preparatory Theological Commission. The impact of this opposition came to dramatic expression on November 20, 1962, when 1,368 Council members voted to remove *The Sources of Revelation* from the immediate agenda. But one should not forget that this was foreshadowed a year before in the Central Preparatory Commission (Bea, König) and that it was definitely helped by the members having before their eyes in autumn 1962 a clear contrast to *The Sources*, namely, the draft text from the Preparatory Commission on Liturgy, which had been assisted by a notable corps of liturgical theologians.

Theologians helped the currents of renewal from original sources to flow more forcefully by their texts that circulated during Vatican II's first weeks (the *Commentary* of Schillebeeckx; Ratzinger-Rahner on revelation) and by their lectures to groups of bishops. Numerous episcopates, like that of Indonesia, resonated with the critical and constructive points made by their theologian-advisors, and this occurred in sufficient numbers so that by the end of 1962 the Council had in effect defined itself as an organ of broad renewal of the Catholic Church.

The new purpose and the themes of renewal, however, did not pass directly from the theologians into the published documents of Vatican II. The theologians drew on scripture and the classic sources to put into circulation numerous valuable ideas. The conciliar situation forced them to concentrate on themes clearly grounded in the sources, but still their proposals had to be accepted positively by the Council's members and then had to mature into texts that would gain the wide acceptance needed to ground a properly conciliar teaching or decree. The bishops and religious superiors, members of the Council, had to study the theological proposals, recognize their value, and judge them worthy of conciliar adoption. Here theology and the magisterium were working in their characteristic manners.

But the general perception is different when one looks back from the end of Vatican Council II in 1965, especially with an eye to the sixteen documents that Vatican II gave to the church and the world. The genesis of these texts demanded countless hours of work from the theologians of Vatican II, as they helped prepare the members' oral and written interventions on the early drafts and on their successive revisions. Many theologians assisted individual bishops or national episcopates by explaining the theology behind the draft texts and proposing directions to take in assessing them (Betti with Archbishop Florit; Smulders with the thirty bishops of Indonesia). Once the members decided the line they would follow, their theologians at times worked out concise Latin texts for delivery in the Aula or longer ones to hand in, over the bishops' signatures, as written comments on drafts under discussion.

Consideration of the breadth of topics taken up at Vatican II makes one grow in esteem for the Council's theologians. They had to quickly become experts in areas outside their own theological specialty. Smulders taught theological anthropology at Maastrict and had just written a well-received book on Teilhard de Chardin, but for the Indonesian bishops he had to first analyze the problematic of scripture/tradition in 1962 and in the following year give accounts of the episcopate as a universal college, of ecumenism, and of the role of the bishop as head of his diocese. Soon, work for the Doctrinal Commission forced him to study the diaconate and God's revelation.

Theologians working for the conciliar commissions had to analyze exactly what the Council members had said on every point in the draft just discussed in the Council hall, which for the Doctrinal Commission's experts often meant studying the notecards prepared for G. Philips. They had to give an accurate report on the overall configuration of the members' thinking, taking care not to omit any intervention, whether substantive or more attentive to particular wordings (Smulders on the diaconate in 1963; Congar, Betti, and Rahner on tradition in early 1964).

When a subcommission found the analysis by the *periti* to be accurate, the theologians moved on to draft a revision of their part of the draft text, trying where possible to introduce the very wording the Council members had used, but not in a way that might set off opposed reactions from bishops who differed. Texts revised by experts had to pass through two approvals, first by the relevant subcommission and then by the full commission. At these stages further changes could be introduced, before the *peritus* retyped the text for delivery to the commission's secretary who would pass it on, through Bishop Felici's central Secretariat, to the Vatican printers who prepared the booklets with revised texts for the Council members.

Vatican II demanded immense hidden labors from its theologian-experts, who made up a component of no small importance in the great ecclesial event that was the Council.

In a global perception, the theologians worked well with the bishops and religious superiors who were the voting members of Vatican Council II. One can see here a well-functioning epistemological duality between (1) the consultative thought of the theologian-experts, that is, their perceptions and concepts drawn from the doctrinal sources, with their provisional judgments, and (2) the decisive judgments by the Council members, who discerned, evaluated, adopted, or rejected the experts' proposals, and so became the responsible authors of Vatican II's teaching and decrees.

This collaboration at Vatican Council II offers us a unique case-study on the relationship between the theologians, with their research and intellectual explanations, and the church's magisterium, with both being bound by the normative contents of the word of God and the tradition of faith and life in the church.

An adequate understanding of this common work by two different components of the church has to take account, also, of the singular situation created at the beginning of the Council by its complex but problematic preparation and by the simple fact that the Council's working periods brought together in intense daily contact so many capable persons from the Catholic world. The stimulus to reflection and dialogue among the theologians was enormous. In this stimulating conversation, we surely find one of the reasons why the overall results of the Second Vatican Council far surpass the aims and purposes set for it as it began and even go beyond the expectations that emerged into formulation in late 1962.[57]

Appendix 6

Interpreting Vatican Council II

Pope Benedict XVI
(December 22, 2005)

INTRODUCTION

On December 22, 2005, Pope Benedict XVI held the traditional pre-Christmas audience for those who work in the offices of the Roman Curia. He took the occasion to review the events of 2005, dwelling on the final days, death, and funeral of Pope John Paul II, on the World Youth Day held in Cologne, Germany, in August 2005, and on the Synod of Bishops on the Eucharist, which met in October.

The pope's fourth point, nearly half of his address, took up the question of how to rightly interpret Vatican Council II, which had concluded forty years before in 1965 and about which different proposals were circulating in 2005 regarding its true significance. Pope Benedict proposed that Vatican II be seen as a Council that exemplified ongoing reform of the church. What follows is the portion of the address devoted to Vatican Council II.[1]

◆ ◆ ◆

The last event of this year on which I wish to reflect here is the celebration of the conclusion of the Second Vatican Council forty years ago. This memory prompts the question, What has been the result of the Council? Was it well received? What, in the acceptance of the Council, was good and what was inadequate or mistaken? What still remains to be done? No one can deny that in vast areas of the church the implementation of the Council has been somewhat difficult, even without wishing to apply to what occurred in these years the description that St. Basil, the great doctor of the church, made of the church's situation after the Council of Nicea: He compares her situation to a naval battle in the darkness of the storm, saying among other things: "The raucous shouting of those who through disagreement rise up against one another, the incomprehensible chatter, the confused din of uninterrupted clamoring, has now filled almost the whole of the Church, falsifying through excess or failure the right doctrine of the faith" (*De Spiritu Sancto*, chapter 30, no. 77; *Patrologia Graeca*, vol. 32, col. 213A).

We do not want to apply precisely this dramatic description to the situation of the postconciliar period, yet something of all that occurred is nevertheless reflected in it. The question arises, Why has the implementation of the Council, in large parts of the church, thus far been so difficult?

Well, it all depends on the correct interpretation of the Council or — as we would say today — on its proper hermeneutics, the correct key to its interpretation and application. The problems in its implementation arose from the fact that two contrary hermeneutics came face to face and quarreled with each other. One caused confusion; the other, silently but more and more visibly, bore and is bearing fruit.

On the one hand, there is an interpretation that I would call "a hermeneutic of discontinuity and rupture"; it has frequently availed itself of the sympathies of the mass media and also one trend of modern theology. On the other, there is the "hermeneutic of reform," of renewal in the continuity of the one subject-church which the Lord has given to us. She is a subject which increases in time and develops, yet always remaining the same, the one subject of the journeying people of God.

The hermeneutic of discontinuity risks ending in a split between the preconciliar church and the postconciliar church. It asserts that the texts of the Council as such do not yet express the true spirit of the Council. It claims that they are the result of compromises in which, to reach unanimity, it was found necessary to keep and reconfirm many old things that are now pointless. However, the true spirit of the Council is not to be found in these compromises but instead in the impulses toward the new that are contained in the texts.

These innovations alone were supposed to represent the true spirit of the Council, and starting from and in conformity with them, it would be possible to move ahead. Precisely because the texts would only imperfectly reflect the true spirit of the Council and its newness, it would be necessary to go courageously beyond the texts and make room for the newness in which the Council's deepest intention would be expressed, even if it were still vague.

In a word, it would be necessary not to follow the texts of the Council but its spirit. In this way, obviously, a vast margin was left open for the question on how this spirit should subsequently be defined and room was consequently made for every whim.

The nature of a Council as such is therefore basically misunderstood. In this way, it is considered as a sort of constituent that eliminates an old constitution and creates a new one.[2] However, the constituent assembly needs a mandator and then confirmation by the mandator, in other words, the people the constitution must serve. The Fathers had no such mandate, and no one had ever given them one; nor could anyone have given them one because the essential constitution of the Church comes from the Lord and was given to us so that we might attain eternal life and, starting from this perspective, be able to illuminate life in time and time itself.

Through the sacrament they have received, bishops are stewards of the Lord's gift. They are "stewards of the mysteries of God" (1 Cor 4:1); as such, they must be found to be "faithful" and "wise" (cf. Luke 12:41–48). This requires them to administer the Lord's gift in the right way, so that it is not left concealed in some hiding place but bears fruit, and the Lord may end by saying to the administrator, "Since you were dependable in a small matter I will put you in charge of larger affairs" (cf. Matt 25:14–30; Luke 19:11–27).

These Gospel parables express the dynamic of fidelity required in the Lord's service; and through them it becomes clear that, as in a Council, the dynamic and fidelity must converge.

The hermeneutic of discontinuity is countered by the hermeneutic of reform, as it was presented first by Pope John XXIII in his speech inaugurating the Council on October 11, 1962, and later by Pope Paul VI in his discourse for the Council's conclusion on December 7, 1965.[3]

Here I shall cite only John XXIII's well-known words, which unequivocally express this hermeneutic when he says that the Council wishes "to transmit the doctrine, pure and integral, without any attenuation or distortion." And he continues: "Our duty is not only to guard this precious treasure, as if we were concerned only with antiquity, but to dedicate ourselves with an earnest will and without fear to that work which our era demands of us." It is necessary that "adherence to all the teaching of the church in its entirety and preciseness" be presented in "faithful and perfect conformity to the authentic doctrine, which, however, should be studied and expounded through the methods of research and through the literary forms of modern thought. The substance of the ancient doctrine of the deposit of faith is one thing, and the way in which it is presented is another," retaining the same meaning and message (*The Documents of Vatican II,* ed. Walter M. Abbott, SJ, 715).

It is clear that this commitment to expressing a specific truth in a new way demands new thinking on this truth and a new and vital relationship with it; it is also clear that new words can only develop if they come from an informed understanding of the truth expressed, and on the other hand, that a reflection on faith also requires that this faith be lived. In this regard, the program that Pope John XXIII proposed was extremely demanding, indeed, just as the synthesis of fidelity and dynamic is demanding.

However, wherever this interpretation guided the implementation of the Council, new life developed and new fruit ripened. Forty years after the Council, we can show that the positive is far greater and livelier than it appeared to be in the turbulent years around 1968. Today, we see that although the good seed developed slowly, it is nonetheless growing; and our deep gratitude for the work done by the Council is likewise growing.

In his discourse closing the Council, Paul VI pointed out a further specific reason why a hermeneutic of discontinuity can seem convincing.

In the great dispute about man which marks the modern epoch, the Council had to focus in particular on the theme of anthropology. It had to question the relationship between the church and her faith on the one hand and man and the contemporary world on the other. The question becomes even clearer if, instead of the generic term *contemporary world,* we opt for another that is more precise: The

Council had to determine in a new way the relationship between the church and the modern era.

This relationship had a somewhat stormy beginning with the Galileo case. It was then totally interrupted when Kant described "religion within pure reason" and when, in the radical phase of the French Revolution, an image of the state and the human being that practically no longer wanted to allow the church any room was disseminated.

In the nineteenth century under Pius IX, the clash between the church's faith and a radical liberalism and the natural sciences, which also claimed to embrace with their knowledge the whole of reality to its limit, stubbornly proposing to make the "hypothesis of God" superfluous, had elicited from the church a bitter and radical condemnation of this spirit of the modern age. Thus, it seemed that there was no longer any milieu open to a positive and fruitful understanding, and the rejection by those who felt they were the representatives of the modern era was also drastic.

In the meantime, however, the modern age had also experienced developments. People came to realize that the American Revolution was offering a model of a modern state that differed from the theoretical model with radical tendencies that had emerged during the second phase of the French Revolution.

The natural sciences were beginning to reflect more and more clearly their own limitations imposed by their own method which despite achieving great things was nevertheless unable to grasp the global nature of reality.

So it was that both parties were gradually beginning to open up to each other. In the period between the two world wars and especially after World War II, Catholic statesmen demonstrated that a modern secular state could exist that was not neutral regarding values but alive, drawing from the great ethical sources opened by Christianity.

Catholic social doctrine, as it gradually developed, became an important model between radical liberalism and the Marxist theory of the state. The natural sciences, which without reservation professed a method of their own to which God was barred access, realized ever more clearly that this method did not include the whole of reality. Hence, they once again opened their doors to God, knowing that reality is greater than the naturalistic method and all that it can encompass.

It might be said that three circles of questions had formed which then, at the time of the Second Vatican Council, were expecting an answer. First of all, the relationship between faith and modern science had to be redefined. Furthermore, this did not only concern the natural sciences but also historical science for, in a certain school, the historical-critical method claimed to have the last word on the interpretation of the Bible and, demanding total exclusivity for its interpretation of sacred scripture, was opposed to important points in the interpretation elaborated by the faith of the church.

Secondly, it was necessary to give a new definition to the relationship between the church and the modern state that would make room impartially for citizens of various religions and ideologies, merely assuming responsibility for an orderly and tolerant coexistence among them and for the freedom to practice their own religion.

Thirdly, linked more generally to this was the problem of religious tolerance — a question that required a new definition of the relationship between the Christian faith and the world religions. In particular, before the recent crimes of the Nazi regime and, in general, with a retrospective look at a long and difficult history, it was necessary to evaluate and define in a new way the relationship between the church and the faith of Israel.

These are all subjects of great importance — they were the great themes of the second part of the Council — on which it is impossible to reflect more broadly in this context. It is clear that in all these sectors, which all together form a single problem, some kind of discontinuity might emerge. Indeed, a discontinuity had been revealed but in which, after the various distinctions between concrete historical situations and their requirements had been made, the continuity of principles proved not to have been abandoned. It is easy to miss this fact at a first glance.

It is precisely in this combination of continuity and discontinuity at different levels that the very nature of true reform consists. In this process of innovation in continuity we must learn to understand more practically than before that the church's decisions on contingent matters — for example, certain practical forms of liberalism or a free interpretation of the Bible — should necessarily be contingent themselves, precisely because they refer to a specific reality that is changeable in itself. It was necessary to learn to recognize that in these decisions it is only the principles that express the permanent aspect, since they remain as an undercurrent, motivating decisions from within.

On the other hand, not so permanent are the practical forms that depend on the historical situation and are therefore subject to change.

Basic decisions, therefore, continue to be well-grounded, whereas the way they are applied to new contexts can change. Thus, for example, if religious freedom were to be considered an expression of the human inability to discover the truth and thus become a canonization of relativism, then this social and historical necessity is raised inappropriately to the metaphysical level and thus stripped of its true meaning. Consequently, it cannot be accepted by those who believe that the human person is capable of knowing the truth about God and, on the basis of the inner dignity of the truth, is bound to this knowledge.

It is quite different, on the other hand, to perceive religious freedom as a need that derives from human coexistence, or indeed, as an intrinsic consequence of the truth that cannot be externally imposed but that the person must adopt only through the process of conviction.

The Second Vatican Council, recognizing and making its own an essential principle of the modern state with the Decree on Religious Freedom, has recovered the deepest patrimony of the church. By so doing she can be conscious of being in full harmony with the teaching of Jesus himself (cf. Matt 22:21), as well as with the church of the martyrs of all time. The ancient church naturally prayed for the emperors and political leaders out of duty (cf. 1 Tim 2:2); but while she prayed for the emperors, she refused to worship them and thereby clearly rejected the religion of the state.

The martyrs of the early church died for their faith in that God who was revealed in Jesus Christ, and for this very reason they also died for freedom of conscience and the freedom to profess one's own faith — a profession that no state can impose but which, instead, can only be claimed with God's grace in freedom of conscience. A missionary Church known for proclaiming her message to all peoples must necessarily work for the freedom of the faith. She desires to transmit the gift of the truth that exists for one and all.

At the same time, she assures peoples and their governments that she does not wish to destroy their identity and culture by doing so, but to give them, on the contrary, a response which, in their innermost depths, they are waiting for — a response with which the multiplicity of cultures is not lost but instead unity between men and women increases and thus also peace between peoples.

The Second Vatican Council, with its new definition of the relationship between the faith of the church and certain essential elements of modern thought, has reviewed or even corrected certain historical decisions, but in this apparent discontinuity it has actually preserved and deepened her inmost nature and true identity.

The church, both before and after the Council, was and is the same church, one, holy, catholic and apostolic, journeying on through time; she continues "her pilgrimage amid the persecutions of the world and the consolations of God," proclaiming the death of the Lord until he comes (cf. *Lumen Gentium*, 8).

Those who expected that with this fundamental yes to the modern era all tensions would be dispelled, and that the "openness towards the world" accordingly achieved would transform everything into pure harmony, had underestimated the inner tensions as well as the contradictions inherent in the modern epoch.

They had underestimated the perilous frailty of human nature which has been a threat to human progress in all the periods of history and in every historical constellation. These dangers, with the new possibilities and new power of man over matter and over himself, did not disappear but instead acquired new dimensions: A look at the history of the present day shows this clearly.

In our time too, the church remains a "sign that will be opposed" (Luke 2:34) — not without reason did Pope John Paul II, then still a cardinal, give this title to the theme for the spiritual exercises that he preached in 1976 to Pope Paul VI and the Roman Curia. The Council could not have intended to abolish the Gospel's opposition to human dangers and errors.

On the contrary, it was certainly the Council's intention to overcome erroneous or superfluous contradictions in order to present to our world the requirement of the Gospel in its full greatness and purity.

The steps the Council took towards the modern era, which had rather vaguely been presented as "openness to the world," belong in short to the perennial problem of the relationship between faith and reason that is reemerging in ever new forms. The situation that the Council had to face can certainly be compared to events of previous epochs.

In his First Letter, St. Peter urged Christians always to be ready to give an answer (*apologia*) to anyone who asked them for the *logos,* the reason for their faith (cf. 3:15).

This meant that biblical faith had to be discussed and come into contact with Greek culture and learn to recognize through interpretation the separating line, but also the convergence and the affinity between them in the one reason, given by God.

When, in the thirteenth century through the Jewish and Arab philosophers, Aristotelian thought came into contact with medieval Christianity formed in the Platonic tradition, and faith and reason risked entering an irreconcilable contradiction, it was above all St. Thomas Aquinas who mediated the new encounter between faith and Aristotelian philosophy, thereby setting faith in a positive relationship with the form of reason prevalent in his time. There is no doubt that the wearing dispute between modern reason and the Christian faith, which had begun negatively with the Galileo case, went through many phases, but with the Second Vatican Council the time came when broad new thinking was required.

Its content was certainly only roughly traced in the conciliar texts, but this determined its essential direction, so that the dialogue between reason and faith, particularly important today, found its bearings on the basis of the Second Vatican Council.

This dialogue must now be developed with great open-mindedness but also with that clear discernment that the world rightly expects of us in this very moment. Thus, today we can look with gratitude at the Second Vatican Council: If we interpret and implement it guided by a right hermeneutic, it can be and can become increasingly powerful for the ever necessary renewal of the church.

Lastly, should I perhaps recall once again that April 19 of this year on which, to my great surprise, the College of Cardinals elected me as the successor of Pope John Paul II, as a successor of St. Peter on the chair of the bishop of Rome? Such an office was far beyond anything I could ever have imagined as my vocation. It was, therefore, only with a great act of trust in God that I was able to say in obedience my yes to this choice. Now as then, I also ask you all for your prayer, on whose power and support I rely.

At the same time, I would like to warmly thank all those who have welcomed me and still welcome me with great trust, goodness and understanding, accompanying me day after day with their prayers.

Christmas is now at hand. The Lord God did not counter the threats of history with external power, as we human beings would expect according to the prospects of our world. His weapon is goodness. He revealed himself as a child, born in a stable. This is precisely how he counters with his power, completely different from the destructive powers of violence. In this very way he saves us. In this very way he shows us what saves.

In these days of Christmas, let us go to meet him full of trust, like the shepherds, like the Wise Men of the East. Let us ask Mary to lead us to the Lord. Let us ask him himself to make his face shine upon us. Let us ask him also to defeat the violence in the world and to make us experience the power of his goodness. With these sentiments, I warmly impart to you all my Apostolic Blessing.

Appendix 7

The Subject Areas
of Catholic Theology

INTRODUCTION

The following chart offers an overview of the areas in which theologians in the Catholic tradition do their work. The five chapters of this book have given an account of the sources and methods of work in the systematic areas that occupy the large central place in the chart below. To use the image of the human body, the foundational areas are like the feet on which theology stands, the dialogical areas are like the arms and hands of outreach and greeting to other worldviews, while the systematic areas with their subdivisions are like the disks of the body's spine by which this theology has its characteristic posture. In the systematic areas theology deals with the understanding that it draws from the witnesses to God's word of truth and that it seeks to explain in an ordered way after reflective questioning on the meaning of God's word for human life.

Foundational Areas

Holy scripture: the collected texts of primary witnesses to God revealing himself (Heb 1:1–2)

Old Testament: Historical Books

Prophets

Psalms and Wisdom Books

New Testament: Synoptic Gospels (Matthew, Mark, Luke)

Pauline Letters

Works of John (Gospel, Epistles, Revelation)

Church Historical Study: on the development of Christian tradition

History of the church's structures and interaction with societies and cultures

Development of doctrines amid the life of the church, especially the general councils

Major figures: for example, Irenaeus, Origen, Augustine, Anselm, Thomas Aquinas, Newman, et al.

Systematic Areas

Fundamental Theology

God's revelation and the response of faith

The credibility (human, historical, rational) of God's revelation

The communication of revelation and faith (scripture, tradition, magisterium, the "sense of the faithful")

Dogmatic Theology

God the Creator: Father, Son, and Holy Spirit

Christology: the person and saving work of Christ

Theological anthropology: the human drama under God's call, in sin, to sanctification

Ecclesiology: in the Holy Spirit, communion and the mission of the church

Liturgy and Sacraments: the church at worship; the events of new life, healing, vocation

Eschatology: the final destiny of creation and human beings

Moral Theology

Fundamental concerns: human vocation, conscience, God's will, sin, the virtues

Personal morality: worship, care of life, sexuality

Social morality: communications, the economy, political obligations

Spiritual Theology

Growth in Christ and in the Holy Spirit to sanctity

Ways of prayer

Vocations and Christian states of life

Dialogical Areas

The ecumenical quest for Christian unity (with other churches and communities)

Theology of religious pluralism (with other religions, for example, Islam, Buddhism)

Faith and philosophical worldviews

Faith and modern scientific accounts of the world and human beings

Encounters with contemporary cultures

Appendix 8

The Levels of Teaching by the Catholic Magisterium

INTRODUCTION

The Vatican Congregation for the Doctrine of the Faith issued in 1990 an Instruction, *The Ecclesial Vocation of the Theologian.*[1] Among other topics, the text sets forth four levels of authority among the doctrines taught officially in the Catholic Church. The levels indicate the different degrees of commitment by the church to the doctrines it teaches, with each looking to a corresponding level of acceptance on the part of the members of the church.[2]

In descending order, these are (1) solemn definitions of the content of God's revelation, which are then articles of faith or dogmas, (2) definitive teachings on other truths closely related to revelation or on truths grounding essential elements of Christian practice, (3) nondefinitive declarations of present doctrine to bring out the further meaning of revelation, in order to support the understanding of and to maintain the truth of God's word, and (4) doctrinal interventions to apply Catholic teaching to issues of particular urgency, in a prudential manner and at times on contingent and changing realities of life.[3]

The following excerpts from the Instruction link together, at each level, passages from its account of the respective magisterial authority (from nos. 15–17) and passages that describe the particular response called for from the Catholic faithful, in correspondence with each level of the magisterium's teaching (nos. 23–24). These English texts are cited, with permission, from *Origins* 20 (1990): 121–23, with headings by J. Wicks in brackets.

237

[LEVEL 1 – SOLEMN DEFINITIONS
OF THE CONTENT OF REVELATION]

This charism [of infallibility] is manifested when the pastors propose a doctrine as contained in revelation and can be exercised in various ways. Thus it is exercised particularly when the bishops in union with their visible head proclaim a doctrine by a collegial act as is the case in an Ecumenical Council, or when the Roman pontiff, fulfilling his mission as supreme pastor and teacher of all Christians, proclaims a doctrine *ex cathedra* ("from the Chair").

When the magisterium of the church makes an infallible pronouncement and solemnly declares that a teaching is found in revelation, the assent called for is that of theological faith.

[LEVEL 2 – DEFINITIVE PRONOUNCEMENTS
RELATED TO TRUTHS OF FAITH]

By its nature, the task of religiously guarding and loyally expounding the deposit of divine revelation in all its integrity and purity implies that the magisterium can make a pronouncement "in a definitive way" (LG 25) on propositions which, even if not contained among the truths of faith, are nonetheless intimately connected with them in such a way that the definitive character of such affirmations derives in the final analysis from revelation itself.

When the magisterium of the church proposes "in a definitive way" truths concerning faith and morals, which, even if not divinely revealed, are nevertheless strictly and intimately connected with revelation, these must be firmly accepted and held.

[LEVEL 3 – NONDEFINITIVE DECLARATIONS
PROMOTING THE UNDERSTANDING
OF REVEALED TRUTH]

Divine assistance is also given to the successors of the apostles teaching in communion with the successor of Peter, and in a particular way to the Roman pontiff as pastor of the whole church, when exercising their ordinary magisterium, even should this not issue in an infallible definition or in a "definitive" pronouncement, but in the proposal of some teaching which leads to a better understanding of revelation in matters of faith or morals and to moral directives derived from such teaching.

When the magisterium, not intending to act "definitively" teaches a doctrine to aid a better understanding of revelation and make explicit its contents, or to recall how some teaching is in conformity with the truths of faith or finally to guard against ideas which are incompatible with these truths, the response called for is that of the religious submission of will and intellect (LG 25).[4] This kind of response cannot be simply exterior or disciplinary, but must be understood within the logic of faith and under the impulse of obedience to the faith.

[LEVEL 4 – PRUDENTIAL AND CONTINGENT APPLICATIONS OF DOCTRINE]

Finally, in order to serve the people of God as well as possible, in particular by warning them of dangerous opinions which could lead to error, the magisterium can intervene in questions under discussion which involve, in addition to solid principles, certain contingent and conjectural elements. It often becomes possible only with the passage of time to distinguish between what is necessary and what is contingent.

The willingness to submit loyally to the teaching of the magisterium in matters per se not irreformable must be the rule. It can happen, however, that a theologian may, according to the case, raise questions regarding the timeliness, the form, or even the contents of magisterial interventions. Here the theologian will need, first of all, to assess accurately the authoritativeness of the interventions, which becomes clear from the nature of the documents, the insistence with which a teaching is repeated, and the very way in which it is expressed.

Notes

Introduction

1. Jared Wicks, *Introduction to Theological Method* and *Introduzione al metodo teologico,* in the two series directed by Rino Fisichella, Introduction to the Theological Disciplines and Introduzione alle discipline teologiche (Casale Monferrato: Piemme, 1994–). Translations of my volume also appeared in Polish, Portuguese, and Spanish.

2. See Maureen Sullivan, OP, *The Road to Vatican II* (New York and Mahwah, NJ: Paulist Press, 2007), for an informative account of Vatican II, which repeatedly charts the movement from preconciliar theologians of renewal to the Council's teaching, beginning with Y. Congar and H. de Lubac (18–20).

3. Pope Benedict XVI to the Cardinal Electors, *Origins* 34 (2005): 724. See also Appendix 6 of this book, which gives Pope Benedict's proposal of interpreting the many-sided event of Vatican II by applying a "hermeneutic of reform."

4. On these and many other teachers of esoteric worldviews, with their revelations of secret knowledge, see David S. Katz, *The Occult Tradition: From the Renaissance to the Present Day* (London: Jonathan Cape, 2006), especially 86–98 (Swedenborg), 98–109 (Mormon origins), and 163–71 (Blavatsky and the Theosophical Societies).

5. Appendix 4 of this book gives the texts on God's revelation and the response of faith issued by Vatican I and Vatican II. The first of these Councils aimed to clarify the mutual relations between faith and reason, based on an account of God's revelation as divine instruction, which had contemporary relevance in 1870. This was part of the starting point ninety-five years later, when Vatican II drew on a wider range of sources, especially scripture, to restate Catholic doctrine on God's word to believers as a saving message in Christ and a loving invitation to personal communion with himself.

6. Behind these paragraphs lies the work of René Latourelle, whose *Theology of Revelation* (Staten Island, NY: Alba House, 1966) is still a classic Catholic account of God's revelation. Latourelle summarized his understanding of God's revealing word in DFT, in the entry "Revelation"

(905–50), especially in section no. 8, "Specific Features of Christian Revelation" (930–47). A marvel of concision on revelation is Gerald O'Collins
and Mario Farrugia, *Catholicism: The Story of Catholic Christianity* (New
York: Oxford University Press, 2003), 96–102.

7. Appendix 1 of this book gives Pope John's opening address to Vatican
Council II, delivered October 11, 1962. In these words the members of the
Council found a convincing sketch of a pastoral renewal, giving them the
aims of their work and the criteria by which they would evaluate, and then
revise, texts proposed for their adoption.

Chapter 1:
Theology in History and the Church

1. René Latourelle and Rino Fisichella explore "meaning" in DFT, 644–
54.

2. The reader may be helped at this point by an initial study of section 1.3, on the two phases of methodical theological activity. The historical
models of section 1.1 and the orientations given by Vatican II in section 1.2
indicate, from different perspectives, the two fundamental phases.

3. Frank L. Cross and Elizabeth A. Livingston, eds., *Oxford Dictionary
of the Christian Church,* 3rd ed. (Oxford: Oxford University Press, 1997),
847. Antonio Orbe offers an introduction to Irenaeus in DFT, 523–29, as
does Richard A. Norris in BDCT, 266–70.

4. Pheme Perkins introduces the gnostic movement in her entry "Gnosis," DFT, 341–46.

5. Alexander Roberts and James Donaldson, eds., *Ante-Nicene Fathers,*
repr. (Grand Rapids: Eerdmans, 1977), 1, 415.

6. *Adversus Haereses,* I, 10, 2; *Ante-Nicene Fathers,* 1, 331.

7. *Adversus Haereses,* I, 10, 2; *Ante-Nicene Fathers,* 1, 311.

8. A short introduction to Origen is Henri Crouzel's presentation in DFT,
743–50. Another is by Joseph W. Trigg in BDCT, 395–99.

9. *On First Principles,* chapter 4, is given in Rowan A. Greer, ed., *Origen,* Classics of Western Spirituality (New York and Mahwah, NJ: Paulist
Press, 1979), 171–205.

10. Origen, "Homily XXVII on Numbers," in Greer, ed., *Origen,* 245–
69.

11. An older collection is Jared Wicks, ed., *Catholic Scholars Dialogue
with Luther* (Chicago: Loyola University Press, 1970). The author's own
further studies are collected in *Luther's Reform: Studies in Conversion and*

the Church (Mainz: Philipp von Zabern, 1992). A more concise presentation is *Luther and His Spiritual Legacy* (Wilmington, DE: Michael Glazier, 1983), especially chapter 7. A short introduction to Luther is by Joan Skocir in BDCT, 336–40.

12. *Luther's Works*, 55 vols. (St. Louis: Concordia Publishing House, and Philadelphia: Fortress Press, 1955–80), 26:9, 10, and 282–83.

13. Ibid., 26:99.

14. From Luther's exposition of Psalm 51, from lectures of 1532, printed in 1538. The translation given here has been adapted from *Luther's Works* 12:371, to agree better with the original Latin.

15. Ibid., 54:7. In these, a person can well be assailed by evil and consoled by the Holy Spirit, he explained in 1539, and so one becomes a true theologian. Ibid., 34:285–87.

16. Luther's *Small Catechism* was for memorizing, while his *Large Catechism* was to guide the teacher. Both are found in the official collection of Lutheran doctrinal texts, Robert Kolb and Timothy Wengert, eds., *The Book of Concord* (Minneapolis: Fortress Press, 2000).

17. I introduced Cano's contribution to theology in "Loci theologici," DFT, 605–7, as did Patrick Carey in BDCT, 114–16.

18. Cano's use of the term *loci* ("places") differs from that of the classic of Protestant theological pedagogy, Philipp Melanchthon's *Loci communes* (1521, revised in 1559). Melanchthon's *loci* are the themes found in scripture, for example, our fallen condition, sin, the Gospel, justification, faith, etc., on which one should garner data and instruction through study of all the canonical books. The *loci* constitute an ordered list of topics or headings that are taken from scripture to define theological formation. The two-volume *Christian Dogmatics*, ed. Carl E. Braaten and Robert W. Jensen (Philadelphia: Fortress Press, 1984), followed this usage by organizing doctrine into twelve treatises, called *loci*. But for Cano, scripture is just one field, although the primary one, in which theologians search. Their *loci* are the fields or areas of theological research on any topic or doctrine.

19. The task of setting forth the credibility of revelation is one work of *fundamental theology*. See the scheme given in Appendix 7 of this book, which shows the place of fundamental theology amid the areas of Catholic theology. In *Fides et ratio* (1999), Pope John Paul II gave a brief but dense description of fundamental theology in no. 67 of the encyclical. Avery Dulles approaches this theological area creatively in "Fundamental Theology and the Dynamics of Conversion," *The Craft of Theology* (New York: Crossroad, 1992), 53–68.

20. *Dei Filius,* no. 16, trans. J. Wicks.

21. The Council sees God in both mysteries adapting himself to our human frailty and limits. "In sacred scripture, without diminishing God's truth and holiness, the marvelous 'condescension' of eternal wisdom is plain to be seen.... For God's words, expressed in human language, are in every way like human speech, just as at one time the Word of the eternal Father, when he assumed the flesh of human weakness, became like human beings" (DV 13).

22. *Summa,* part III, q. 1, art. 2.

23. A good introduction to St. Thomas Aquinas as a theologian is by Brian Davies in BDCT, 501–5.

24. *Humani generis,* no. 18, from Claudia Carlen, ed., *The Papal Encyclicals, 1939–58* (Ann Arbor, MI: Pierian Press, 1990), 177.

25. *Humani generis,* no. 21, from Carlen, *The Papal Encyclicals,* 178. Pius XII's insistence on the theological sources, that is, the biblical, patristic, and liturgical expressions of Christian life, was central in works by theologians of special influence on the renewal worked out at Vatican II (1962–65). Good examples of this pioneering work, deeply indebted to the Church Fathers, are Henri de Lubac, *Catholicism: Christ and the Common Destiny of Man* (San Francisco: Ignatius Press, 1988; French original, 1937), and Yves Congar, *Divided Christendom: A Catholic Study of the Problem of Reunion* (London: G. Bles, 1939; French original, 1937).

26. *Humani generis,* no. 21, from Carlen, 178.

27. A lucid formulation of this "regressive" method was given by René Latourelle, *Theology: Science of Salvation* (Staten Island, NY: Alba House, 1969), 71–75. Further, Jared Wicks, "Theology, Manualistic," in DFT, 1102–5.

28. Initial orientations to Vatican II are given by Norman Tanner, *The Councils of the Church: A Short History* (New York: Crossroad, 2001), 96–113, and in the entry by Robert Trisco and Joseph Komonchak in *New Catholic Encyclopedia,* rev. ed. (Detroit: Thompson & Gale, 2002), 14, 407–18. The Appendices of this book give important discourses at the Council by Popes John XXIII and Paul VI, along with sections of the Council's fundamental statement on God's revelation and on the Bible in Catholic life. Appendix 7 is an account of the work of theologians in service of the Council. But, the main study has to be of the documents issued by Vatican II, as in the revised, inclusive-language edition of the sixteen texts, overseen by Austin Flannery, OP (Northport, NY: Costello, and Dublin: Dominican Publications, 1996).

29. In his remarks about interpreting Vatican II, on December 22, 2005, Pope Benedict XVI cited this statement of Pope John as one basis for seeing the Council as basically issuing a program of church reform (see Appendix 6 below).

30. See the text below in Appendix 4. On the further communication of God's revealed and revealing word, see Avery Dulles, "Revelation, Scripture, and Tradition," in *Your Word Is Truth,* ed. Charles Colson and Richard J. Neuhaus (Grand Rapids: Eerdmans, 2002), 35–58. Also Gerald O'Collins and Mario Farrugia, *Catholicism* (Oxford: Oxford University Press, 2003), 96–123.

31. Chapter 5 of OT, nos. 13–18, bears the title, "The Revision of Ecclesiastical Studies." Twenty-five verbs of the Latin text of no. 16, on dogmatic theology, are in the subjunctive mood. This means that they are not describing what is being done, with indicative verbs, but are instead prescribing what should be done in a new type of practice in theology.

32. OT 16, translated by the author from the Latin text of the decree.

33. UR 11, in the author's own translation. The comments in this section owe much to the writings of William Henn in *The Hierarchy of Truths according to Yves Congar* (Rome: Gregorian University Press, 1987); also "The Hierarchy of Truths Twenty Years Later," *Theological Studies* 48 (1987): 439–71; and in compact form, "Hierarchy of Truths," DFT, 425–27.

34. Congar, in the entry "Théologie," in the *Dictionnaire de Théologie catholique,* vol. 15 (1946), made an explicit statement of the two phases of theology in col. 462, which he developed in cols. 447–77. For an introduction to this major Catholic theologian of the twentieth century, see the short account by Susan Wood in BDCT, 131–35. After Congar's diaries of 1946 to 1966 were published, the author of this book wrote "Yves Congar's Doctrinal Service of the People of God," *Gregorianum* 84 (2003): 499–550. The diaries shed brilliant light on Catholic theology in the twentieth century and especially on the many-sided event that was Vatican Council II.

35. Bernard Lonergan, *Method in Theology* (New York: Herder and Herder, 1972), 133. Matthew Lamb introduces B. Lonergan in BDCT, 324–29.

36. *The Craft of Theology* (as in note 19 above), 52.

37. At this point the reader could study section 5.1 below on "Theology as Methodical Discipline and Wisdom," for a further development of the two phases sketched here. The intervening chapters 2, 3, and 4 lay the foundations of the more developed account offered in section 5.1.

Chapter 2:
Doing Theology by Listening to the Biblical Word

1. DV 21, translated by J. Wicks. This text follows the words cited above on page 25.

2. On this topic: Jared Wicks, "Canon of Scripture," in DFT, 94–100. More at length: Joseph T. Lienhard, *The Bible, the Church, and Authority: The Canon of the Christian Bible in History and Theology* (Collegeville, MN: Liturgical Press, 1995), and Lee M. McDonald, *The Formation of the Christian Biblical Canon*, 2nd ed. (Peabody, MA: Hendrickson, 1995).

3. *On the Decrees of the Council of Nicea*, no. 18; in *Nicene and Post-Nicene Fathers*, Series II, vol. 4, reprint, ed. Philip Schaff and Henry Wace (Grand Rapids: Eerdmans, 1978), 160.

4. Letter 39, in *Nicene and Post-Nicene Fathers*, ed. Schaff and Wace, II/4, 551–52.

5. *Summa of Theology*, part I, q. 1, art. 8.

6. Letter 82, to St. Jerome, no. 3, in St. Augustine, *Letters*, vol. 1, trans. Wilfred Parsons, Fathers of the Church (Washington, DC: Catholic University of America Press, 1951), 392.

7. Augustine gave the canon in chapter 8, no. 13, of Book II. He wrote further, on seeking in scripture as the guide of faith, life, hope, and charity, in chapter 9, no. 14. *Christian Instruction*, trans. J. J. Gavigan, in *Writings of St. Augustine*, vol. 4, Fathers of the Church (New York: Cima, 1947), 71–72.

8. Ellen F. Davis and Richard B. Hays, *The Art of Reading Scripture* (Grand Rapids: Eerdmans, 2003), 2.

9. Albert Sundberg, *The Old Testament of the Early Church* (Cambridge, MA: Harvard University Press, 1964); Rowan A. Greer, "The Christian Transformation of the Hebrew Scriptures," in *Early Biblical Interpretation*, ed. J. L. Kugel (Philadelphia: Westminster, 1986), 126–54; Craig A. Evans, "The Scriptures of Jesus and His Earliest Followers," in *The Canon Debate*, ed. Lee M. McDonald and James A. Sanders (Peabody, MA: Hendrickson, 2002), 185–95; and Daniel J. Harrington, "The Old Testament Apocrypha in the Early Church and Today," in *Canon Debate*, 196–210.

10. On Marcion, see the entry by Joseph Lienhard in BDCT, 349.

11. BDCT gives introductions to each of these early Christian writers.

12. ND, 211, and Dean Béchard, ed., *The Scripture Documents: An Anthology of Official Catholic Teachings* (Collegeville, MN: Liturgical Press, 2002), 3–4. Early canons including the deuterocanonical books were

issued by the Councils of Hippo in AD 393 and Carthage in 397, which Pope Innocent I confirmed in 405. The Protestant–Catholic argument over the deuterocanonical books is sketched by the author in the DFT entry "Canon of Scripture," already mentioned in note 2 above in this chapter.

13. A concise introduction is the entry "Gnosticism" in Frank L. Cross and Elizabeth A. Livingston, eds., *Oxford Dictionary of the Christian Church*, 3rd ed. (Oxford: Oxford University Press, 1997), 683–85.

14. The gnostic scriptures are much studied in our day, especially those works discovered in 1945 where they had been buried, at Nag Hammadi in Egypt, most likely after the letter on the canon from Athanasius in 367. See James M. Robinson, ed., *The Nag Hammadi Library in English* (New York: Harper & Row, 1977); Bentley Layton, ed. and trans., *The Gnostic Scriptures*, 2nd ed. (Garden City, NY: Doubleday, 1995); Bart Ehrman, *Lost Scriptures: Books That Did Not Make It into the New Testament* (New York: Oxford University Press, 2003). The most recent such discovery is presented in Rodolphe Kasser, Marvin Meyer, and Gregor Wust, eds., *The Gospel of Judas* (Washington, DC: National Geographic Press, 2006). A contemporary personal testimony to the attraction of these books is given by Princeton professor Elaine Pagels, *Beyond Belief: The Secret Gospel of Thomas* (New York: Random House, 2003).

15. This ancient manuscript bears the name of Lodovico Muratori, who discovered it in the Ambrosian Library of Milan in the eighteenth century. The original Latin text is found in *Enchiridion Biblicum* (Bologna: Dehoniane, 1993), 2–6. In English translation: in Raymond F. Collins, *Introduction to the New Testament* (Garden City, NY: Doubleday, 1983), 33–34, and in Harry Gamble, *The New Testament Canon, Its Making and Meaning* (Philadelphia: Fortress, 1985), 93–95.

16. An exposition of the criteria applied in the canonical selection process for the New Testament, that is, use in the liturgy, coherence with the rule of faith, and apostolic origin of the books, is given in the DFT entry, "Canon of Scripture," indicated in note 2 above in this chapter.

17. Vatican II concludes its chapter on biblical inspiration and interpretation, in DV 13, by citing a homily on Genesis by St. John Chrysostom, who speaks of God's accommodation in the Bible of his biblical revelation to our human weakness, limitations, and fragility. The text was cited in chapter 1, note 21, above.

18. A good recent exposition of the bases of faith in inspiration and of the paths taken by the theological quest of its meaning is Raymond F. Collins, "Inspiration," in *The New Jerome Biblical Commentary*, ed. Raymond E.

Brown, Joseph A. Fitzmyer, Roland E. Murphy (Englewood Cliffs, NJ: Prentice Hall, 1990), 1023–33. More briefly, R. Fisichella in DFT, 515–18.

19. See the second text, cited on page 38, above.

20. Ambrose, *Exposition of the Gospel according to Luke,* Book VII, in Arthur A. Just, ed., *Luke,* Ancient Christian Commentary on Scripture, ed. Thomas C. Oden, New Testament, vol. 3 (Downers Grove, IL: InterVarsity Press, 2003), 177–81.

21. We treated this aspect of Vatican II on pages 27–29, above.

22. *Providentissimus Deus,* named from the opening words, "The God of all providence." The encyclical is given in Béchard, ed., *Scripture Documents* (as in note 12 above), 37–59.

23. *Providentissimus,* no. 42, in Béchard, 55–56. The formulation follows closely the descriptive definition of inspiration given in the textbook of J. B. Franzelin, longtime teacher at the Roman College (the Gregorian University of today), *De divina Traditione et Scriptura* (Rome, 1870, with new editions in 1875, 1882, and 1896), in which Franzelin speaks of the biblical authors as subordinated instrumental causes of the divine principal cause, who carries out his purposes with infallible truthfulness.

24. Pius XII's encyclical, *Divino afflante Spiritu,* from the opening words, "Inspired by the Divine Spirit," is given in Béchard, ed., *Scripture Documents,* 115–35. Pius XII oriented Catholic interpreters away from the argumentative defense of Scripture against charges that it taught errors, a task highlighted by Leo XIII in 1893, toward the retrieval of what the inspired authors of the biblical texts intended to say to their first readers. This encyclical will appear again in section 2.3 below in this chapter, on rightly interpreting Scripture.

25. In *The New Jerome Biblical Commentary* (as in note 18 of this chapter above), Raymond E. Brown and Sandra M. Schneiders explain biblical interpretation in the topical entry "Hermeneutics," 1146–65. A major recent summary is by the Catholic Pontifical Biblical Commission, "The Interpretation of the Bible in the Church" (1993), given in Béchard, ed., *Scripture Documents,* 244–315. From the viewpoint of an experienced interpreter of Israel's Psalms and Wisdom books, we have the book of Luis Alonso Schökel, co-authored with J. M. Bravo, *A Manual of Hermeneutics* (Sheffield, UK: Sheffield Academic Press, 1988). The last-named work treats the two moments or phases of interpretation, which will appear just ahead, as "author-hermeneutics" (retrieval of what the original writer *meant*) and "text-hermeneutics" (exploration of the text as it lives on in tradition, to find out what it *means*).

26. Good examples of New Testament commentaries are at hand in the series Sacra Pagina, now being brought out by Liturgical Press, such as the commentary on the Gospel of Luke by Luke Timothy Johnson, on the Letter to the Romans by Brendan Byrne, and on Colossians and Ephesians by Margaret McDonald. Also, based on the work of such commentaries, helpful annotations in some Bibles, such as the New Jerusalem Bible or the New American Bible, guide readers toward a better understanding of the original meaning of the texts.

27. This statement should be seen in its context in chapter 6 of the constitution, given below in Appendix 4. The notion of biblical study as "the soul of theology" occurred in Leo XIII's *Providentissimus Deus,* no. 33 (Béchard, *Scripture Documents,* 50), on the study of Scripture animating, like the soul in the human body, all teaching of theology. Vatican II's Decree on Priestly Formation, *Optatum totius,* also uses this phrase, in no. 16, on theological studies. J. M. Lera traced the phrase to a decree on studies issued by the Thirteenth General Congregation of the Society of Jesus in 1687. Rudolph Cornely cited it on the opening page of his *Introductio in Veteris Testamenti Libros* (Paris: Lethielleux, 1885), from which it was taken over in *Providentissimus.* J. M. Lera, "Sacrae Paginae studium sit veluti anima sacrae theologiae...," in *Palabra y vida,* ed. A. Vargas Machuca and G. Ruis (Madrid: Comillas, 1983), 409–22.

28. A helpful, yet concise, treatment of these matters is given by R. E. Brown, in the topical article "Hermeneutics," *The New Jerome Biblical Commentary* (as in note 18 above), nos. 14–29, with references to the New Testament volumes in the Fortress Press series Guides to Biblical Scholarship, such as E. V. McKnight, *What Is Form Criticism?* (1971), and N. Perrin, *What Is Redaction Criticism?* (1969). Also: Alonso Schökel and Bravo, *Manual of Hermeneutics,* indicated in note 25 above in this chapter.

29. During the preparation of this book, Joseph A. Fitzmyer, SJ, brought out *The Interpretation of Scripture: In Defense of the Historical-Critical Method* (New York and Mahwah, NJ: Paulist Press, 2008). On the retrieval of textual meanings, see especially Fitzmyer's chapter 4, "Historical Criticism: Its Role in Biblical Interpretation and Church Life," 59–73, in which pages 61–66 (on four steps of interpretation) and 68–69 (on "exegesis") are especially helpful. A decade ago, Gerald O'Collins and Daniel Kendall pointed theology in this direction in their book *The Bible for Theology: Ten Principles for the Theological Use of Scripture* (New York and Mahwah, NJ: Paulist, 1997) by making "faithful hearing" of Scripture their first principle of theological work, as stated on page 6 and expanded on pages 19–21.

O'Collins's recent work, *Jesus Our Redeemer: A Christian Approach to Salvation* (New York: Oxford Unversity Press, 2007), illustrates such faithful hearing by constantly probing biblical accounts of the human condition, redemption, sacrifice, God's transforming love, and several other themes of the doctrine of salvation.

30. We recall how the philosopher Hans-Georg Gadamer expressed this principle of hermeneutics: "What is fixed in writing has detached itself from the contingency of its origin and its author and made itself free for new relationships." *Truth and Method,* trans. Joel Weinsheimer and Donald G. Marshall (New York: Crossroad, 1989), 395.

31. The final phrase, "the analogy of faith," is well explained in the *Catechism of the Catholic Church,* no. 114, as "the coherence of the truths of faith among themselves and within the whole plan of Revelation." This passage of DV 12 was studied by Ignace de la Potterie in "Interpretation of Holy Scripture in the Spirit in Which It Was Written (*Dei Verbum* 12c)," in René Latourelle, ed., *Vatican II Assessment and Perspectives,* 3 vols. (New York: Paulist, 1988), 1:220–66.

32. The principal notion here is that of type/antitype, by which a person, place, or event (the type) comes to be grasped as foreshadowing a later person, place, or event (the antitype) in God's economy. Obvious examples are the bronze serpent raised on high by Moses (Num 21:9) as foreshadowing Jesus' being lifted up on the cross (John 3:14), and the passage of Israel to freedom through the sea as foreshadowing baptism (1 Cor 10:1–2). Early Christians saw Susanna as a type of Christ, since she was accused by two false witnesses of a sin punishable by death, just as was Jesus, and under accusation she remained silent as did Jesus after her (Dan 13:34–41 / Matt 26:60–63).

33. A new journal, *Letter and Spirit,* an annual begun in 2005 by the St. Paul Center for Biblical Theology, Steubenville, Ohio, has an approach to Scripture and an interpretive aim akin to the approach just set forth. It takes the Bible as having everywhere an essentially religious message, for the recovery of which one must apply historical and literary analyses. But Scripture is also to be read "in the Spirit," with attention to the canon and Christian tradition.

Chapter 3:
Doing Theology in the Stream of Catholic Tradition

1. Birger Gerhardsson developed this thesis in his *Memory and Manuscript: Oral Tradition and Written Transmission in Rabbinic Judaism and*

Early Christianity, 2nd ed. (Grand Rapids: Eerdmans, 1998), treating the rabbinical schools, 71–189, and then Paul, 262–323. The same author treated the matter more succinctly, but with further analytical refinement, in *The Gospel Tradition* (Malmö, Sweden: Gleerup, 1986).

2. On tradition, Hermann J. Pottmeyer gives a good orientation in the entry "Tradition," in DFT, 1119–26. Also Avery Dulles, "Tradition as a Theological Source," *The Craft of Theology* (New York: Crossroad, 1992), 87–104.

3. Tertullian, *On the Crown*, III, 4, given in J. Stevenson, ed., *A New Eusebius*, revised by William H. C. Frend (London: SPCK, 1987), 171–72. On Tertullian: Kenneth B. Steinhauser, in BDCT, 495–96.

4. The term "deposit" entered Catholic parlance by way of the Latin Vulgate translations of the imperatives of 1 Timothy 6:20 (*depositum custodisce*) and 2 Timothy 1:14 (*bonum depositum custode*). Vatican I spoke of "the deposit of faith" as that which the teaching office is charged to preserve. Vatican II speaks of "the deposit of revelation" in specifying that which the charism of infallibility is given to protect and preserve (LG 25, par. 3). Also in Vatican II Scripture and tradition are "a single deposit of the word of God" entrusted to the whole church (DV 10).

5. The author developed the biblical notion of "deposit" in the entry "Deposit of Faith," in DFT, 229–39. The notion goes together with active traditioning, that is, "receiving and handing on," to indicate the content, in a global sense, of what is received, preserved, and further passed on as a precious heritage or legacy.

6. Other late works of the New Testament share the concern that the churches remain rooted in the life-giving soil of the apostolic tradition. An emblematic text is the last discourse of Paul's missionary work in the Acts of the Apostles (20:17–35), which will be treated in the next chapter, section 4.1.

7. On this, the author wrote the entry "Rule of Faith," in DFT, 959–61.

8. *Adversus Haereses*, I, 10, 1–2; similar formulations are in I, 9, 4; III, 4, 2; IV, 33, 7, and in Irenaeus's *Demonstration of the Apostolic Preaching*, 3. In North Africa, Tertullian also gave similar summaries of the rule of faith: *On the Prescription of Heretics*, 13 and 36; *On the Veil of Virgins*, 1; *Against Praxeas*, 2, 1–2. Clement of Alexandria speaks of the "ecclesiastical rule," given by the apostles, that is "the understanding and practice of the divine tradition." *Stromata* VI, 124, 4–5, 125, 2–3; VI, 90, 2, 95, 3–8. BDCT gives concise entries on all these early Fathers.

9. See the entry "Creed," in DFT, 209–11, and the chapter, "The Ecclesiastical Form of Faith," in Joseph Ratzinger, *Introduction to Christianity* (San Francisco: Ignatius, 2004), 82–100. Henri de Lubac presents an abundance of insights, going well beyond the modesty of his subtitle, in *The Christian Faith: An Essay on the Structure of the Apostles' Creed* (San Francisco: Ignatius, 1986).

10. Hippolytus of Rome, *The Apostolic Tradition,* no. 21; given in ND, 3–4. The dialogue creed is still part of the rite of baptism and of the renewal of baptismal faith in the liturgy of the Easter Vigil.

11. On this Council, see Norman Tanner's chapter, "Ecumenical Councils of the Early Church," in *The Councils of the Church: A Short History* (New York: Crossroad, 2001), 13–45. In the Sistine Hall in the Vatican Museum, a sixteenth-century depiction of the Council of Nicea shows an altar in the midst of the gathered bishops, before which an open book of the Gospels rests on a chair, to indicate that Christ, presented in the Gospels as incarnate Son, teacher, and savior, is presiding at the Council.

12. On Arius, K. M. Spoerl has a short entry in BDCT, 29–30. Michel R. Barnes introduces Athanasius, Arius's adversary and the defender of Nicea's teaching, on pages 33–36.

13. ND 11 gives the Arian sayings that were excluded. Every dogma, thus, leads to "language rules" regarding communication between members of the church. What we commonly call the "Nicene Creed" today, and recite in the liturgy, is the revised form promulgated by the First Council of Constantinople in AD 381, without the added condemnation of specific Arian formulations.

14. Short introductions to St. Thomas are given by René Latourelle in DFT, 1105–9, and by Brian Davies in BDCT, 501–5.

15. *Summa of Theology,* part II-II, q. 1, art. 7.

16. "Truth," q. 14, art. 8, answers to the 5th and 12th objections. In *The Christian Faith* (as in note 9 above in this chapter), H. de Lubac has an enlightening chapter on "The Dynamism of Faith," based on patristic insights into "believing *in*" God as the movement of the believing person into union with God, who is revealed in the content of what we profess (291–316).

17. Paraphrase of *Summa,* II-II, 1, 2 ad 2.

18. Paraphrase of a text quoted approvingly by St. Thomas in *Summa,* II, 1, 6.

19. *An Essay on the Development of Christian Doctrine,* originally from 1845 (and frequently republished), is the fruit of Newman's four years of

anguished study and prayerful reassessment that led to his reception into the Roman Catholic Church. As recently as 1990, Newman's thought on development was singled out by the International Theological Commission in its study, "On the Interpretation of Dogmas," given in *Origins* 20 (1990): 1–14, where Newman's criteria of genuine past developments are set forth as fruitful principles to apply in any contemporary interpretation (p. 13). William J. Kelly introduces Newman in BDCT, 378–80.

20. Conventionally, the age of the Fathers who wrote in Latin ended with Isidore of Seville, who died in AD 636, while the Greek patristic period extended to the death of John of Damascus in AD 749. These are approximations, and should not obscure a view of the golden age between AD 350 and 450, when, in the East, major works were written by Athanasius, Ephrem, Basil, Gregory Nazianzen, Gregory of Nyssa, John Chrysostom, and Cyril of Alexandria. In the West there were at the same time Hilary of Poitiers, Ambrose, Jerome, Augustine, and Leo the Great. Still some towering figures are not of the golden age, including such earlier thinkers as Irenaeus (d. ca. 200) and Origen (d. 254) and the later contributors Gregory the Great (d. 604) and Maximus the Confessor (d. 662). BDCT gives helpful short introductions to all of these Fathers of the Church.

21. For initial contact with writings of the Fathers, two older collections serve well: Adalbert Hamman, ed., *Early Christian Prayers* (Chicago: Regnery, 1961), and William A. Jurgens, *The Faith of the Early Fathers* (Collegeville, MN: Liturgical Press, 1970). St. Ignatius Loyola stated why we should esteem the Fathers: "It is characteristic of the positive doctors, such as St. Augustine, St. Jerome, St. Gregory, and others, to rouse the affections so that we are moved to love and serve God our Lord in all things." *Spiritual Exercises,* no. 363. On this and other aspects of the Fathers, we now have the thoughtful work of Robert Louis Wilken, *The Spirit of Early Christian Thought* (New Haven: Yale University Press, 2003).

22. Again, short introductions are in BDCT. On the first two of these, see F. Kerr, "French Theology: Yves Congar and Henri de Lubac," in *The Modern Theologians: An Introduction to Christian Theology in the 20th Century,* ed. David Ford, 2nd ed. (Oxford: Blackwell, 1997), 105–17. Congar is *the* expert on the notion of tradition, expressed concisely in *Tradition and the Life of the Church* (originally 1964, now San Francisco: Ignatius Press, 2004) and at length in *Tradition and Traditions* (London: Burns and Oates, 1967). J. Ratzinger wrote on the importance of the Fathers in a section of his *Principles of Catholic Theology* (San Francisco: Ignatius Press, 1987), 133–52.

23. Two publication projects in North America are making the biblical interpretations of the Fathers more accessible. Thomas C. Oden is general editor of *Ancient Christian Commentary on Scripture,* a series begun in 1998 which will cover the whole Bible in volumes coming out from InterVarsity Press. Robert Louis Wilken is general editor of *The Church's Bible,* which will give longer patristic texts on fewer books of Scripture in volumes which began appearing in 2003 from Eerdmans.

24. These problems have been treated by J. Ratzinger, in the section mentioned in note 22, and by Antonio Orbe, "The Study of the Fathers of the Church in Priestly Formation," in *Vatican II: Assessment and Perspectives,* ed. René Latourelle, vol. 3 (New York: Paulist, 1989), 361–77.

25. The enrichment of theology from the Fathers is demonstrated by the readings collected in the twenty-two-volume series *Message of the Fathers of the Church* (Collegeville, MN: Liturgical Press). We note vol. 4, *The Church,* ed. Thomas Halton (1985), vol. 10, *The Gospel and Its Proclamation,* ed. Ronald Sider (1983), and vol. 13, *Women in the Early Church,* ed. Elizabeth A. Clark (1983).

26. The best known early apologists are Justin Martyr (d. ca. AD 165), Tertullian (d. after AD 220), and the unknown author of the charming *Letter to Diognetus.* The chart given in Appendix 7 below locates fundamental theology in the scheme of areas of theological study.

27. In the original Latin, "Cum altari assistitur, semper ad Patrem dirigitur oratio." Canon 21 of the North African Council of Hippo of 393, later confirmed by a Council of Carthage, cited from *Concilia Africae, An. 345 ad An. 525,* ed. C. Munier, Corpus Christianorum, Series Latina, 149 (Turnholt, Belgium: Brepols, 1974), 39; also 264 and 305.

28. *The Bondage of the Will* (1525), cited from *Luther's Works,* vol. 33, 76–77. J. Patrick Donnelly introduces Erasmus in BDCT, 181–83, as does Joan Skocir for Luther, on pages 336–40.

29. *Confessions,* X, 28, cited from the translation of R. S. Pine-Coffin (Harmondsworth: Penguin Books, 1961), 232. On Augustine, see J. Kevin Coyle's introduction in BDCT, 36–40.

30. *St. Thérèse of Lisieux. Her Last Conversations* (Washington, DC: Institute of Carmelite Studies, 1977), 147. Thèrése, we recall, was declared a Doctor of the Church by Pope John Paul II in 1997.

31. John O'Malley treated Ignatius in Carter Lindberg, ed., *The Reformation Theologians: An Introduction to Theology in the Early Modern Period* (Oxford: Blackwell, 2002), 298–310, to which J. Patrick Donnelly adds a short account in BDCT, 265–66. The Ignatian religious style was set in relief

by H. Outram Evennett, in *The Spirit of the Counter-Reformation* (Notre Dame, IN: University of Notre Dame Press, 1970), 23–66.

32. On this Council, see Tanner, *The Councils* (as in note 11 above in this chapter), 75–87, and Jared Wicks, in DFT, 1126–29.

33. These selected points come from the preface of Fisher's 1523 *Confutation* of Luther.

34. The text is ND 210 and Dean Béchard, ed., *The Scripture Documents: An Anthology of Official Catholic Teachings* (Collegeville, MN: Liturgical Press, 2002), 3–4. Its concern with books and practices should not obscure the primacy of believing assent that the Holy Spirit instills in human hearts, as this was stated in the programmatic address of Cardinal Marcello Cervini on February 18, 1546 (*Concilium Tridentinum*, 1, 484–85). Joseph Ratzinger featured Cervini's presentation in Karl Rahner and Joseph Ratzinger, *Revelation and Tradition* (New York: Herder and Herder, 1966), 50–78.

35. Many at Trent did hold that for knowing God's revelation the content of Scripture must be supplemented by other contents given only in tradition. But the Council did not say this, leaving open to different explanations the interrelation of the biblical books and what the apostles left as teaching and practices in the churches. Because of this openness Vatican II took up the question and favored the view that tradition is the way in which believers come to know, not new truths but all the implications of Scripture for them. Tradition, furthermore, adds a certainty coming from the lived practices of community life and worship.

36. ND 215 and Béchard, *Scripture Documents*, 4–5 (no. 2 of the decree). This topic will come back in the next chapter, in section 4.3, on the church's magisterium as interpreter of Scripture.

37. "Apostolical Tradition," *Essays Critical and Historical*, vol. 1 (London: Longmans, 1895), 126–27. For basic presentations on Newman, see Rino Fisichella in DFT, 734–38, and William J. Kelly in BDCT, 378–80.

38. Newman's criteria were restated by the Catholic International Theological Commission in its 1990 document, "On the Interpretation of Dogmas," *Origins* 20 (1990): 13. These principles of true development are: preservation of type or overall structure, continuity of underlying principles, power of assimilating other ideas, logical coherence in development, anticipation of later data, conservation of the past, and chronic vitality.

39. These two understood tradition in ways like those of Newman: the Tübingen theologian Johann Adam Möhler (1796–1838) and the French philosopher Maurice Blondel (1861–1949). Both are introduced in BDCT, Möhler by Bradford Hinze, 365–68, and Blondel by Jamie LeGrys, 77–78.

From Blondel, see especially his chapter, "The Vital Role and the Philosophical Basis of Tradition," in the longer essay, "History and Dogma," in *The Letter on Apologetics and History and Dogma*, ed. Alexander Dru and Illtyd Trethowan (Grand Rapids: Eerdmans, 1994), 264–87. On Blondel, René Latourelle wrote the entry in DFT, 78–84. See also Avery Dulles, "Tradition and Creativity in Theology," in *First Things*, no. 27 (November 1992): 20–27.

40. The text is in Béchard, *Scripture Documents*, 21–25. For a commentary, see Joseph Ratzinger, in *Commentary on the Documents of Vatican II*, ed. Herbert Vorgrimler, vol. 3 (New York: Herder and Herder, 1969), 181–98.

41. The text is my translation of DV 8, second paragraph.

42. On the "sense of the faith," Salvador Pie-Ninot contributed the entry in DFT, 992–95. Below, in section 5.1, it will return as a key aspect of doing theology in the midst of life.

Chapter 4:
Doing Theology in the Light of Church Teaching

1. A balanced and much read account of this part of ecclesiology is Francis A. Sullivan, *Magisterium: Teaching Authority in the Catholic Church* (New York: Paulist Press, 1983), to which one should add Ladislas Örsy, *The Church: Learning and Teaching* (Collegeville, MN: Liturgical Press, 1987); Avery Dulles, chapters 7, 10, 11 of *The Craft of Theology* (New York: Crossroad, 1992); and Richard R. Gaillardetz, *Teaching with Authority: A Theology of the Magisterium in the Church* (Collegeville, MN: Liturgical Press, 1997).

2. To make this point concrete, Appendix 5 below, "Theologians at Vatican Council II," shows the interaction of the bishops of the magisterium with the well-qualified theologians who assisted them in a variety of ways in the work of the Council.

3. See Francis A. Sullivan, *From Apostles to Bishops* (New York: Newman Press, 2001), treating the apostles, their immediate co-workers, and the later church leaders who make their appearance in the later writings of the New Testament (chapters 2–4).

4. Sullivan treats the pastoral letters to Timothy and Titus in *From Apostles to Bishops*, 70–76.

5. On this discourse of Paul as rendered by St. Luke, see Sullivan, *From Apostles to Bishops*, 64–66. More in detail: William S. Kurz, *Farewell Addresses in the New Testament* (Collegeville, MN: Liturgical Press, 1990),

33–51, and Jan Lambrecht, "Paul's Farewell-Address at Miletus," in *Pauline Studies* (Leuven, Belgium: Leuven University Press, 1994), 369–400.

6. For a comparative study of how different early communities dealt with these threats, see the survey by Raymond E. Brown, *The Churches the Apostles Left Behind* (New York: Paulist Press, 1984).

7. DV 7, in the author's translation. The inserted citation is from Irenaeus, *Adversus Haereses*, III, 3, 1.

8. See the list given above in note 20 on page 253.

9. See above the subsections on "Canon and Canonicity" (page 39) and "The New Testament Canon" (page 44).

10. Norman Tanner gives a succinct presentation of the major early Councils in *The Councils of the Church: A Brief History* (New York: Crossroad, 2001), 13–45.

11. See above page 74, "St. Thomas on 'Articles of Faith.' "

12. Innocent's letter to North Africa is Epistle no. 181 in the correspondence of St. Augustine, given in ND, 801, and James Stevenson, ed., *Creeds, Councils, and Controversies*, 2nd ed. (London: SPCK, 1989), 220–21. See Klaus Schatz, *Papal Primacy* (Collegeville, MN: Liturgical Press, 1996), 28–40, on the circumstances surrounding the emergence in the fourth and fifth centuries of the special primatial role of the successor of Peter in Rome.

13. North Africa was a zone of more active oversight by the bishops of Rome, while the canonically autonomous Eastern churches accepted interventions of the Petrine see only when controversy touched central issues of faith and worship, as over the veneration of images in the eighth century. See William Henn, *For the Honor of My Brothers: A Short History of the Relation between the Pope and the Bishops* (New York: Crossroad, 2000), 62–63, note 13, and 96–97.

14. Excerpts from Leo's *Tome* are given in ND, 609–12, followed by the dogmatic definition of the Council of Chalcedon in ND, 613–16. W. Henn relates this, with an account of the prehistory, in his chapter 3, "Peter Has Spoken through Leo," in *For the Honor of My Bothers*, 51–83.

15. *Summa of Theology*, Part II-II, q. 1, art. 10. Thomas speaks of the pope being by right able "to settle authoritatively [*sententialiter determinare*] what is of faith," suggesting by the terminology an analogy with the role of a medieval university professor presiding over a disputation. Advanced students would debate by giving arguments for and against a given position, but near the end, the professor would give his "determination" of what he held to be the best resolution of the point at issue. This points to a magisterium that is not particularly creative, but is instead discerning

and discriminating of the views of others, as it adjudicates a controversy or discussion over how to best express God's word of revelation, which the church has received in faith.

16. In the thirteenth century, the pastoral teaching office of bishops and pope was not yet called "magisterium," for the powers of those in pastoral office were of two kinds, namely, orders or sacramental power and jurisdiction for governance. Only in the nineteenth century did it become clear that teaching did not fit under either of these, but was a third power with a distinct contribution to the life of the faithful. Teaching does not serve directly sanctification or good order in the community, but instead promotes faith's grasp of the truth of God's word already received.

17. St. Thomas's text on the two *magisteria* is in his third *Quodlibet*, Art. 9. Ladislas Örsy gives the text and analyzes it in *The Church: Learning and Teaching* (as in note 1, this chapter), 70–73. Avery Dulles treats the "two chairs" in "The Magisterium in History: Theological Considerations," *A Church to Believe In* (New York: Crossroad, 1982), 109–11, and in "The Two Magisteria: An Interim Reflection," ibid., 118–32. The two magisteria recur in F. Sullivan, *Magisterium* (as in note 1, this chapter), 24–25, 45, 54, 149–50, 200, 204, and 218.

18. L. Örsy gives Gratian's text and analyzes it in *The Church: Learning and Teaching*, 67–70.

19. A recent study treated seventy doctrinal cases examined by the theology faculty of Paris in the early sixteenth century: James K. Farge, *Orthodoxy and Reform in Early Reformation France: The Faculty of Theology of Paris, 1500–1530* (Leiden: Brill, 1985). In Luther's case, the earliest censures of his positions came from the university faculties of Cologne (1519) and Louvain (1520), from which Pope Leo X then took over numerous condemnations in his bull *Exsurge Domine* (June 1520), in which he called on Luther to recant forty-one listed propositions, taken from Luther's works, within six months or face excommunication.

20. A recent survey is by David Bagchi, "Catholic Theologians of the Reformation Period before Trent," in *Cambridge Companion to Reformation Theology,* ed. David Bagchi and David Steinmetz (Cambridge: Cambridge University Press, 2004), 221–32, with a select bibliography on pages 275–76.

21. Norman Tanner presents the Council of Trent in a concise manner in *The Councils of the Church* (as in note 10 above), 75–87.

22. *Catechism of the Council of Trent for Parish Priests,* trans. John A. McHugh, OP, and Charles J. Callan, OP (New York: Wagner, and London:

B. Herder, 1923; reissue South Bend, IN: Marian Publishers, 1972). Also, *The Roman Catechism,* trans. Robert I. Bradley and Eugene Kevane (Boston: St. Paul, 1985). The reader will note the similarity with Vatican II and the preparation under Pope John Paul II of the *Catechism of the Catholic Church,* first issued in 1992.

   23. For the modern encyclicals down to 1981, see the stately volumes edited by Claudia Carlen, IHM, *The Papal Encyclicals,* 5 vols. (Ann Arbor: Perian Press, 1990). The encyclicals of Pope John Paul II were first published together by J. Michael Miller, CSB, ed., *The Encyclicals of Pope John Paul II* (Huntington, IN: Our Sunday Visitor, 1996). Pope Benedict XVI's encyclicals, *Deus caritas est* (February 2006) and *Spe salvi* (November 2007) are given in *Origins* 35 (February 2, 2006): 541–57, and 37 (December 13, 2007): 421–39.

   24. See the account of Pius XII's *Humani generis* above in chapter 1, pages 20–21.

   25. To date the "Considerations" have appeared in Italian in a volume in the Congregation's series Documenti e studi, in *Il primato del successore di Pietro nel mistero della chiesa* (Vatican City: Liberia Editrice Vaticana, 2002), 9–21, and in French in *Documentation catholique* 95 (1998): 1016–20. *Dominus Iesus* is given in *Origins* 30 (2000): 209–19.

   26. Some examples are Joseph Komonchak and others, eds., *The New Dictionary of Theology* (Collegeville, MN: Liturgical Press, 1987); Peter Fink, ed., *The New Dictionary of Sacramental Worship* (Collegeville, MN: Liturgical Press, 1990); Michael Downey, ed., *The New Dictionary of Catholic Spirituality* (Collegeville, MN: Liturgical Press, 1993); René Latourelle and Rino Fisichella, eds., *Dictionary of Fundamental Theology* (New York: Crossroad, 1994); and Wolfgang Beinert and Francis Schüssler Fiorenza, eds., *Handbook of Catholic Theology* (New York: Crossroad, 1995).

   27. The documents published by the commission were collected in Michael Sharkey, ed., *Texts and Documents* (San Francisco: Ignatius Press, 1989), which include the 1976 "theses" on the relation between the magisterium and theology. Francis Sullivan gives the theses with added commentary in chapter 8 of *Magisterium* (as in note 1 of this chapter). Some of the commission's further publications since the year 2000 are offered online by the Vatican, under "Roman Curia/Congregations/Congregation of the Doctrine of the Faith." One publication of special relevance to those doing theology is "The Interpretation of Dogmas," given in *Origins* 20 (1990): 1–14.

   28. Trent's decrees are in ND, 1512, 1636, and 1656. I treated this topic in the entry "The Church as Interpreter of Scripture," DFT, 175–77.

29. To make this last point concrete, I would urge theologians in North America to read regularly the articles, often incisively secular but always informative of actual intellectual currents, in such a publication as the bi-weekly *New York Review of Books*.

30. For a comprehensive and detailed presentation of this phase of theological work, one should study Francis A. Sullivan's *Creative Fidelity: Weighing and Interpreting Documents of the Magisterium* (New York and Mahwah, NJ: Paulist Press, 1996), which treats in detail the nature of dogma, definitions, and teachings by Councils and popes, and a five-step process of interpreting doctrinal texts, before then offering numerous applications of the process on doctrinal and moral topics (e.g., to Pope John Paul II's *Evangelium vitae* of 1995) and adding a well-grounded approach to weighing and interpreting the teachings of Vatican Council II. What follows in our introductory text works from less comprehensive accounts.

31. Given in *Origins* 20 (1990–91): 1–14. Walter Kasper, now cardinal-president of the Pontifical Council for Promoting Christian Unity, directed the group entrusted with preparing the text. Members included Carl Peter (then professor at the Catholic University of America) and Christoph von Schönborn (now cardinal-archbishop of Vienna). Other drafters were Catholic theologians from Belgium, Germany, India, Italy, Lebanon, Poland, and Portugal.

32. J. Alfaro, "Theology and the Magisterium," in René Latourelle and Gerald O'Collins, eds., *Problems and Perspectives in Fundamental Theology* (New York: Paulist Press, 1982), 340–56. The International Theological Commission gives in section B.III of its document a set of systematic theological considerations on the foundations of dogmatic teaching in the church.

33. The third of these topics is not a new idea about theology, but was advanced by John Henry Newman in the nineteenth century, when he spoke of the corporate body of Catholic theologians, called the *schola theologorum* (school of the theologians), who were expected "to determine the force of Papal and Synodal utterances." *Letter to the Duke of Norfolk* (London: Pickering, 1875), 4 and 121. For more on Newman on this topic, see Sullivan, *Creative Fidelity* (as in note 30 above), 175–80.

34. Appendix 4, giving Catholic teaching on revelation and faith in dogmatic texts of 1870 (Vatican I) and of 1965 (Vatican II), opens up one possibility of charting change and development. A good example of study of a development of teaching within a Council is Joseph Ratzinger, "On the Interpretation of the Tridentine Decree on Tradition," in Karl Rahner

and J. Ratzinger, *Revelation and Tradition* (New York: Herder and Herder, 1966), 50–78. One learns regularly of the genetic development of Vatican II documents from the initial draft to the promulgated text in Herbert Vorgrimler, ed., *Commentary on the Documents of Vatican II,* 5 vols. (New York: Herder and Herder, 1967–69).

35. Dean Béchard's collection, *The Scripture Documents* (Collegeville, MN: Liturgical Press, 2002), gives one the possibility of charting continuities and noting innovations in official Catholic teaching on the Bible and its interpretation, for example, in encyclicals of Leo XIII (1893), Pius XII (1943), and then in Vatican II's constitution *Dei Verbum,* chapters 3 and 6.

36. See the contributions to John A. Coleman, ed., *One Hundred Years of Catholic Social Teaching* (Maryknoll, NY: Orbis Books, 1999), and the introductions to the texts given in David O'Brien and Thomas A. Shannon, eds., *Catholic Social Thought: The Documentary Heritage* (Maryknoll, NY: Orbis Books, 1992).

37. Appendix 8 below gives the graded scale of four levels of teaching, as the Congregation for the Doctrine of the Faith presented these in 1990. For further clarification, Richard Gaillardetz gives a careful analysis in *Teaching with Authority: A Theology of the Magisterium in the Church* (Collegeville, MN: Liturgical Press, 1997), 101–28, "What the Church Teaches: Gradations of Church Doctrine," with a diagram on page 102, and 255–73, "Receiving and Responding to the Word: Personal Reception of Church Teaching," with a chart on page 271.

Chapter 5:
Doing Theology amidst Life

1. BDCT offers concise presentations of these three theologians, while other twentieth-century architects of theological systems are presented more at length in David F. Ford, ed., *The Modern Theologians,* 2 vols. (Oxford: Blackwell, 1989).

2. In DFT, the lead editor, René Latourelle, presents first the "Fundamental Theologian" and then the history and specific character of "Fundamental Theology" (320–32), while Rino Fisichella takes up this systematic theological area from the angle of the question, "Whom Is It For?" (332–36). A variation appears in a recent call to reinsert an argumentative approach in fundamental theology: Avery Dulles, "The Rebirth of Apologetics," *First Things,* no. 143 (May 2004): 18–23.

3. Karl Rahner gives an account of dogmatic theology in the entry "Dogma, IV. Dogmatics," in Karl Rahner, ed., *Encyclopedia of Theology:*

The Concise Sacramentum Mundi (New York: Seabury Press, 1975), 366–70, which completes Rahner's compressed entry, "Dogma, I. Theological Meaning of Dogma," ibid., 352–56. A more ample treatment is Guy F. Mansini's entry "Dogma," DFT, 239–47.

4. A basic-level work that illustrates well the fundamental topics of Catholic moral theology is Elizabeth Willems, *Understanding Catholic Morality* (New York: Crossroad, 1997).

5. A good orientation is the entry by Walter H. Principe, "Spirituality, Christian," in *New Dictionary of Catholic Spirituality,* ed. Michael Downey (Collegeville, MN: Liturgical Press, 1993), 931–38.

6. *Summa of Theology,* part I, q. 1, art. 6, response to the 3rd objection.

7. In his epilogue to two volumes on contemporary theologians, the editor David F. Ford speaks of the common thread running through the many projects and proposals of these authors. This is their search for wisdom, a search that makes considerable demands on a person in gaining knowledge and skills, so that he or she can approach deep mysteries and gradually move toward wisdom by intense thought and ongoing, careful discernment. *The Modern Theologians* (as in note 1 of this chapter), 2:296.

8. Bernard Lonergan, *Method in Theology* (New York: Herder & Herder, 1972), 127–32, after which individual chapters explain each specialty in greater detail. Vernon Gregson sets forth the specialties in chapters on "theological method and collaboration" in V. Gregson, ed., *Desires of the Human Heart* (New York: Paulist, 1988), 74–119.

9. See the elegant response of Richard R. Gaillardetz to the question "What Is the Sense of the Faithful?" in *By What Authority? A Primer on Scripture, the Magisterium, and the Sense of the Faithful* (Collegeville, MN: Liturgical Press, 2003), 107–20.Ormond Rush has treated this topic comprehensively in *The Eyes of Faith: The Sense of the Faithful and the Church's Reception of Revelation* (Washington, DC: Catholic University of America Press, 2009).

10. See the text in ND, 714.

11. See A. Dulles, *Models of the Church,* rev. and expanded ed. (Garden City, NY: Doubleday, 1987); *Models of Revelation* (Garden City, NY: Doubleday, 1983); *The Assurance of Things Hoped For: A Theology of Christian Faith* (New York: Oxford University Press, 1994), chapter 8, "Models and Issues," 170–84. For an account of the method, see A. Dulles, *The Craft of Theology* (New York: Crossroad, 1992), 41–52.

12. A *bilateral* dialogue is "two-sided," between appointed representatives of two churches or communions, as in Lutheran–Catholic, Pentecostal–

Catholic, or Lutheran–Orthodox. The aim is to identify and overcome particular obstacles to ecclesial communion between the two bodies. A *multilateral* dialogue involves participating representatives from numerous confessions, as in the Faith and Order Commission, with its 120 members drawn from the whole spectrum of Christian churches. A good example of theology in a multilateral dialogue is the recently published Faith and Order paper *The Nature and Mission of the Church: A Stage on the Way to a Common Statement* (Geneva: World Council of Churches, 2005). The dialogues continue to be remarkably productive, as shown by the standard collections, Harding Meyer and Lukas Vischer, eds., *Growth in Agreement: Reports and Agreed Statements of Ecumenical Conversations on a World Level* (New York: Paulist, and Geneva: World Council of Churches, 1984); Jeffrey Gros, Harding Meyer, and William G. Rusch, eds., *Growth in Agreement II: Reports and Agreed Statements of Ecumenical Conversations on a World Level, 1982–1998* (Geneva: World Council of Churches, and Grand Rapids: Eerdmans, 2000); and Jeffrey Gros, Thomas F. Best, and Lorelei F. Fuchs, eds., *Growth in Agreement III: International Dialogue Texts and Agreed Statements 1998–2005* (Geneva: World Council of Churches, and Grand Rapids: Eerdmans: 2007).

13. A particularly profound consensus paper is the 1982 document of the Catholic–Orthodox dialogue on "The Church, the Eucharist, and the Trinity," given in *Origins* 12 (1982): 157–60, and *Growth in Agreement II,* 652–59. The most dramatic product of the Lutheran–Catholic theological dialogues is the *Joint Declaration on the Doctrine of Justification* (Grand Rapids: Eerdmans, 2000), formally accepted by the churches at Augsburg, Germany, October 31, 1999. The declaration draws its conclusions from numerous Lutheran–Catholic bilateral conversations conducted since Vatican Council II.

14. While this book was being revised, the Lutheran–Catholic dialogue in the United States brought out a new statement: Randall Lee and Jeffrey Gros, eds., *The Church as Koinonia of Salvation: Its Structures and Ministries,* Lutherans and Catholics in Dialogue, X (Washington, DC: United States Conference of Catholic Bishops, 2005). The latest work of the Anglican–Roman Catholic International Commission appeared in Donald Bolen and Gregory Cameron, eds., *Mary: Grace and Hope in Christ. The Text with Commentaries and Study Guide* (London and New York: Continuum, 2006).

15. This programmatic mandate given by the Council was taken up and elaborated by Robert J. Schreiter, in *Constructing Local Theologies* (Maryknoll, NY: Orbis Books, 1985).

16. Based on Yves Congar's diaries of the years 1946 to 1966, the author set forth something of the drama of his life and work in "Yves Congar's Doctrinal Service of the People of God," *Gregorianum* 84 (2003): 499–550. On J. C. Murray: Donald E. Pelotte, *John Courtney Murray: Theologian in Conflict* (New York: Paulist, 1976), and J. Leon Hooper and Todd D. Whitmore, eds., *John Courtney Murray and the Growth of the Tradition* (Kansas City, MO: Sheed & Ward, 1996).

17. See above at the end of section 1.1.

18. Chapter 2, "Human Experience," in Gerald O'Collins, *Fundamental Theology* (New York: Paulist, 1981), 32–52. When he reached age seventy, O'Collins was honored by a volume of twenty-one essays, of which nos. 8–15 bring out experiential themes under the heading "Fundamental Theology and Spirituality," in *The Convergence of Theology*, ed. Daniel Kendall and Stephen T. Davis (New York: Paulist, 2001), 139–269.

19. What this paragraph states is well exemplified in the texts of Karl Rahner, in *The Practice of Faith: A Handbook of Contemporary Spirituality*, ed. Karl Lehmann and Albert Raffelt (New York: Crossroad, 1983).

20. What the text asserts arises from the author's formation under St. Ignatius Loyola, who left a unique text giving "rules for understanding the different movements produced in the soul and for recognizing those that are good to admit them, and those that are bad, to reject them." *Spiritual Exercises*, no. 313, in the introduction to the two sets of "Rules for the Discernment of Spirits" (nos. 313–36). The New Testament is the basis of the rules, but the formulation by Ignatius goes on from Scripture to formulate the outcome of his attentive review of his own personal experiences in prayer and living.

Appendix 1:
Opening Address of the Second Vatican Council, Pope John XXIII

1. The translation has been moderately revised, in inclusive language style and correcting a few errors, from the English text in *Council Daybook: Vatican II, Session 1, 1962, and Session 2, 1963*, ed. Floyd Anderson (Washington, DC: National Catholic Welfare Conference, 1965), 25–29. The Latin text is in *Acta Apostolicae Sedis* 54 (1962): 786–95. Biblical citations follow the Latin Vulgate, from which Pope John cited. The section headings, not in the Latin original, are from *Council Daybook,* while the paragraph numbers are added by J. Wicks for ease of reference.

Appendix 2:
Opening of the Second Period of Vatican Council II, Pope Paul VI

1. The full text, in the original Latin, is in *Acta Apostolicae Sedis* 55 (1963): 841–59. It is given in English in the volume of *Council Daybook, Sessions 1 and 2* (as in the previous note), 143–50.

2. In one of his first actions regarding the Council, Pope Paul VI appointed four cardinals as "moderators" to set the schedule of topics of debate, to preside over the daily assemblies, to call for votes on the draft texts, etc. These were Cardinals Gregory P. Agagianian (prefect of the Congregation for the Missions in the Curia), Julius Döpfner (archbishop of Munich), Giacomo Lecaro (archbishop of Bologna), and Leo Jozef Seunens (archbishop of Malines-Brussels). Pope Paul met with these four regularly and through them he was able to guide the Council. The board of ten presidents, mostly older cardinals, remained but now had less influence over the direction of the Council.

3. On Vatican Council I (1869–70), see the introduction to Appendix 4 below. Vatican I issued two Dogmatic Constitutions: *The Catholic Faith* (*Dei Filius*), on revelation, faith, and the relation of faith and reason, and *The Eternal Shepherd* (*Pastor aeternus*), on the pope as successor of Peter, with supreme ruling power of jurisdiction and in teaching solemnly the truths of divine revelation being endowed with the protective charism of infallibility. A longer draft text on the Church itself, on bishops, etc., had been drawn up, but the outbreak of the Franco-Prussian war in July 1870, followed by the occupation of Rome by Italian troops on September 20, ending papal rule over the papal states, caused the suspension of the Council before it could elaborate a more ample teaching on the church in which the pope holds supreme authority.

4. As Pope Paul read this part of his address, he turned toward his left to face the non-Catholic observers of Vatican II. In 1962 they had been fifty-four in number, but grew to over one hundred by the time the Council ended in 1965. Some were sent by the independent Orthodox Churches, while many represented the world organizations of Anglican and Protestant confessions, as well as the World Council of Churches in Geneva. Their regular reports to those who commissioned them are valuable sources of Vatican II history. The observers were given the documents and draft texts of the Council, while the officials of the Vatican Secretariat for the Promotion of Christian Unity had regular contacts with them, even to the point of receiving from them proposed emendations of the texts under discussion.

5. The Church's outlook on the modern world had come onto the Council's agenda through the efforts of the Belgian cardinal L. J. Suenens, with the backing of Pope John XXIII. As Pope Paul spoke in September 1963, different drafting groups were at work on a text which, after discussion by the Council members and numerous revisions, became the Pastoral Constitution on the Church in the Modern World, *Gaudium et spes*, promulgated at the Council's final meeting, December 7, 1965.

6. What Pope Paul said here on other religions led to Vatican II's Declaration on the Relation of the Church to Non-Christian Religions (*Nostra aetate*), with its notable no. 4 on Christian–Jewish relations, after appreciative words on Hindus, Buddhists, and Muslims.

Appendix 3:
Address at the Last Meeting of Vatican Council II, Pope Paul VI

1. The text is reprinted with permission from the copyright holder, the Vatican Information Service, which offers such texts at *www.vatican.va/ holyfather/paulvi/speeches*. The original Latin text is given in *Acta Apostolicae Sedis* 58 (1966): 51–59, and the English translation is printed in the *Council Daybook: Vatican II, Session 4, 1965,* ed. Floyd Anderson (Washington, DC: National Catholic Welfare Conference, 1966), 359–62.

Appendix 4:
Catholic Doctrine on Revelation and Faith: The Conciliar Texts

1. See the accounts of the Councils of Nicea (AD 325), Constantinople (381), Ephesus (431), and Chalcedon (451), in Norman P. Tanner, *The Councils of the Church: A Short History* (New York: Crossroad, 2001), 13–33.

2. The text is reprinted, by kind permission of the copyright holder, Continuum International, from the English translation given in *Decrees of the Ecumenical Councils,* vol. 2, *Trent to Vatican II,* ed. Giuseppe Alberigo and Norman P. Tanner, SJ (London: Sheed & Ward, and Washington, DC: Georgetown University Press, 1990), 804–8.

3. The Preface was not discussed by the bishops of Vatican I as they reviewed and amended the preliminary drafts of the constitution, but it was added by the Council leadership, with the approval of Pope Pius IX, to express how the Council understood its place in history. The Preface is not part of the official teaching of Vatican Council I on revelation and faith, but

it shows the understanding of modern history and of the church's role which was widespread in Catholicism during the nineteenth century and well into the twentieth century.

4. Lateran Council IV (AD 1215), *Constitution on the Catholic Faith,* in Alberigo and Tanner, eds., *Decrees,* citing from page 230.

5. The Council of Trent (1547), *Decree on Justification,* chapter 8, given in Alberigo and Tanner, eds., *Decrees,* 674.

6. The Second Council of Orange (AD 529), Canon 7 on grace, given in ND, 1919.

7. This topic was treated in chapter 1, section 2, pages 17–19, above.

8. The translation given here cites with permission the revised and inclusive-language translation, edited by Austin Flannery, OP, *Vatican Council II: Constitutions, Decrees, Declarations* (Northport, NY: Costello, and Dublin: Dominican Publications, 1996), 97–100 and 111–15. The author has added in brackets the paragraph headings.

9. Cf. St. Augustine, *De catechizandis rudibus,* chapter 4, no. 8; *Patrologia Latina,* 40, 316.

10. Cf. Matt 11:27; John 1:14 and 17, 14:6, 17:1–3; 2 Cor 3:16 and 4:6; Eph 1:3–14.

11. Epistle to Diognetus, chapter 7, no. 4; given in Funk, *Apostolic Fathers,* 1:403.

12. Vatican Council I, Dogmatic Constitution *Dei Filius,* chapter 3, "Faith."

13. Second Council of Orange, Canon 7, cited by Vatican Council I, *Dei Filius,* chapter 3.

14. Vatican Council I, Dogmatic Constitution *Dei Filius,* chapter 2, "Revelation."

15. Ibid.

16. This was set forth in chapter 1, section 3 above. See pages 24–27.

17. Chapter 2 above treated this, in sections 2–3, on biblical inspiration and interpretation. See pages 48–54.

18. See Pius XII, encyclical *Divino Afflante Spiritu,* in selected paragraphs, given in D. Béchard, ed., *The Scripture Documents* (Collegeville, MN: Liturgical Press, 2002), 125–26 and 133–34 (nos. 15, 16, and 27). Also, Pontifical Biblical Commission, "Instruction on Proper Teaching of Sacred Scripture in Seminaries and Religious Colleges," May 13, 1950, in *Acta Apostolicae Sedis* 42 (1950): 495–505.

19. See Pius XII, *Divino afflante,* in Béchard, 135–36 (no. 29).

20. See Leo XIII, encyclical *Providentissimus Deus*, in Béchard, 50 (no. 33). Also, Benedict XV, encyclical *Spiritus Paraclitus*, in Béchard, 100 (in no. 13).

21. St. Augustine, Sermon 179, no. 1, in *Patrologia Latina*, 38, 966.

22. St. Jerome, *Commentary on Isaiah*, Prologue, in *Patrologia Latina*, vol. 24, col. 17. Cf. Benedict XV, *Spiritus Paraclitus*, in Béchard, 96–99 (nos. 11–12), and Pius XII, *Divino Afflante Spiritu*, in Béchard, 119f. (no. 9).

23. St. Ambrose, *On the Duties of Ministers*, I, 20, 88, in *Patrologia Latina*, 16, 50.

24. St. Irenaeus, *Against Heresies*, IV, 32, 1, in *Patrologia Graeca*, 7, 1071.

Appendix 5:
Theologians at Vatican Council II, Jared Wicks, SJ

1. J. Wicks, "I teologi al Vaticano II: Momenti e modalità del loro contributo al concilio," *Humanitas* (Brescia, Italy) 59 (2004): 1012–38.

2. Étienne Fouilloux mentioned a tendency to legendary amplification of the influence of the theologians in the first lines of his paper, "Comment devient-on expert à Vatican II? Le cas du Père Yves Congar," in *Le duxième Concile du Vatican 1959–1965* (Rome: École Français, 1989), 307–31.

3. "Les conciles dans la vie de l'Église," in *Informations catholiques internationales*, no. 90 (February 15, 1959): 17–26. The article was unsigned, but É. Fouilloux, in the article mentioned in note 2, related that it was by Congar.

4. *Le Concile et les conciles* (Chevetogne: Abbaye de Chevetogne, 1960), 75–109, 285–334. Congar's sketch of the ecumenical possibilities of the coming Council appeared as "The Council, the Church, and the 'Others,'" *Cross Currents* 11 (1961): 241–54.

5. H. Jedin, *Ecumenical Councils of the Catholic Church: An Historical Outline* (New York: Herder & Herder, 1960). By 1962 *Conciliorum oecumenicorum Decreta* was published, edited by Giuseppe Alberigo and others, from which we now have the bilingual edition with English translations, including the documents of Vatican II, *Decrees of the Ecumenical Councils*, ed. Norman P. Tanner, 2 vols. (London: Sheed & Ward, and Washington DC: Georgetown University Press, 1990).

6. In English: *The Council, Reform, and Reunion* (New York: Sheed & Ward, 1961). Just before Vatican II opened, Küng's *Strukturen der Kirche* appeared, translated as *Structures of the Church* (London: Burns & Oates,

1965), with extensive treatment of the Councils. Küng narrates the circumstances surrounding the preparation of both works in the first volume of his memoirs, *My Struggle for Freedom* (Grand Rapids: Eerdmans, 2004).

7. "Zur Theologie des Konzils," *Catholica* 15 (1961): 292–304, originally a lecture of February 25, 1961.

8. J. Jacobs, "Les *vota* des évêques néerlandais pour le concile," in *A la veille du Concile Vatican II,* ed. Mathijs Lamberigts and Claude Soetens (Leuven: Leuven University Press, 1992), 99–110. The history of the Catholic Committee has been sketched by Mauro Velati in chapters 1–5 of *Una difficile transizione: Il cattolicesimo tra unionismo ed ecumenismo (1950–1964)* (Bologna: Il Mulino, 1996).

9. This and future references to Yves Congar as Vatican II theologian come from his Council diary, *Mon Journal du Concile,* ed. E. Mahieu, 2 vols. (Paris: Cerf, 2002), which I presented in "Yves Congar's Doctrinal Service of the People of God," *Gregorianum* 84 (2003): 499–550.

10. J. Komonchak, "U.S. Bishops' Suggestions for Vatican II," *Cristianesimo nella storia* 15 (1994): 313–71.

11. Cardinal Montini's proposal is given in *Acta et Documenta Concilio Oecumenico Vaticano Secondo Apparando,* series 1 (Antepraeparatoria), 2/3, 374–81. The faculty wanted the Council to clarify the supernatural destiny of humans in relation to life in this world and to work out doctrine on the role of bishops in the church (ibid., 4/2, 667–96). On Montini's preparation: A. Rimoldi, "La preparazione del Concilio," in *Giovanni Battista Montini Arcivescovo di Milano e il Concilio Ecumenico Vaticano II. Preparazione e primo periodo* (Brescia: Istituto Paolo VI, 1985), 202–41, especially 212–22.

12. Bishop Keller's proposal: *Acta et Documenta,* series 1, 2/2, 629–33. The faculty's suggestions: ibid., 4/2, 799–803. H. Volk published "Wort Gottes Gabe und Aufgabe," *Catholica* 16 (1962): 241–51, and *Zur Theologie des Wortes Gottes* (Münster, 1962).

13. The incident at the October 1965 meeting of the Doctrinal Commission was recorded in the diary of Father Umberto Betti, OFM, *Diario del Concilio* (Bologna: Dehoniane, 2003), 71.

14. *Acta et Documenta,* series 1, 4/1, 189–94.

15. *Acta et Documenta,* series 1, 4/1, 248–63. The passage of Pius XII's *Humani generis* to which Piolanti referred is given in *The Papal Encyclicals 1939–1958,* ed. C. Carlen (Ann Arbor: Pierian Press, 1990), 178–79, esp. no. 21.

16. É. Fouilloux studied the Lateran University proposals, along with publications of its professors, in the journal *Divinitas,* in "Théologiens romains et Vatican II (1959–1962)," *Cristianesimo nella storia* 15 (1994): 373–90, concluding that this group took as its starting point the authoritative documents of the current magisterium and frequently called attention to contemporary deviations from such authoritative teaching. The proposal of the Congregation for Seminaries, incorporating Piolanti's critical essay, is in *Acta et Documenta,* series 1, 3, 321–28.

17. *Acta et Documenta,* series 1, 4/1, 263–70.

18. The Montreal faculty proposal is given in *Acta et Documenta,* series 1, 4/2, 461–62.

19. *Acta et Documenta,* series 1, 4/1/1, 125–36.

20. Ibid., series 1, 4/2, 223–26.

21. Preparatory Commissions were founded for these areas: theology, bishops and the governance of dioceses, the clergy and Christian people, religious orders, the sacraments, liturgy, seminaries and studies, the Catholic Oriental churches, missions, and the lay apostolate. Their work is studied by Joseph Komonchak in his long chapter in Giuseppe Alberigo, ed., *History of Vatican II,* vol. 1, *Announcing and Preparing Vatican Council II: Toward a New Era in Catholicism* (Maryknoll, NY: Orbis Books, and Leuven: Peeters, 1995), 167–356.

22. M. Velati related the founding and conciliar action of the Secretariat in *Una difficile transizione* (as in note 8 above), chapters 8–13. One of Cardinal Bea's first co-workers told the story from his personal experience: Thomas Stransky, "The Foundation of the Secretariat for Promoting Christian Unity," in Alberic Stacpoole, ed., *Vatican II Revisited. By Those Who Were There* (Minneapolis: Winston, 1986), 62–87.

23. The *Conspectus* is given in an Appendix volume to *Acta et Documenta,* series 1. É. Fouilloux studied the process by which the proposals were filtered into established schemes of theological textbooks and of canon law. Alberigo, *History of Vatican II,* 1 (as in note 21 above), 140–49.

24. Cardinal Carlo Confalonieri, at the June 19, 1962, meeting of the Central Preparatory Commission, when draft texts, sharply differing with each other, were presented by the Theological Commission and the Secretariat for Promoting Christian Unity on the question of church-state relations. *Acta et Documenta,* series 2 (Praeparatoria), 4, 731.

25. We have a narrative of the sessions of the Central Commission, including the moments of sharp debate that broke out, from A. Indelicato, *Difendere*

la dottrina o annunciare l'evangelo: Il dibattito nella Commissione central preparatoria del Vaticano II (Genoa: Il Mulino, 1992).

26. Jedin related in his autobiography that in favoring reform he was often allied with Father Paolo Dezza, SJ, and Father Pierre Girard, general superior of the Sulpicians, but they were regularly outvoted by the Rome-based members of the commission. Lebensbericht, ed., K. Repgen (Mainz: Grünewald, 1984), 200–201.

27. Early in 1961, the archbishop of Munich, Cardinal Julius Döpfner, proposed Rahner as a consultor of the Preparatory Theological Commission, but the President, Cardinal Ottaviani, was reluctant, since the Holy Office, which Ottaviani headed, was then processing accusations against Rahner's fidelity to Catholic doctrine. See K. Wittstadt, Julius Kardinal Döpfner (1913–1976) (Munich: Don Bosco, 2001), 183. Rahner threw himself into research on the diaconate and gathered thirty-eight contributions from all over the Catholic world for publication in what became a basic text of reference on the subject of the diaconate: Diaconia in Christo: Über die Erneuerung des Diakonats (Freiburg: Herder, 1962). See also H. Vorgrimler, "Karl Rahner: The Theologian's Contribution," in Vatican II Revisited (as in note 22 above), 39–40.

28. The first volume, in two parts, of Father Tromp's diary of his work as commission secretary has appeared: Alexandra von Teuffenbach, ed., Konzilstagebuch Sebastian Tromp SJ (Rome: Gregorian University Press, 2006). This 965-page publication covers the preparatory period of 1960–62, giving with helpful annotations Father Tromp's record of his work as secretary, both in the original Latin and with a German translation, adding letters and numerous other documents preserved along with the diary in the Vatican Secret Archive from this phase of work by Vatican II's Preparatory Theological Commission.

29. Cardinal Ernesto Ruffini, who had been both secretary of the Congregation for Seminaries and rector of the Lateran University and then, after World War II, became archbishop of Palermo, had expressed just this hope for Vatican II's work in a discourse in October 1959. The Council would render definitively valid the principal teachings of the popes from Leo XIII through Pius XII, by adding to their own magisterial authority the greater authority of an Ecumenical Council, so as to raise these doctrines above any possible questioning. See Angelo Romano, Ernesto Ruffini: Cardinale arcivescovo di Palermo (Caltanissetta-Rome: Centro A. Cammarata, 2002), 492.

30. Mon Journal du Concile (note 9 above), 1, 55, 67, 71, 96.

31. In 1961, it was an open question how the coming Council would address itself to Catholic Scripture scholars. The approach of admonition and censure of error, because of new opinions about the kind of history given in Genesis and in the Gospels, had been in effect urged by Msgr. Antonino Romeo, in a long article published in the Roman journal *Divinitas* at the beginning of the year. Romeo offered a scathing criticism of the professors and graduates of the Pontifical Biblical Institute, accusing them of undermining the Catholic faith, which led to two of them being temporarily suspended from teaching. See, on this, J. Fitzmyer, "A Recent Roman Scriptural Controversy," *Theological Studies* 22 (1961): 426–44. Another account, relating as well the repercussions in the United States, is Gerald P. Fogarty, *American Catholic Biblical Scholarship: A History from the Early Republic to Vatican II* (San Francisco: Harper & Row, 1989), 281–96.

32. Rahner's often devastating comments were published in "Konzilsgutachten für Kardinal König," in *Sehnsucht nach dem geheimnisvollen Gott,* ed. Herbert Vorgrimler (Freiburg: Herder, 1990), 95–149.

33. "Kardinal Frings über das moderne Gedankenwelt," *Herder Korrespondenz* 16 (1961/62): 168–74. One theme is the impact of technology on much of the reality surrounding people's lives, leaving them with only few encounters with God's natural creation. So the Council should show that human beings are still prepared for God's word, if not by the wonders of nature, still by the restless yearnings that well up from their hearts, which are satisfied only ultimately by resting in God. A further analysis of this and five other Vatican II texts prepared by *peritus* J. Ratzinger appeared in *Gregorianum* 89 (2008): 233–311.

34. H. Jedin, *Lebensbericht* (note 26 above), 203f.

35. I read O. Semmelroth's diary, *Konzilstagebuch,* in the Archive of the Jesuit Province of Northern Germany, now at Berchmans College in Munich.

36. Concerning P. Smulders's Vatican II activity, I draw on his diary, letters to the Maastrict Jesuit community, and many other papers now in the Smulders-Archive of the Katholiek Documentatie Centrum, Nijmegen, The Netherlands, where the staff was very helpful in assisting my Vatican II research.

37. A sample is given in *Sehnsucht* (note 32 above), 149–63. On the four theological texts, Rahner commented: "Here there's no radiance at all of the victorious power of the Gospel" (155). The text on protecting the deposit of faith is asking the Council to treat many topics well below the dignity of an Ecumenical Council of the Catholic Church.

38. I gave further details in "Congar's Doctrinal Service" (note 9 above): 519–20.

39. Pietro Pizzuto, *La teologia della rivelazione di Jean Daniélou. Influsso su Dei Verbum e valore attuale* (Rome: Gregorian University Press, 2003), 32–39, giving the texts on 505–23.

40. The letter, signed by Cardinal Frings, is in Appendix I of the Vatican II *Acta Synodalia,* 74–77. A presentation and English translation is given in *Gregorianum* 89 (2008): 239–41 and 264–68.

41. I am grateful to Father Paolino Zilio, OFMCap, for copies of material by Stegmüller that he found in the Freiburg diocesan archive. The draft text, entitled *Schema de Deo,* is in the Vatican Archive's huge collection of Vatican II material, in the box *Animadversiones Patrum ante Concilii Initium,* as Bishop Schäuffele's contribution sent in a month before the Council opened.

42. I presented this in "Pieter Smulders and *Dei Verbum:* A Consultation on the Eve of Vatican II," *Gregorianum* 82 (2001): 241–97, giving texts by Smulders on 283–97.

43. Jan Brouwers, "Vatican II, derniers préparatifs et première session: Activités conciliares en coulisses," in *Vatican II commence... Approaches francophones,* ed. É. Fouilloux (Leuven: Peeters, 1993), 353–78.

44. [E. Schillebeeckx,] *Commentary on the "prima series" of "Schemata Constitutionum et Decretorum de quibus disceptabitur in Concilii sessionibus"* (1962), in a photocopy given me by E. Schillebeeckx, whom I thank for his help and discussions during my visits to Nijmegen.

45. *De revelatione Dei et hominis in Jesu Christo facta,* distributed in two thousand copies. The Latin text with English translation is in B. Cahill, *The Renewal of Revelation Theology* (Rome: Gregorian University Press, 1999), 300–317.

46. Published in the original Latin, with a German translation, in Elmar Klinger and Klaus Wittstadt, eds., *Glaube im Prozess,* Festschrift K. Rahner (Freiburg: Herder, 1984), 51–64.

47. Published as an Appendix in U. Betti, *La dottrina del Concilio Vaticano II sulla trasmissione della rivelazione* (Rome: Pontifical Athaenum Antonianum, 1985), 303–6.

48. "Bemerkungen zum Schema De fontibus revelationis," in a sixteen-page copy in the Smulders-Archive (note 36 above), in folder no. 100. Ratzinger told how classical Catholic figures, like Thomas Aquinas and Bonaventure, held that all the truths of faith are in some way present in the inspired Scriptures, a notion that *The Sources* proposed to condemn

as a Protestant error now infiltrating Catholic theology. The original text and an English translation of this address are given in *Gregorianum* 89 (2008): 269–85 and 295–309.

49. I told about this in "Pieter Smulders and *Dei Verbum*: 2. On *De fontibus* during Vatican II's First Period," *Gregorianum* 82 (2001): 559–93.

50. Betti, *Diario* (note 13 above), 22–25.

51. I told in "Congar's Doctrinal Service" (note 9 above), 537f. of how Congar saw the gestures of Pope Paul VI during ecumenical encounters with Orthodox bishops as being equivalent to recognition of them as bishops in the proper sense. But his *modus* on this, after discussion in the doctrinal commission, was not accepted, although it was not denied outright, as we read in the final paragraph, introduced by "N.B.," of the "Preliminary Explanatory Note" appended to the Council's dogmatic constitution on the church. See, for example, the revised edition of Vatican II Documents, ed. A. Flannery (Northport, NY: Costello, 1996), 94–95.

52. Jan Grootaers relates this turning point in Giuseppe Alberigo, ed., *History of Vatican II*, vol. 2, *The Formation of the Council's Identity: First Period and Intersession* (Maryknoll, NY: Orbis Books, and Leuwen: Peeters, 1997), 391–410.

53. Congar wrote in his diary that the German text was too long, too scholarly, too much like a short university course rather than a conciliar text. *Mon Journal* (note 9 above), 1, 321. This German text has recently been studied in its depth and for further influence on the Council by Guenther Wassilowsky, *Universales Heilssakrament Kirche: Karl Rahners Beitrag zur Ekklesiologie des II. Vaticanums* (Innsbruck and Vienna: Tyrolia Verlag, 2001).

54. Congar, *Mon Journal*, 1, 336–37, on the commission meeting of March 4, 1963.

55. Ibid., 2, 202, and 281.

56. One group that had considerable theological significance at Vatican II, also omitted here, is the corps of delegated observers from the other churches and ecclesial communities. Thomas Stransky introduced them and noted their influence on the Council's Decree on Ecumenism in "Paul VI and the Delegated Observers/Guests to Vatican Council II," in *Paolo VI e l'ecumenismo* (Brescia: Istituto Paolo VI, 2001), 118–58, especially 146f. A more recent study is Carmen Aparicio, "Contributo di Lukas Vischer alla *Gaudium et spes*," in *Sapere teologico e unità della fede*, ed. Carmen Aparicio Valls, Carmelo Dotolo, Gianluigi Pasquale (Rome: Gregorian University Press, 2004), 3–19.

57. A principal historian of the Council, Giuseppe Alberigo of Bologna, gave a positive answer to the question of whether Vatican II exceeded the expectations of its initiators. The change of direction (*svolta*) was deep, yet organically configured, and went well beyond what anyone could have foreseen or proposed at the start. "Il Vaticano II dalle attese ai risultati: una svolta?" in *Volti di fine concilio,* ed. Joseph Doré and Alberto Melloni (Bologna: Il Mulino, 2000), 395–415, especially the concluding words on page 415.

Appendix 6:
Interpreting Vatican Council II, Pope Benedict XVI

1. The full text of the papal address is given in English translation in *Origins* 35, no. 32 (January 26, 2006): 534–39, from which the following portion is reprinted with the kind permission of the copyright holder, Liberia Editrice Vaticana. The issue treated has been studied by Joseph A. Komonchak in "Benedict XVI and the Interpretation of Vatican II," *Cristianesimo nell storia* 28 (2007): 323–37.

2. What the translator rendered as "constituent" in this passage is known in American English as a "constitutional convention."

3. These texts of Popes John XXIII and Paul VI are given as Appendices 1 and 3 above in this book.

Appendix 8:
The Levels of Teaching by the Catholic Magisterium

1. Given in *Origins* 20 (July 5, 1990): 118–26, from which the following excerpts are reprinted with the kind permission of CNS–Catholic News Service.

2. For commentary, see Avery Dulles, *The Craft of Theology* (New York: Crossroad, 1992), 108–16. Levels 1–3, along with the respective responses, were treated by Francis A. Sullivan, in *Magisterium: Teaching Authority in the Catholic Church* (New York: Paulist, 1983), chaps. 5–7, and then in more detail in *Creative Fidelity: Weighing and Interpreting Documents of the Magisterium* (New York: Paulist, 1996). Richard R. Gaillardetz describes the four levels in *Teaching with Authority: A Theology of the Magisterium in the Church* (Collegeville, MN: Liturgical Press, 1997), chapter 4, "What the Church Teaches: Gradations of Church Doctrine," pages 101–28.

3. In his address on December 22, 2005, Pope Benedict XVI spoke of this level regarding certain earlier Catholic teachings, on political liberalism and interpretation of Scripture, as "decisions on contingent matters" which then must change when new contexts arise. See Appendix 6, above.

4. On this submission (*obsequium religiosum*) as taught by Vatican Council II in LG 25, see Sullivan, *Magisterium*, 158–66.

Recommended Further Reading

Theology in History and the Church

Carey, Patrick W., and Joseph T. Lienhard, eds. *Biographical Dictionary of Christian Theologians.* Peabody, MA: Hendrickson, 2002.

Congar, Yves. *A History of Theology.* Garden City, NY: Doubleday, 1968.

Ford, David F., ed. *The Modern Theologians.* 2nd ed. Oxford: Blackwell, 1997.

Latourelle, René, and Rino Fisichella, eds. *Dictionary of Fundamental Theology.* New York: Crossroad, 1994. Note especially the entries on Apologists (41–44), Augustine of Hippo (59–68), Karl Barth (74–77), Maurice Blondel (78–84), Henri de Lubac (224–29), John Henry Newman (734–38), Origen (743–50), Karl Rahner (804–06), Manualistic Theology (1102–05), Thomas Aquinas (1105–09), Council of Trent (1126–32), Vatican I (1147–51), and Vatican II (1151–62).

Pelikan, Jaroslav. *The Christian Tradition.* 5 vols. Chicago: University of Chicago Press, 1971–1989.

Tanner, Norman. *The Councils of the Church: A Short History.* New York: Crossroad, 2001.

Listening to the Biblical Word

Alonso Schökel, Luis. *The Inspired Word: Scripture in the Light of Language and Literature.* New York: Herder and Herder, 1965.

———. and J. M. Bravo. *A Manual of Hermeneutics.* Sheffield: Sheffield Academic Press, 1998.

Béchard, Dean, ed. *The Scripture Documents. An Anthology of Official Catholic Teaching.* Collegeville, MN: Liturgical Press, 2002.

Brown, Raymond E., Joseph A. Fitzmyer, and Roland E. Murphy, eds. *The New Jerome Biblical Commentary.* Edgewood Cliffs, NJ: Prentice-Hall, 1990. Note especially the topical articles on Inspiration (pages 1023–33), Canonicity (1034–54), and Hermeneutics (1146–65).

Davis, Ellen, and Richard B. Hays, eds. *The Art of Reading Scripture.* Grand Rapids: Eerdmans, 2003.

Fitzmyer, Joseph A., SJ. *The Interpretation of Scripture: In Defense of the Historical-Critical Method.* New York and Mahwah, NJ: Paulist Press, 2008.

Gamble, Harry. *The New Testament Canon: Its Making and Meaning.* Philadelphia: Fortress Press, 1985.

Hahn, Scott W., ed. *Letter and Spirit.* Steubenville, OH: St. Paul Center for Biblical Theology, 2005–. Annual publication of book-length volumes, for example, *Reading Salvation. Word, Worship, and the Mysteries* (2005), *The Authority of Mystery. The Word of God and the People of God* (2006), and *The Hermeneutic of Continuity. Christ, Kingdom, and Creation* (2007).

Latourelle, René, and Rino Fisichella, eds. *Dictionary of Fundamental Theology.* New York: Crossroad, 1994. Note especially the entries on Canon of Scripture (pages 94–101), Church as Interpreter of Scripture (175–77), Inspiration (515–18), and Integral Exegesis (291–98).

Lienhard, Joseph T. *The Bible, the Church, and Authority.* Collegeville, MN: Liturgical Press, 1995.

McDonald, Lee M. *The Formation of the Biblical Canon.* Rev. ed. Peabody, MA: Hendrickson, 1995.

———, and James A. Sanders, eds. *The Canon Debate.* Peabody, MA: Hendrickson, 2002.

O'Collins, Gerald, and Daniel Kendall. *The Bible for Theology: Ten Principles for the Theological Use of Scripture.* New York and Mahwah, NJ: Paulist Press, 1997.

Rahner, Karl. *Inspiration in the Bible.* Freiburg: Herder, 1961.

Theology in the Catholic Tradition

Congar, Yves. *Tradition and Traditions: An Historical and Theological Essay.* New York: Macmillan, 1967.

———. *The Meaning of Tradition.* New ed. San Francisco: Ignatius Press, 2004.

Dulles, Avery R. "Tradition as a Theological Source." In *The Craft of Theology,* 87–104. New York: Crossroad, 1992.

Latourelle, René, and Rino Fisichella, eds. *Dictionary of Fundamental Theology.* New York: Crossroad, 1994. Note especially the entries on the Creed (pages 209–11), Deposit of Faith (229–39), Rule of Faith (959–61), and Tradition (1119–26).

Wilken, Robert Louis. *The Spirit of Early Christian Thought.* New Haven: Yale University Press, 2003.

Theology in the Light of Church Teaching

Alfaro, Juan. "Theology and the Magisterium." In *Problems and Perspectives in Fundamental Theology*, ed. René Latourelle and Gerald O'Collins, 340–56. New York: Paulist Press, 1982.

Dulles, Avery R. "The Magisterium in History: Theological Considerations." In *A Church to Believe In*, 103–17. New York: Crossroad, 1982.

———. "The Two Magisteria: An Interim Reflection." Ibid., 118–32.

———. *The Magisterium: Teacher and Guardian of the Faith*. Naples, FL: Sapientia Press, 2007.

Gaillardetz, Richard. *Teaching with Authority: A Theology of the Magisterium in the Church*. Collegeville, MN: Liturgical Press, 1997.

International Theological Commission. "The Interpretation of Dogmas." *Origins* 20 (1990–91): 1–14.

Kelly, Joseph F. *The Ecumenical Councils of the Catholic Church: A History*. Collegeville, MN: Liturgical Press, 2009.

Latourelle, René, and Rino Fisichella, eds. *Dictionary of Fundamental Theology*. New York: Crossroad, 1994. Note especially the entries on Apostle (page 48), Church as Interpreter of Scripture (175–77), Dogma (239–47), and Magisterium (614–20).

Örsy, Ladislas. *The Church: Learning and Teaching*. Wilmington, DE: Michael Glazier, 1987.

O'Malley, John W. *What Happened at Vatican II*. Cambridge, MA: Belknap Press of Harvard University Press, 2008.

Rush, Ormond. *The Eyes of Faith: The Sense of the Faithful and the Church's Reception of Revelation*. Washington, DC: Catholic University of America Press, 2009.

Schatz, Klaus. *The Papal Primacy: From its Origins to the Present*. Collegeville, MN: Liturgical Press, 1996.

Sullivan, Francis A. *Magisterium: Teaching Authority in the Catholic Church*. New York: Paulist Press, 1983.

———. *Creative Fidelity. Weighing and Interpreting Documents of the Magisterium*. New York and Mahwah, NJ: Paulist Press, 1996.

———. *From Apostles to Bishops: The Development of the Episcopacy in the Early Church*. New York and Mahwah, NJ: Newman Press, 2001.

Theology and Its Methods

Dulles, Avery R. *The Craft of Theology.* New York: Crossroad, 1992.

Latourelle, René, and Rino Fisichella, eds. *Dictionary of Fundamental Theology.* New York: Crossroad, 1994. Note especially the entries on Experience (pages 306–08), Fundamental Theology (324–36), Quest for Meaning (648–51), Method in Systematic Theology (670–84), Method in Fundamental Theology (684–90), Theological Pluralism (783–85), Theology (1060–81), Contextual Theology (1097–1102), and Manualistic Theology (1102–05).

Lonergan, Bernard. *Method in Theology.* New York: Herder and Herder, 1972.

Louth, Andrew. *Discerning the Mystery: An Essay on the Nature of Theology.* Oxford: Oxford University Press, 1983.

Nichols, Aidan. *The Shape of Catholic Theology.* Collegeville, MN: Liturgical Press, 1991.

Ratzinger, Joseph. *The Nature and Mission of Theology: Essays to Orient Theology in Today's Debates.* San Francisco: Ignatius Press, 1995.

Schreiter, Robert. *Constructing Local Theologies.* Maryknoll, NY: Orbis Books, 1985.

Index

reform, needed, in church and teaching, 89–90
ressourcement (drawing afresh on early sources), 1, 20
revelation
    conveys meaning, 7
    culminates in the gospel, 8
    and doctrine, 4–5
    in events, 57, 88
    of God's saving work, 2–3, 241n5
    leads to communion, 3–5, 8, 24, 241n5
    meets human yearnings, 19
    nature and content (Vatican II text), 181–83
    nature of (Vatican I text), 176, 241n5
    stages of, 8
    unity
        organic, 30
        shown in rule of faith, 71
    theology of (R. Latourelle), 241n6
    See also credibility, fundamental theology, gospel
Roman Catechism: See Trent, Council of, *Catechism*
Romeo, Antonino, 272n31
Ruffini, Ernesto, 212, 215, 271n29
rule of faith, 71–72, 251n8
    in Irenaeus, 9, 71
    in Origen, 11,
    trinitarian structure, 71
Rush, Ormond, 262n9

Schillebeeckx, Eduard, 187, 210–11, 221, 273n44
Sant'Egidio, Community of, 137
Saulchoir, Dominican School (Paris), 205
Schäuffele, Hermann, 210, 273n41
Schatz, Klaus, 257n12
Schmidt, Hermann, 212
Schreiter, Robert J., 263n15
scripture
    analogous with incarnation, 18, 244n21
    authenticity, literary, of books, 40–41

scripture (*continued*)
    centered in epiphany and passover of Christ, 63
    in church's life, 25–26, 46, 62–63, 184–86 (Vatican II text)
    as inerrant, 51–53
    spiritual senses (Origen), 11, 12
    in Vatican II, 25–26, 27, 183–86
    veneration of, 36
    See also canon of scripture, inspiration, interpretation of scripture
Secretariat for Promoting Christian Unity, 195, 198, 200, 201, 206, 212, 218, 270n22
    See also Vatican Council II, preparatory commissions
Semmelroth, Otto, 209, 216
sensus fidei (sense of the faith), 126–27, 130, 262n9
sensus fidelium (sense of the faithful), 126–27
Seper, Franjo, 203
Septuagint, 43, 44, 184
Smith, Joseph, 2
Smulders, Pieter, 209, 219, 222, 272n36
    comments on Vatican II early draft texts (1962), 210, 211
    drafting for *Gaudium et spes* (1965), 218
    drafting on permanent diaconate, 216–17
    drafting on revelation (1964), 218
    serving bishops of Indonesia, 213, 221
Spadafora, Francesco, 197
Spellman, Francis, 193
spiritual theology, 123, 236
Stegmüller, Friedrich, 210, 273n41
Suenens, Leo Josef, 188, 199, 215, 266n5
Sullivan, Francis A., 256nn.3–5, 260nn.30, 33, 275n2 (of Appendix 8)
Sullivan, Maureen, 241n2
Swedenborg, Emanuel, 2